Urbanism Under Sail

An archaeology of fluit ships
in early modern everyday life

Niklas Eriksson

Södertörns högskola

©Niklas Eriksson

Södertörn University
SE-141 89 Huddinge

Cover Images: based on sketches by Niklas Eriksson
Cover Design: Jonathan Robson
Layout: Per Lindblom & Jonathan Robson

Printed by Elanders, Stockholm 2014

Södertörn Doctoral Dissertations 95
ISSN 1652-7399
Södertörn Archaeological Studies 10
ISSN 1652-2559

ISBN 978-91-87843-02-0
ISBN 978-91-87843-03-7 (digital)

Abstract

In the seventeenth- and early eighteenth centuries, *fluits* were the most common type of merchant ship used in Baltic trade. Originally a Dutch design, the majority of all goods transported between Sweden and the Republic was carried on board such vessels. Far from all voyages reached their destination. Down in the cold brackish water of the Baltic, the preservation conditions are optimal, and several of these unfortunate vessels remain nearly intact today.

Although thousands of more or less identical *fluits* were built, surprisingly little is known about the arrangement of space on board, their sculptural embellishment and other aspects that formed the physical component of everyday life on and alongside these ships. *Fluits* were a fixture in early modern society, so numerous that they became almost invisible. The study of wrecks thus holds great potential for revealing vital components of early modern life. Inspired by phenomenological approaches in archaeology, this thesis aims to focus on the lived experience of *fluits*. It sets out to grasp for seemingly mundane everyday activities relating to these ships, from the physical arrangements for eating, sleeping and answering nature's call, to their rearrangement for naval use, and ends with a consideration of the architectonical contribution of the *fluit* to the urban landscape.

Keywords: Seventeenth century, Urbanism, Shipwrecks, Historical Archaeology, Buildings Archaeology, Nautical Archaeology, Sweden, the Netherlands, *Fluit*

Acknowledgments

Above all, it has been great fun writing this thesis. Numerous people, companies, institutions, museums and so on have contributed to this positive experience. First of all I wish to thank my supervisor, Johan Rönnby, for his great support, not only with this thesis, but also for always offering the opportunity to join and participate in different projects. I also wish to thank my second supervisor, Anders Andrén, for valuable comments on the manuscript and suggestions for relevant literature.

Many people have been involved in the archaeological surveys that laid the foundation for this study. I therefore wish to thank all my colleges at the Unit for Archaeology at the Swedish National Maritime Museum, in particular Trevor Draeske, Mikael Fredholm, Jim Hansson, Patrik Höglund, Jens Lindström and Eduardo Roa Brynhildsen, for excellent cooperation at the 'Jutholmen Wreck' as well as on the *Anna Maria* sites in Dalarö. Thanks also go to Anders Backström and Markus Hårde, who both discovered the 'Lion Wreck'and surveyed it with me, Jonas Rydin and Tommy Hallberg.

This dissertation would have looked very different if Johan Rönnby had not invited me to participate in the 'Ghost Ship' project. It was a cooperative endeavour carried out by MARIS, The Vasa Museum and the two companies, Deep Sea Productions and Marin Mätteknik. Many people have thus contributed to the project, but in particular I would like to acknowledge Malcolm Dixelius, Carl Douglas, Björn Hagberg, Joakim Holmlund, Fred Hocker, Ola Oscarsson and Martin Widman.

Archaeological fieldwork is something you learn by doing. Through the years I have had the opportunity to work with Jonathan Adams and Harry Alopaeus, from whom I have learned a lot about wreck-recording. Harry's words of wisdom – that 'every wreck has its own method' – have been running through my head while writing this book, especially while finishing chapter 3.

Of course this thesis was not written out at sea or underwater, but within the solid walls of Södertörn University. I definitely must express my gratitude to *The Foundation for Baltic and East European Studies* for financing my project. Great support including navigating all the practicalities has been provided by the administrative staff at the Baltic and East European Graduate School (BEEGS) and later at the Institution for History and Contemporary Studies. Not least, Jorid Palm has done a fantastic job with the necessary paperwork.

I am very grateful for all the feedback on drafts of the manuscript. In addition to my supervisors, Anna Mc Williams, Patrik Höglund and Oscar Törnqvist have read and commented. I also want to thank Kerstin Cassel for delivering some really important notes and observations at the final seminar. The book has greatly benefited from these. I also appreciated the discussions with the abovementioned colleagues, as well as Björn Nilsson and Hans Bolin and others at seminars, in corridors and while indulging in breaded fish at Matmakarna. Thanks also to Ingvar Sjöblom for helping me with the archive material concerning the *Constantia*.

I also want to thank those anonymous peer reviewers for commenting on papers related to this thesis. These have sometimes been positive, but sometimes also very negative and harsh. Irrespective of which, I have learnt a lot from these, not least how delicate the relationship can sometimes be between archaeology, history and historical archaeology. I would also like to thank Leos Müller for taking his time and offering an historian's view on these matters.

Kristin Bornholdt Collins deserves to be acknowledged for a fantastic job with the language. In the same way, I wish to thank Per Lindblom, Jonathan Robson and everyone else involved at the library for turning the manuscript into a book.

Special thanks go to my wife, Mirja Arnshav, for continuous discussions, comments on texts and general encouragement along the way, which has been of invaluable help. Finally, I thank my kids – Astrid, Torun and Ivar – for constantly reminding me that there are more important things in life than old, half-rotten ships.

Flemingsberg, 5 August 2014.

Contents

Abstract	3
Acknowledgments	5
1. Introduction	9
Sources that describe *fluits*	12
The *Mother of all Trades*	13
Aim of thesis	14
2. Historical archaeology and the Baltic Sea	21
A maritime perspective	28
Between artefact and text	30
Ship Archaeology and Naval Architecture	31
Well-preserved wrecks	34
3. From wrecks to everyday life	37
Things in everyday life	37
Method	40
Recording shipwrecks	41
In dialogue with ship-timbers	47
To present ships	49
4. Everyday *fluits*	53
The 'Jutholmen Wreck'	53
A contrasting picture	76
The *Anna Maria*	77
Clues from other sources	81
The 'Ghost Ship'	85
Quarters	88
The 'Lion Wreck'	92
Conclusion	96
5. Embarking *fluits*	101
Being-in-the-*fluit*	102
Sleeping	104
Eating	105
The privy	110

Social structure	114
The *Fluit* as lodging for the town	118

6. *Fluits* at war — 125

The armed merchantman	126
The *Constantia*	127
The *Spanienfararen*	135
Manning the naval *fluit*.	139
Before the mast	142
Approaching the stern	147
Conclusion	148

7. Urbanism under sail – the exterior of the *fluit* — 151

A view of Stockholm	154
Name	155
Who is the Hoekman?	165
Knightheads	170
Fluits in Stockholm	175
Swedish attitudes towards trade	176

8. Conclusions — 181

Sammanfattning (Swedish Summary) — 189

Glossary — 201

References — 205

1. Introduction

Shipbuilders, skippers and other curious people, from near and from far, travelled to Hoorn in Nord Holland to look at the new ship. A prominent merchant, Pieter Janszoon Liorne, had turned his view of the ideal merchant vessel into reality. According to D. Velius, the city's chronicler, it had resulted in a 'crazy and unusual design'. For instance the length-to-beam ratio of Liorne's new ship, was 4:1, which was considered exceptionally long in 1595 when it all took place (De Vries &Van Der Woude 1997:357, Hoving 1995:47f, Hoving & Emke 2000:34, Ketting 2006:9–13, Unger 1978:36ff, 1994:121, Wegener 2003:20).

This popular and often cited account regarding the 'invention' of the *fluit* portrays its introduction as if it were a sudden 'flash of genius'. Most writers on the matter agree that the development of the type had a much longer prelude, and was in fact the result of gradual improvements over time. Irrespective of its validity the account clearly reveals that by the end of the sixteenth century there existed a ship type called a *fluit*, which had some specific characteristics.

Seen from the side a *fluit* looks just like any old three-masted sailing ship. The mainmast and the foremast have square sails and the aftermost mizzenmast has a triangular lateen-sail occasionally supplemented with some smaller sails on the bowsprit and mizzenmast.

The particularities of the hull of a *fluit's* hull become apparent when seen from above or from astern. From above the outline of the hull appears as a rectangle box with slightly rounded corners. Seen in cross section the sides of the hull slope inwards, so-called 'tumble-home', which result in very narrow upper works. The rounded lower parts of the stern are crowned by a narrow flat transom, giving it a pronounced pear-shape (Fig. 1.1). It might be that this shape, which stern-on gave the impression that the after works looked something like a thinly shaped glass, a flute, is the origin of the name (Unger 1992:121). Others have argued that the name, which is spelled *fluit* or *fluyt* is related to the English word fluid (which is related to *flow*), meaning 'floating' (Cederlund 1988:45–55). The English used the word *flyboats* (Barbour 1930:279f). Below I have decided to spell it *fluit*, simply because this is a frequently used and universally accepted spelling.

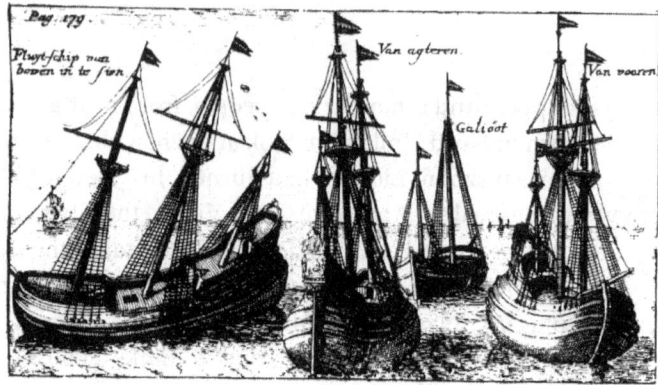

Figure 1.1: Fluits depicted from three angles in Nicolaes Witsen's treatise on shipbuilding, the 1690 edition (after Cederlund 1982b:36).

It is sometimes argued that the hull-shape, with the prominent 'tumblehome' and the narrow deck, was a response to the Sound Toll (cf. Hoving 1995:47, De Vries & Van Der Woude 1997:357), which was calculated on the basis of the breadth of the upper deck. There are however several other reasons for building a hull with this shape. Keeping the centre of gravity low is perhaps the most obvious. The idea that the hull shape of the *fluit* was adjusted to cut costs probably derives from the general reputation of the Dutch merchants at the time. Creating a ship type that kept costs to a minimum becomes just another way to confirm their superiority and skill when it came to making profit. There are several reasons to return to these ideas in the following chapters.

The *fluit* was a total success. From the end of the sixteenth century to the mid eighteenth century *fluits* were amongst the most common type of merchant vessels in Northern Europe and the Baltic Sea. They were easy and cheap to build thanks to standardization of design as well as a technological improvements, such as the sawmill (Unger 1978:7). Another important advantage of the type was that it could be sailed and operated with proportionally small crews. While a *fluit* might be handled by twelve or thirteen men, another ship of similar size could not be managed with fewer than seventeen (Kirby & Hinkkanen 2000:189, Lucassen & Unger 2011:3–44, for discussion regarding ton-to-man ratio, see Van Tielhof & Van Zanden 2011:49, Van Zanden & Van Tielhof 2009:289–403).

1. INTRODUCTION

The *fluit* was a 'multi-purpose' vessel, a ship that with slight adjustments could meet a wide range of demands. Even if the term embraces a range of ships which share some important characteristics, there are variations with important differences. The size of *fluits* varied considerably. The smallest versions, sometimes referred to as the *boot*, were 86 feet at most (around 24 m), whereas the largest versions were 140 feet (just over 39 m) (Hoving 1995:49) and larger. Others claim that a *fluit* could be as short as 78 feet (around 21.8 m) (Cederlund 1983:33).

Variations of the basic concept did not only affect the size, but included some special features connected to the trades in which these ships were used. A lengthened version, dubbed *Noortsvaarders*, was developed with orts in the bow and stern for loading long beams and timbers; and there was also the *Ostervaarders*, especially designed for the shallow harbours of the Baltic Sea (Cederlund 1983:33ff, 1995:68ff). Other 'specials' were the *Spaensvaerder* and the *Straetsvaerder*, so called because they were used in the trade with Portugal or Spain and the Mediterranean (through the straits). From the exterior, they differed from the other varieties through the beakhead (Hoving 1995:49f, Unger 1992:126ff). The *Vereenigde Oost-Indische Compagnie, VOC,* (United East India Company), employed a number of *fluits* (see overview in Ketting 2006). *Fluits* were also used as whalers which are easy to distinguish in depictions as they have davits on the sides for lifting whaling boats.

There are also a number of ships which are very similar but which are not always labelled as *fluits*. The *katschip* for instance was a cheaper version of the *fluit*, with a shallower draught and a simplified rig (Cederlund 1995:68, Hoving 1995:51f, Ketting 2006:100ff). The versions of the *fluit* mentioned above were relatively lightly armed and most often they did not carry guns at all, which was one of the prerequisites for having a small crew. According to Richard Unger, '(t)he lightly built fluyt was of little use in war. It was almost defenseless and when *fluits* carried guns the complement was small. In wartime, rather than build stronger merchant ships, the Dutch resorted to convoys' (Unger 1978:38, 2011:257).

A common expression within the navy was that ships were armed 'en flute'. This means that most guns were removed in order to clear deckspace, for example to transport troops. Some *fluits* however, were really heavily armed, with a number of gunports along the hull side. These *fluits* sailed along the specialized warships in several European navies, from the

French to the Swedish (Lavery 1992:111ff, Unger 1992:122, 2011:257). In Sweden merchant vessels were entitled to a reduction in customs rates if they could be used by the navy in wartime (Ahlström 1997:103–104, Glete 2010:434ff). This is something we have reason to return to in chapter 7.

Sources that describe *fluits*

Accounts that describe *fluits* with any detail or accuracy are remarkably few, particularly considering the vast quantity of ships built. They appear to have been so numerous that they became almost invisible. Constructional drawings of *fluits* have never existed as these ships were designed and built by rule of thumb and through copying previously built ships. The reason for this was the inability to theoretically calculate and to predict the qualities and sailing performance in beforehand. The 'same ship' was built repeatedly, over and over again, but in different sizes. This of course was a coincidence that obstructed elaboration and development of new designs (Hoving 2012:15ff, Landström 1980).

The few drawings that have survived up to our time were produced for the basis of discussion or as illustrations to literature (Witsen 1979:160ff, Rålamb 1943: 25, plate G.). In the *Scheepwartsmuseum* in Amsterdam there is a preserved seventeenth-century drawing of a *fluit*, signed F. C. Keyzer. Of particular interest on this drawing is the presence of five different scale bars, meaning that the drawing could be used to describe *fluits* in five different sizes – from 90 to 130 feet (Hoving 1995:48, Hoving & Emke 2000:45).

To the depictions one should also add models. Slightly more than a handful of contemporary models of *fluits* and associated types have survived. How representative these models are, when compared to the real thing, may of course be questioned (Hoving & Emke 2000:49, Hoving 2005:17ff, Petrejus 1967:81ff). The majority of the votive ships that are preserved from the seventeenth century are generally correct regarding details, whereas the proportions are naive. There are a few *fluits* among these votive ships, which I will return to in chapter 7.

But neither drawings nor models provide any thorough account on how the interiors of these ships were arranged. The few preserved drawings commonly reveal the location of bulkheads and deck levels, but they do not reveal what facilities were installed in these rooms, how the *fluit* functioned as lodging for the people aboard and what they were doing in there. *Fluits* are often present in depictions of seventeenth-century urban harbour views, as well as in the background of dramatic sea battle scenes. They are easily identified by their characteristic pear-shaped stern. But, as noted by Ab Hoving, *fluits* are 'seldom portrayed with the loving attention to detail expended on men-of-war or East Indianmen' (1995:47).

The *Mother of all Trades*

In the seventeenth century the Dutch Republic was Sweden's main trading partner. The Baltic trade was referred to as the *Moedernegotie* (the Mother of all Trades) (Noldus 2005: 8, Fahlborg 1923:206, van Tielhof 2002). The Dutch dominance is illustrated through the fact that the English, the competing economic superpower, regarded the Baltic as 'the lost trades' (Barbour 1930: 267). *Fluits* formed the tool in the story of economic success in the period later known as *De Gouden Eeuw* (the Golden Age) of the Dutch Republic and *stormaktstiden* (the Swedish Empire) in Sweden. In fact, the economic growth during the period is sometimes explained through the 'invention' of this very ship type (Hansson 2002:216–218, Hoving & Emke 2000:35, van Royen 1992:153, Van Zanden & Van Tielhof 2009:389–403).

The cooperation between Sweden and the Dutch Republic relied on mutual dependency. The Swedish territory stretched over a huge landmass, nearly surrounding the Baltic Sea, and consisted of sparsely populated districts and countries conquered by war. The economy relied on the export of raw materials such as iron, tar and copper. The Dutch Republic consisted of a small, densely populated area with an economy relying on massive foreign trade and of colonies. Raw material was exported to the Republic, while finished products and skilled labour and know-how were brought back (Fahlborg 1923: 205–281, Fahlström 1947, Noldus, 2002:14, 2005, Müller 1998, van Zanden and van Tielhof, 2009: 389–403). The shipbuilding industry was typical of this co-operation. Wood, iron and tar were exported to the Low Countries, where these products were turned into ships. In return, ships or shipbuilders were imported to the Baltic area.

But the Dutch influence on Swedish society was much more profound than that. The art, architecture and clothing styles, indeed taste in general, that arrived in Sweden, either through production skills or finished products, are all quite revealing. The influence was also of a more ideological or cultural character. The Dutch merchants, the burghers of cities like Amsterdam, Enkhuisen, or Lieden, were a powerful and influential force in their home country as well as overseas. During the course of the seventeenth century their wealth alongside their societal influence increased considerably in Sweden too. The term 'Skeppsbro nobility', which derives from the name of the main quay for merchant ships in Stockholm, is used to define these merchants, who had grown prosperous from trade. Many of these were Dutch immigrants. The influence of Dutch attitudes towards trade and commerce in Swedish society was not unproblematic as it progressed down a collision course with the ideology of Swedish estate society. Not least, the Swedish aristocracy was for instance very anti-mercantile in the early seventeenth century (cf. Englund 1989, Noldus 2004:7ff, Stadin 2009:421, Nováky 1993:215ff). The vast majority of goods, commodities, ideas, people, competence and so on, everything that moved in between these two countries, travelled aboard *fluits*.

Aim of thesis

The Swedish and Dutch relationships during the period, the Dutch dominance in the Baltic trade, the Swedish raw material export, the emergence of nascent capitalism, the Dutch influence on Swedish society in the seventeenth century, the Dutch engagement in the conflicts that threatened the Baltic trade and so on, are all quite familiar stories, which have been told by writers from various academic disciplines in the past (for example see Fahlborg 1923, Fahlström 1947, Heckscher 1940, Müller 1998, Noldus 2002, 2005, Van Tielhof 2002, Van Tielhof & Van Zanden 2011, Van Zanden & Van Tielhof 2009, Unger 2011).

Besides its economic significance the *fluit* has achieved a great deal of attention from authors, model builders and ship-enthusiasts in general. Thus, there are several texts that perfectly fulfil the objective to describe the development and history of this iconic ship type (see for instance Emke 2001, 2004, Hoving 1995:34–54, Hoving & Emke 2000, Ketting 2006, Landström 1961:154, Lavery 1992:106–115, Unger 1978, 1994, van Beylen 1970:101–109, Wegener 2003). There is no need to repeat it all here.

1. INTRODUCTION

Several archaeologists and others have thoroughly discussed different techniques employed in seventeenth-century Dutch shipbuilding, including *fluits* and associated old ship types (cf. Cederlund 1988:45–55, 1995, Hoving 2012, Lemeé 2006, Maarleveld 1994:153–163, 2013:348–357). Hence there exists what one may refer to as a 'grand narrative' of this type of vessel, including how they were built and the trade in which they were used. The question, then, is what else is there to add?

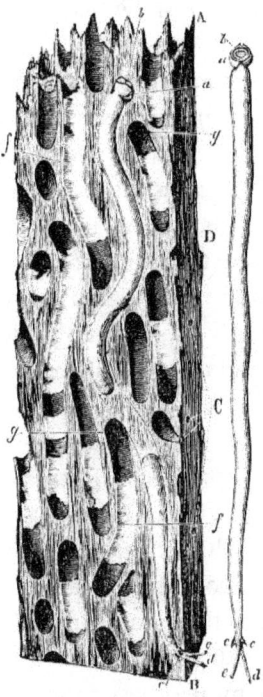

Figure 1.2: An illustration showing the Teredo Navalis, commonly referred to as the shipworm, and what it does to wood (after Baumhauer 1878).

It goes without saying that all of the thousands of voyages that were made on the Baltic Sea did not reach their aimed for destination. Regardless of whether the foundering was due to storms, navigational failings, rotten planking, icing or anything else, a certain number of *fluits* have ended up at the bottom of the sea. Down in this dusky cold environment, the conditions for preservation are optimal. The shipworm (Fig. 1.2), which can erase an entire wooden ship in a few years, cannot survive in this environment due to low salinity. As a consequence many of the *fluits*, and a lot of other unfortunate vessels, still remain intact at the seafloor after hundreds of years.

The aim of this thesis is to develop a new approach to studying well-preserved wrecks, like the ones found in the Baltic Sea. Through the coincidence that in some cases these can be reconstructed to more or less complete buildings, they can also be analysed as such. Inspired by archaeology, which asserts and studies use, everyday life and practice in buildings and houses, I wish to show that such approaches also are valid on board ships.

Through examining a number of wrecked *fluits* I wish to show that these can be used to highlight aspects which are not accessible through other sources. Wrecks can also provide insights, nuances and new perspectives on relatively familiar historical episodes. They can also be used to refine and correct some errors in previous assumptions.

It has been recognized for quite some time (see chapter 2) that conditions for preservation in the Baltic are uniquely favourable, a fact often cited by journalists, divers, museum professionals, cultural heritage bureaucrats, academics and others. This being so, it is quite remarkable how little archaeological research that has been carried out using these well-preserved shipwrecks. Despite claims of maritime archaeologists being obsessed with shipwrecks (Flatman 2003:143–157, Ransley 2005:621–629) the effort put into recording and trying to understand the still standing hulls of the Baltic Sea has been negligible.

In most cases the names of these vessels, their crews, where they were heading, what happened as they sank and so on has been long forgotten. When the wrecks are rediscovered on the seafloor, they are large, manifest, well-preserved, more or less complete, buildings from a period traditionally highlighted by historians.

This thesis does not set out to *explain* these seemingly silent physical remains through reading written accounts. There are definitely competent historians more suited for such tasks. As will be described in more detail in chapter 2, when archaeology is applied to periods where written sources are available it sometimes has a tendency of becoming an expensive way of repeating what the historians already knew (cf. Andrén 1997:13, 1998:3, citing Peter Sawyer).

Instead this study springs from the conviction that material culture, things, like for instance ships, has the capacity to contribute with a dimension to our understanding of human life and experience which is not directly accessible in documents. Such recognition may be argued to run along a general trend within the humanities to 'return to things' (cf. Hicks & Beadry 2010, Knappet & Malafouris 2008, Latour 2005, Trentmann 2009:283–307) and archaeology may be argued to be 'The discipline of Things' *par excellance* (Olsen et al. 2012, Olsen 2010).

Being-in-the-world involves an immediate engagement with things. Things 'sneak upon us' and become so integrated in our lives that we often don not even recognize their existence. Hence, the things that have greatest impact upon us are the ones we probably are not aware of. The *fluit*, the most common merchant ship on the Baltic Sea, the workhorse in the 'Mother Trade', the everyday setting for thousands of sailors and a self-evident feature in any North European harbour city, definitely was one of the fundamental components in the formation of seventeenth and early eighteenth-century society. They were crucial, but at the same time mundane, aspects of this society; components that have been long forgotten and lost in the mists of time. They were so common that they were essentially taken for granted; they were ubiquitous. Nobody found it necessary to waste time and effort describing them.

Even if shipwrecks form the departure point, this thesis does not set out to make a detailed account of how these ships were built or their sailing performance, which are common research topics within the archaeology of ships (see chapter 2). Instead, this study studies these ships as representing humanized space. The space where all those trivial, more or less unconscious, actions of everyday life took place. The reconstructed ship allows us to 'go aboard' and experience the vessel as a setting for all those activities that form the everyday.

Thanks to the ideal conditions for preservation in the Baltic Sea, several of these ships have the capacity to bring aspects of everyday life of the past into the present. Beginning with a discussion on human life and its everyday entanglement with things, chapter 3 deals with some considerations on how to transform the remains at the seabed into a format suitable for archaeological analysis. As it is never possible to record it all, the chapter aims to sort out what aspects of the wreck are needed in order to utilize the source for discussions concerning the lived experience of ships. Surveying, recording and reconstructing wrecks is here undertaken with the objective to recreate everyday human environments.

Taking four surveyed wrecks as its material evidence, chapter 4 aims to reconstruct the everyday environment on board *fluits*. The focus is on the location of decks, bulkheads, windows, ports, hatches and similar physical structures that define rooms and direct human action. Besides reconstructing these rooms, the chapter also sets out to discuss what features were present and what kinds of activities were carried out in them. It also consders where people were lodged, where they ate, and so on. In this account it is necessary to review a few earlier statements and interpretations of spatial arrangements on board these ships. More information such as drawings, photos, measurements and other descriptions exist concerning the wrecks covered in this chapter. However, as these details have been published in reports and papers elsewhere, which are referred to in the text, there is no attempt to present a full catalogue to accompany this section of the study.

In order to reach a more thorough understanding of everyday life aboard *fluits* it is necessary to add action to the reconstructed vessels. It is argued that humans always have some sort of spatial consciousness. Being in a ship, or any other environment for that matter, is always a matter of submitting to the conditions set by the surrounding world. The wrecks provide an opportunity to discuss working, eating, sleeping and visiting the vital seat, the more or less unconscious rituals of the everyday. What kind of life is revealed from these reconstructed ships? Or, to put it slightly differently: what kind of human life could be lived inside these ships? The aim of chapter 5 is thus not just to discuss what people did with *fluits*, but even more importantly: what *fluits* made people do.

Besides fulfilling the perhaps quite obvious and familiar tasks such as transporting goods and people, a ship holds together its crew, directs their movement patterns and controls their interaction and upholds a social order. The fully working ship consists of hull, rig, provisions, crew, and a whole lot of other actors that together form a functioning unit that may be described as a network of human and non-human actors (Law 2000). Through their interaction they constantly reproduce the fully working ship. In its moored form the *fluit* becomes a part of the urban environment, whereas conditions on board the sailing ship differ. When ships are moored they are part of the town, together with houses, churches, streets, quays and so forth. The network around a *fluit* reshapes and the ship works in a way that differs from the 'same' ship when it sails.

1. INTRODUCTION

As argued in the chapters 4 and 5, the spatial arrangement as revealed from wrecks differs from how *fluits* have been reconstructed before. But they also reveal a picture of a social environment that differs in several ways from the hierarchical structures on board naval ships. Chapter 6 aims to highlight this further through discussing the means that were taken when transforming a merchant *fluit* into a fully-fledged naval ship. Together with the greater number of people and guns that embark comes abstract notions such as hierarchy and duty. These become evident through a discussion drawn from the lived experience of a ship transformed for war service. All on board have to be arranged and held together to transform into a lethal unit, the warship. The purpose of the interior of the naval *fluit* is partly to make people behave in ways, and carry out acts, that they perhaps do not want to.

Fluits, together with many other objects, materialize the urban merchant's culture of the seventeenth and early eighteenth centuries. But in contrast to other forms of architecture, like the famous Dutch 'halsgevel' (neck gable) house, *fluits* are mobile architectural units. Chapter 7 focuses on the exterior of *fluits*, and highlights the appearance of these ships. The discussion concerns the kinds of sculptures these ships carried and what they mean. The analysis then continues with an attempt to place these ships in an urban setting in order to discern what insights the awareness of the sculptural messages expressed in the exteriors of *fluits* adds to our understanding of the early modern urban landscape. *Fluits* set sail and move between different ports, clearly signalling the specific ideology and attitudes towards trade for which the Dutch had become famous (cf. Schama 1988, Weber 1978).

During the seventeenth century the attitudes towards commerce and trade changed thoroughly in Swedish society as well (see Englund 1989, Noldus 2002, 2005, Nováky 1993). Cities like Amsterdam, Stockholm, Lisbon and other metropolises all compressed their own versions of urbanism and commerce. The *fluits*, though, are the 'same objects' that moved between these ports, hence the title 'Urbanism under Sail'. How were they perceived in their different ports? What did they do to the societies, towns, harbours and municipalities into which they sailed and were moored?

The study is grounded upon the recognition that human life and society as a whole is dependent on the things and other non-human actors in it. Despite claims that Actor-Network-Theory, or ANT, and phenomenology are sometimes argued to be irreconcilable (see discussion with Dolwick 2009, Latour 2005, Riis 2008, Olsen 2010:13,73f) references to both schools of thought will appear as guides along the way.

The thesis is written from a Swedish vantage point, which may be worth pointing out as the *fluit* was originally developed in, and is associated with, the Dutch Republic. The thesis does not include any previously unpublished archival records from either Sweden or the Netherlands. As mentioned already, there are certainly historians better suited for such tasks.

My hope is that it will show that shipwrecks can reveal aspects of past societies that are not directly accessible through other sources. And, that wrecks are valuable resources worthy of study even if there are no historical documents relating to that specific vessel.

2. Historical archaeology and the Baltic Sea

As mentioned above, the conditions for preservation of shipwrecks are favourable in the brackish water of the Baltic Sea. Nowhere else are there so many well-preserved early modern wrecks. With this in mind it is somewhat puzzling that there have not been more attempts to undertake practical archaeological fieldwork aiming to record these remains. Whereas raised artefacts, guns and ship timbers have been used as illustrations for texts, the still standing ship-structures, the really unique aspect of these wrecks, have attracted surprisingly little attention.

The aim of this chapter is to provide an overview of the kinds of surveys that, nevertheless, have been conducted in the past. The account does not aspire to be complete. It is rather an attempt to assess how previous wreck-researchers have used the archaeological potential of shipwrecks. The account is divided into two sections. The first section aims to sort out the relation between archaeology and shipwrecks on the one hand and written sources and history on the other. The focus here is mainly on research carried out in the Baltic Sea (for a more general overview see for instance Adams 2003:2–46, 2013a:1–51, Bass 2011:3–21). The second section concerns the archaeology of post-mediaeval wrecks from a naval architectonical point of view. For example, how they are used as sources for studying methods of ship construction and similar. Here, we will have to go on some excursions to other corners of the world.

Important to bear in mind is that the well-preserved wrecks of the Baltic Sea are from a period traditionally studied by historians. Prehistoric ships and boats, either found in graves, carved on stone, or occurring elsewhere, have been studied by archaeologists since the very introduction of the discipline. At the beginning of the twentieth century neither of the sub-disciplines, Historical Archaeology nor Maritime Archaeology, was established in Sweden (cf. Andrén 1997, 1998, Cederlund 1983, 1997, Lovén 1996:11–18, Mogren et al. 2009). A long time elapsed before post-medieval ships achieved the status and treatment in terms of antiquarian protection and archaeological attention as the prehistoric sites. In spite of this, several surveys of medieval and post-medieval ships and boats were carried out in Sweden and the Baltic Sea area before the Second World War.

For instance building-antiquarian Tord Nordberg led the survey of the 'Riddarholmen ship' in the middle of Stockholm 1930 (Nordberg 1930, 1931, Fischer 1983, Hansson 1960:42ff) and a clinker-built ship, dated to the sixteenth century, was found and surveyed in Västerås in 1935 (Eriksson 2004:15-17).

Perhaps the best known pre-war survey was carried out in Kalmar harbour between 1933 and 1934. An area identical to the medieval harbour was totally emptied from water and no less than 18 hulls and fragments of some additional boats were discovered. These were dated to the medieval period up to the sixteenth and seventeenth centuries (Åkerlund 1951). Harald Åkerlund, a draughtsman, supervised the survey and later he also built scale models for reconstruction purposes. He may be regarded as a forerunner in this field as similar methods are still in use today (Cederlund 1981a, 1983:44, compare Lemée 2006, Steffy 1994), primarily when it comes to studies in boat- and shipbuilding techniques, see below.

The interest in Åkerlund's boat-surveys appears to have been minimal among contemporary professional archaeologists, which may be regarded to run along the general scope to focus on prehistory. Ruins and similar medieval remains started to achieve antiquarian interest, but from the point of view of architectural and art historians (Andrén 1997, 1998, Lovén 1996:11-18, Mogren et al. 2009).

Even if the post-medieval shipwrecks did not appeal to archaeologists at that time, there were others that did embrace these relics with more enthusiasm. In fact, in the early twentieth century there was generally an increasing interest in maritime and nautical objects; a tendency that may be seen all over the world. A number of old sailing ships, obsolete since the introduction of steam, were rescued and turned into museum ships. Several maritime museums were opened showing objects from naval model chambers (Nordlinder 1988:25-35). Together with paintings of famous sea battles, cannons, sculptures and flag exhibitions were assembled, commemorating a heroic naval past (cf. Sigmound & Wouter 2007).

In England the Society for Nautical Research was founded in 1911, encouraging research into seafaring and shipbuilding. Their journal *Mariner's Mirror* has published many articles concerning wrecks of post-medieval ships (for an overview, see Mc Grail 2011:37–62), written by authors from several nations, including Sweden.

Figure 2.1: Director of 'Olschanski's Salvage and Diving Enterprises on Sunken Ships' Leonard Olschanski (1882–1943) to the left and Commanding Officer Lenny Stackell (1875–1957) to the right, posing together with a raised iron cannon and other objects recovered from Riksäpplet, sunk in 1676. The picture was taken in 1921 on deck of the salvage vessel Sigrid (SMM Fo86859C).

Several salvage operations on early modern warships had already been carried out in Sweden by the late nineteenth century. Artefacts, such as cannons, gun-carriages and cannon balls, were either sold to private collectors or included in what was to become the National Maritime Museum. An early example of the salvage operations is the work carried out on *Riksäpplet* (1676). In 1868 three iron guns and an anchor was raised from the wreck (Cederlund 1983:39). At the beginning of the following century many similar operations were carried out. The practical salvage work was carried out by commercial diving companies but was supervised by naval officers with an interest in history. For instance Commanding Officer, marine painter and naval historian Jacob Hägg (1839–1931) was involved in the salvage work carried out at the Danish ship *Enigheden* (1979) in 1909. Another naval officer, Lenny Stackell (1876–1957), was involved in the salvage of *Riksäpplet* in the 1920s (Fig. 2.1). The practical underwater work was carried out by the salvage company Olschanski, and the purpose was to recover black oak, which was a popular material for manufacturing furniture (Cederlund 1983:38, 1997, 2006, 2012).

The raised artefacts were either sold to private collectors or to what later became museums. The cannon balls, deadeyes, gun carriages and similar were used as illustrations for the grand narrative of the Swedish Navy in exhibitions as well as publications. Among the latter the substantial publication *Svenska flottans historia* (History of the Swedish Navy) consisting of three volumes, each over 500 pages long, has a prominent position. It is richly illustrated with preserved drawings, paintings and ship-models, alongside photos of various artefacts, blocks and deadeyes, guns and ammunition raised from sunken naval ships. From an archaeological point of view, it is important to note that the artefacts are illustrations, a material curiosity, to confirm an already existing story written on the basis of historical sources, one that essentially could be told without the things (cf. Lybeck 1942).

Among the pioneer investigations on early modern wrecks in Sweden one must mention Commanding Officer Carl Ekman as he is sometimes referred to as an early underwater archaeologist. Most notably he surveyed the remains of Swedish sixteenth-century man-of-war *Elefanten* (the Elephant), between the years 1933 and 1939, and employed several innovative methods during fieldwork (Adams 2003:3, 2013a:3, 87–99, Gould 2000:234f). Ekman saw great potential in the study of wrecks, possibilities beyond the mere tautological and illustrative role they were given by his contemporary researchers in the field. Perhaps the most notable expression of this is the fact that his fieldwork included a not insignificant amount of recording under water (cf. ibid., also Cederlund 1983:188–200, Ekman 1934:6, 1942:89–98).

To sum up there existed some researchers who had an interest in and knew a great deal about the terminology of rigs, construction of hulls, names of various ship-types and similar by the mid twentieth century. These were modellers, naval officers, marine painters, retired seamen and others – not archaeologists. Their prime source material consisted of preserved models, paintings as well as the few historical ships that were still afloat or towed into dry-docks as museum ships. To some extent, remains of sunken ships were taken into account, as Ekman and Åkerlund did with the *Elefanten* and Kalmar surveys. The common practice however was to use raised effects from sunken ships as illustrations and to add a little extra flavouring to historical sources. The story itself was told on the basis of written texts and to a large extent centred on the glorious deeds of the navy.

After the Second World War the clearance, reconstruction and rebuilding of the demolished cities of Europe was an important factor in the evolution of historical archaeologies in general (Andrén 1997:41, 1998:31ff, Larsson 2009:147–160). The study of post-medieval ships was no exception. For instance, the outspoken purpose of the *Centralne Muzeum Morskie* (CMM) situated in Gdansk, Poland was to salvage artefacts from the sea as a way to redress the losses of material cultural heritage sustained during the War. Most historic districts in Poland's coastal towns and cities were reduced to ruins. Sunken ships were used to enrich museum collections with valuable new artefact assemblages (Ossowski 2008:35, 1985:421–435). In a similar way the land reclamation projects in the Netherlands, from 1930s onwards, have revealed several hundreds of shipwrecks, dated from the fourteenth to the nineteenth centuries (cf. Hocker & Vlierman 1996, Maarleveld & Van Ginkel 1990, Oosting 1991, Oosting & Van Holk 1994, Vlierman 1997a, 1997b, 2003:44–48).

The post-war period saw another important factor in the evolution of the study of wrecks, namely the development of the modern, self-contained diving equipment. In the late 1950s Jacques Cousteau (a French naval officer this time!) and his Undersea Research group excavated a wreck outside Marseilles using the new aqualung he had developed together with engineer Emile Cagnan (Adams 2003:3, Bass 1966:125, 2011:5f). Even if the techniques used were by no means up to archaeological standards, Cousteau's excavation, but most notably, his popular films and books regarding the exploration of the underwater world, provided a consciousness about 'its treasures' in a sphere that stretched far beyond archaeology.

But there were archaeological initiatives to follow. In 1960 American archaeologist George Bass and a team excavated a wreck at Cape Galedonia outside Greece. The site, located at 30 m deep, was surveyed according to archaeological standards. When Bass recruited his team, he sought archaeological skills rather than diving skills. Bass thought that it was easier to teach someone with professional skills to dive than the other way around (Adams 2003:4, Bass 1966:125, Muckelroy 1978:15). I think that the fact that they were surveying a prehistoric site was of prime importance for Bass' decision to employ archaeologists rather than divers. This was classical archaeology carried out under water. To a large extent, the topics discussed from the results of these surveys revolve around trade, influences and connections across the Mediterranean (see Bass et al. 1972), but also, which we have reason to get back to, ship construction.

The 1960s were the decennium when the potential of underwater archaeology was realized internationally, and on a large scale. In addition to the project mentioned there were several other notable projects formed around recent discoveries. For example, the cog in Bremerhaven, excavated and salvaged in its entirety in 1962 (Ellmers 1994:29–46), and the Viking ships discovered in Roskilde Denmark 1957–62 (Olsen & Crumlin-Pedersen 1978, Crumlin-Pedersen & Olsen 2002).

Vasa and Riks-Wasa

Here one cannot avoid mentioning the relocation and salvaging of *Vasa* (1628). The prelude to this project may be traced in the pre-War salvage operations on sunken warships described above. These were continued after the War as the navy conducted their diving training at the sites of famous naval ships. For instance the *Riksäpplet* site was revisited (Hamilton 1957:163–183). The individuals initially involved in salvaging *Vasa* were mariners not archaeologists.

2. HISTORICAL ARCHAEOLOGY AND THE BALTIC SEA

Figure 2.2: In the 1960s archaeology was still more or less synonymous with the study of prehistory. The picture shows a commercial salvage company demolishing the remains of the Riks-Wasa in 1967 (SMM, Fo 1449AB).

One important person who engaged in the post-medieval shipwrecks in Sweden, after the Second World War, was engineer Anders Franzén (1918–1993) (see Cederlund & Hocker 2006:140ff). Franzén was involved in the diving and salvage operations at the *Riksäpplet* and *Gröne Jägaren* (1676) sites in the 1950s, and had formulated a research programme consisting of 12 wrecks that he regarded of prime interest. All twelve were warships. Franzén was in fact quite extraordinary in his disinterest in merchant vessels. Among the reasons he mentions is that merchant ships 'primarily consist of their cargo', but also that the captains were illiterate (Franzén 1981:8ff, 1982:6–9, 1985:15, my translation). According to this perspective the potential of a wreck is *always* limited as no more than an illustration to a history told from texts. The *Vasa* project started out as an event aiming to illustrate the grand narrative of a period of great power in Sweden and later evolved into an archaeological project (cf. Cederlund 1994, 1997, 2006).

The uncertainty that still prevailed in the 1960s regarding the archaeological potential of post-medieval shipwrecks is illustrated by a fascinating paradox. While the *Vasa* (1628) was raised, conserved and put on display as a national icon, her precursor, known as *Riks-Wasa*, built in 1599 and sunk in 1623, was blown up and salvaged in pieces (Fig. 2.2). The work was carried out by a private company making money out of trade in black oak. *Riks-Wasa* was the last wreck to meet this fate as the National Heritage Act was extended in 1967, so that shipwrecks, if an estimated 100 years had passed since wreckage, achieved legal protection (Arnshav 2011:39ff, Cederlund 1983:224–225).

A maritime perspective

Parallel to the introduction of juridical antiquarian protection of post-medieval shipwrecks, academic research into different maritime fields developed. Perhaps this should be seen as a response to the spontaneously grown interest in old ships and maritime matters in general among museum institutions, initiated by naval officers, retired captains, model builders and similar ship-enthusiasts. Important for this professionalization has been the introduction of *The International Journal of Nautical Archaeology and Underwater Exploration* (IJNA) (from 1984, renamed *International Journal of Nautical Archaeology*) in 1972 and the International Symposium on Boat and Ship Archaeology (ISBSA) held every third year since 1976.

In the Baltic Sea area, The Scandinavian Maritime History working group was initiated in 1966 and consisted of researchers from several disciplines. In the anthology *Ships and Shipyards, Sailors and Fishermen*, which formed a kind of manifesto, it is argued that maritime ethnology and its associated disciplines, such as archaeology, may provide a vernacular perspective challenging traditional history writing, which tends to be focused on wars and kings (Hasslöf 1970:9–20, Hasslöf 1972:9–19). Maritime material culture provided something beyond mere confirmation of 'normative' written accounts and could be used to study the broad illiterate masses of people. It was thus an approach that stood in contrast to the naval perspective as articulated by for instance Anders Franzén as cited above (also Franzén 1981:8ff, 1982:6-9, 1985:15).

With the Act of 1967 old wrecks also became a concern for the antiquarian authorities instead of being an activity that consisted of mere salvaging, initially carried out by the divers of the navy, and later on, in reduced scale, by recreational divers (Arnshav 2011:39-44). With the boom of recreational diving in the Baltic Sea, new discoveries of old wrecks were reported to the SMM (Swedish National Maritime Museum), who had become the preferred authority in matters that concerned monuments under water. In order to build up knowledge, and to develop methods, the SMM conducted underwater fieldworks on some selected wrecks (cf. Cederlund 1981b, 1982b, Kaijser 1981, 1983). The 'Jutholmen Wreck', which we will return to in chapter 4, was one of those.

Carl Olof Cederlund's dissertation entitled *The Old Wrecks of the Baltic Sea* (1983) aimed to lay the foundation for the archaeology of the well-preserved post-medieval wrecks. In an attempt to structure the possibilities as well as the informative qualities and archaeological potential he proposes a standard for wreck investigations. One point is underlined, and this is the matter of identification (Cederlund 1983, also 1997:126). Archaeological fieldwork, to some extent, became a matter of collecting clues that would enable the identification of the ship's original identity in written sources. 'The identity of a ship is like the key that unlocks this information by linking a given ship together with a particular historical circumstance' (Cederlund 1983:69).

While the identities of sunken warships tended to remain in memory, the names of smaller craft, but also large merchant and transport vessels, tended to be long forgotten (ibid., also Ahlström 1995:24ff, 1997:30ff). The search for the lost identities of the sunken merchant ships was considered as a way to go beyond traditional history writing about wars and the kings (cf. Cederlund 1982a, 1983, 1997, compare Franzén 1982). The study of merchant ships, it was argued, was a way to reveal the history of ordinary people and the wordless illiterate masses (see discussion with Little 1994, Moreland 2001:94). From the 1970s up until the 1990s fieldwork under water that aimed to collect information leading to the identification of shipwrecks was carried out by private individuals, most notably recreational divers supervised by the SMM and Stockholm University (SU) (Cederlund 1983:49). An important actor for the development of maritime archaeology in Sweden was – and still is – the

Swedish Maritime Archaeological Society (Sw. *Marinarkeologiska Sällskapet*, or MAS), founded in 1978, where semi-professional diving archaeologists are organized on a non-profit basis.

The conditions for preservation are more or less the same on the east coast of the Baltic, and several wrecks were investigated in Finnish waters in the same way and with similar objectives as in Sweden, from the 1950s and onwards (cf. Ahlström 1995:132–165, 1997:157–198, Nurmio-Lahdenmäki 2006). Finnish historian Christian Ahlström picked up the task defined by Cederlund and developed methods for identifying anonymous shipwrecks, in Swedish and Finnish waters, through searching among documents in archives. Thanks to his careful work several wrecks of merchant ships were identified. We will return to one of these in chapter 5, the large *fluit Anna Maria*, sunk in 1709. Ahlström wrote his dissertation on the subject (1995, translated into English 1997) and together with Cederlund's dissertation these books formed a kind of research programme for Baltic Sea ship archaeology. Several wrecks were examined according to the same premises, and some of these shipwrecks did get their original names back (Ahlström 1995, 1997, Cederlund 1997, Eriksson 1995, Rönnby 2003:123–130, Rönnby & Adams 1994).

Between artefact and text

To recapitulate: the early surveys of naval vessels derived from an interest in naval history. Naval officers raised objects from the seabed to remember a history told by historical documents. The 1960s and '70s witnessed a reaction to these grand historical narratives that focused on wars, kings and 'the great men'. Instead, the new focus was on the anonymous wrecks of merchant ships. Through identifying these ships, other activities and categories of people from the past became visible.

But even if the categories of ships differed, and even if focus was on merchants rather than the king and nobility, on trading routes rather than naval and famous battles, the two schools of Baltic Sea wreck research had one particular thing in common, namely how they handled written sources in relation to the material remains. Irrespective of whether the story is known beforehand, as with a celebrated naval ship, or if the research started with an unknown wreck of a merchant vessel, written sources were used to *explain* the mute material remains at the seabed (for a similar discussion see Harpster 2013:588–622).

The situation is not unique for the study of wrecks or ships. Quite the contrary: indeed the relationship between the material remains of archaeology on the one hand, and the written sources of history on the other, is quite commonly described as that between servant and master (Adams 2003:42, Muckelroy 1978:6, referring to Clarke 1968:13). In this model the basic facts of history and the important questions about the past tend to be established by historians from the written sources. The role of archaeology in the reconstruction of the past is restricted to presentation (Andrén 1997:13ff, 1998:3, Moreland 2001:10). The basic facts of history, the historical network and the important questions about the past were all established by historians from the written sources (Moreland 2001:10).

The role of the material remains, the things dug up from the soil or salvaged from the seabed, tends to be an ancillary or supportive role only, basically reduced to illustrations. As a result, the large well-preserved wrecks at the bottom of the Baltic Sea have been left without further attention. The coherent hulls, the really unique feature of the Baltic shipwrecks, have attracted very little attention. They are seldom documented at all. The historical events can be told by written accounts alone.

This does not mean that *all* nautical or maritime archaeologists are totally uninterested in and seldom record wrecks. Indeed, at an international level there is significant interest in the detailed empirical studies of ship-remains, which are regarded as a vital field of research.

Ship Archaeology and Naval Architecture

The term 'naval architecture' is at least as old as the wrecks studied in this thesis, and was in use at least as early as in 1570 (Lemée 2006:95, Ferreiro 2007:xiii). One early example of a treatise on this topic is Joseph Furtenbach's *Architectura Navalis*, published in 1629, and covers hull design, rig and armament of ships. The treatises that followed, during the seventeenth and eighteenth centuries, had titles that altered Furtenbach's example. The second edition of Nicolaes Witsen's *Aeoloude En Hedendaegshe Scheeps-Bouw en Bestier, first published in 1671 (second edition in 1690), is entitled Architectura Navalis et Regimen (Hoving 2012, Witsen 1979).* English examples are master shipbuilder, Anthony Deane's *Doctrine on naval architecture* from 1670 (Lavery 1981) and William Sutherland's *The Ship-builders Assistant*, subtitled '*Or some essays towards completing the ART of Marine Architecture'* (1711). The latter treatises, describe, besides the methods used for shaping and erecting the hulls, how to calculate costs and similar practical matters associated with ship construction.

Perhaps the best known is Fredrik Henrik af Chapman's (1721–1808) *Architectura Navalis et Mercatoria*, a collection of drawings of different ships published in 1769. The supplementary and explaining treatise *'Tractat om skeppsbyggeriet'*, was published in 1772. Chapman is sometimes referred to as 'the inventor of naval architecture' (Lemée 2006:95, Harris 1998). The reason for this honour is the mathematical methods he developed for predicting the stability of a ship, its sailing characteristics and cargo capacity and so forth. To the topics described in the previously mentioned treatises, Chapman added the calculation of sailing qualities. Thus, what dwells in the term 'naval architecture' is about the erecting and construction of hulls and estimating sailing performance.

The topics discussed within these old treatises have a prominent position within the archaeological study of boats and ships as well. How was the hull shape determined during construction? How did the shipbuilder implement the abstract idea of the hull shape into a realized ship? Was it through using drawings or by rule of thumb? Inherent in these discussions are thus the sequence of events when the hull was assembled. Whether the hull-form was predetermined by the frames or the planking is a crucial part within this discussion – an archaeology of shipwright's problem solving so to speak (for a more thorough account on the subject shell versus skeleton, see for instance Hasslöf 1970, 1972, Hocker 2004:1–11, Lemée 2006, Maarleveld 1994:153–163, Pomey 2011:25–46).

Skimming through the proceedings of the International Symposium on Boat and Ship archaeology (ISBSA), reveals that the study of the sequence of a ship's construction has evolved to what may be regarded as a ship-archaeological paradigm. It includes detailed recording of ship timbers in order to reconstruct the construction sequence. In accordance Danish archaeologist Christian Lemée labels his recording and analysis of Renaissance shipwrecks as 'reverse naval architecture'. With such a term he wishes to encapsulate the process of producing drawings of existing ships as a parallel to the term 'reverse engineering' (Lemée 2006:97).

The vast majority of all ships and boats have a life between their 'construction sequence' and ending up as wrecks at the seabed or in the landfill. In most cases they have had an assignment-life. To a large extent, the archaeology of ships consists of discussions concerning the ability of a vessel to fulfil its tasks as gun-platform, transport-, trading-, fishing-vessel and so on. Discussions concerning sailing performance, carrying capacity and hydrodynamics are aspects added to the concept of naval architecture by persons such as Chapman. Within the archaeology of ships and boats such discussions have partially been highlighted through the aid of building replicas and experimental archaeology, which tests the methods used for construction, sailing performance as well as investigating the old sailing routes (see for instance Edberg 2002).

The technical character of ship archaeology has led to the work of boat and ship archaeology experts being seen as separate from the general archaeological debate. Ship-archaeologists are said to be obsessed with the mere source material (cf. Flatman 2003:143-157, Hocker 2003:4), screened off from the wider societal contexts (Dolwick 2009: 21–49) or stuck with discussions concerning diving, treasure-hunting and different high-tech apparatus (cf. Adams 2003:6, Ransley 2005, Wijkander 2007:66).

Some argue that the focus on describing the material, on typologies and methods for ship construction, is due to the relative youth of the discipline. According to George Bass (1983:97) the emphasis on data collection and classification is both inevitable and necessary for a new area of enquiry assembling its database (Adams 2003:7 for similar discussions see Cederlund1983:119, Hocker 2003, Muckelroy 1978:10).

Irrespective of the substance in the critique, the so often claimed obsession with ship-timbers may, at least to some extent, derive from the condition that the archaeology of naval architecture constitutes a self-limiting 'text-free zone' where archaeologists can work without competition from historians (Andrén 1997:132ff, 185, 1998:101ff,181, Moreland 2001: 21). The identity of specific vessels, the trades they were involved in, the battles fought, the biographies of the ship's owners, captains or admirals are aspects that historians are much better equipped to reveal than archaeologists (see also Harpster 2012). On the contrary, tool marks, joints, trunnels and similar, are not visible in the written documentary sources that the historians are trained to master. But, such aspects are perfectly accessible from almost the slightest fragment of a ship.

It has also been suggested that the preoccupation with the techniques used for building ships and boats is springs from the fact that the pioneers within the field came from branches and disciplines other than the humanities. Naval officers were mentioned, but researchers with a background within engineering as well as wooden ship-building have also held prominent positions within the study of naval architecture, which may have had consequences for the topics raised within the study of ship remains (Cederlund 1997:31ff, 107ff).

The underwater location of many wrecks is another factor that contributes to the reputation of maritime archaeology focusing largely on research methods. The public's interest in wrecks and other artefacts lost at sea is sometimes confused with activities such as treasure hunting. The author has noticed that it is more common to be called 'diver' than 'archaeologist' when newspapers and television, but also museums, report about different underwater archaeological projects. Underwater archaeology tends to be described in terms of Indiana Jones-inspired archaeology (Wijkander 2007:66).

Archaeologist Jesse Ransley has argued that maritime archaeology to a large extent consists of men who are researching traditionally masculine activities. Shipbuilding, naval warfare, technology, fishing, trading and colonizing within maritime archaeology is due to a more or less all-pervading masculine perspective within the sub-discipline (Ransley 2005:625). Others have suggested that underwater archaeology attracts men of action rather than men of contemplation (Adams 2003:6, or 2013a:5, citing Lenihan 1983:39).

The criticism might be explored further, but the point seems to be made. Regardless of whether there is substance in the accusations towards ship-archaeology, it is worth observing that methodology as well as naval architecture, with a focus on construction and sailing performance, appear to be hot research-topics within the sub-discipline.

Well-preserved wrecks

The well-preserved shipwrecks of the Baltic Sea, like the *fluits* in this book, are underrepresented within the archaeological studies of naval architecture. One reason for this is that they are simply not so informative from a construction sequence point of view. They do not reveal the clues necessary to build such a discussion. The relevant questions concerning constructional methods tend to bounce against the intact hull side; most notably when those queries are addressed in low visibility by a diving archaeologist, who is always, more or less, under time stress (also Eriksson 2012a:193–198).

As pointed out by building archaeologist Gunhild Eriksdotter regarding houses, 'a building can only be fully documented if it is torn apart' (Eriksdotter 2005:71, my translation). Baltic Sea shipwrecks may in this sense be compared to coherent, still standing, buildings. It is seldom possible – or desirable – to dismantle them. When wrecks are found on land, however, or in shallow water and excavated in cofferdams, dismantling the construction is fairly common (for examples see Bruseth & Turner 2005, Crumlin-Pedersen & Olsen 2002, Hocker & Vlierman 1996, Lemée 2006, Pedersen 1996, Åkerlund 1951).

An illustrative example of just how inscrutable a coherent shipwreck may be from a construction- sequence point of view, is *Vasa* (1628). As I write this text, more than fifty years have passed since her intact hull was raised from the Stockholm harbour. Despite the fact that the hull has been accessible on land for decades, archaeologists are still figuring out the methods used when the hull was built. The clues for such discussions are well hidden and sealed inside the intact hull (cf. Hocker 2011:195ff).

But, while *Vasa* may be recorded under relaxed and convenient conditions inside a museum building, an intact hull, situated under 30 m of water or more, is a far more demanding task. The conditions for gathering information for construction sequence analysis or detailed hull shape recording for calculating sailing performance and similar aspects, is further obstructed through limited access due to the underwater location. The more well-preserved the less naval architectonical information is accessible (cf. Eriksson 2012a:197).

However, even if it is of interest to the majority of ship-archaeologists today whether a *fluit* was built using shell-first or skeleton-first construction technique, this must have been of limited consideration within the ship's contemporary society. The ship-owners who ordered the vessel, the people who sailed it, those who were lodged in it, or the persons who saw the ship moored along the quay, did not see whether the hull was built using one technique or the other. Ludolf Bakhuysen, the van der Veldes, Abraham Storck and all the other artists that have depicted *fluit*s during the seventeenth century, most likely had quite vague notions about all those ship-constructional matters, which for different reasons have become the focus for decades of boat and ship archaeological research.

As a parallel, most of us have quite limited familiarity with the techniques employed when our homes were built. Even without this knowledge, we are perfectly competent to inhabit these buildings. What I would like to stress in the following chapters is that the house itself and all the things inside it, have a crucial impact on everyday life lived inside and around these buildings. The location of walls, doors and similar, set the limits for our behavioural action. The building is inherent in all those seemingly trivial routines and practices of the everyday. For this reason we shall leave the discussion about construction techniques for now. The focus of the book now turns to the finished ship, analysed with the objective of unpacking how humans interact with ships and what ships make humans do.

3. From wrecks to everyday life

Recording a large coherent shipwreck under water almost presupposes an idea of how to use, discuss and analyse the gathered information. It is a matter of searching for features considered relevant to highlight a specific issue or question, as it is never possible to record everything. The aim of this chapter is thus not to formulate an approach that is suitable for all shipwrecks at all times, answering all imaginable queries. This is an attempt to devise a strategy to unveil aspects of the lived experience of ships using wrecks as a point of departure.

In the previous chapter it was argued that intact and unidentified wrecks tend to end up in a gap between research focuses. On the one hand they are too coherent to reveal the clues necessary to discuss technical issues such as ship construction and sailing performance. On the other hand they are too 'wordless' to be used to retell or illustrate the history of a dramatic foundering, a specific trading route or journey, the fate of a particular captain, a naval battle or similar. However, just as they are problematic to use for some discussions they are more appropriate for others. Some well-preserved wrecks can be assembled into buildings.

Things in everyday life

As argued amongst for instance *Annales* historians, true understanding of past societies does not derive from description of particular events, but from a recognition of long, deep structures. Even kings, wars and battles must be understood from the background and the mentality that created them (for an overview see Burke 1990). Things, everyday life and consumption studies have become central within such approaches (cf. Forssberg & Sennefelt 2014, Roche 2000, Trentmann 2009). Shipwrecks have the potential to provide an idea of how everyday life was lived in the Early Modern period.

According to the grand narrative of archaeological thought the processual, and most notably the post-processual, archaeologies developed as a reaction to an alleged unreflective antiquarian study of 'just things'. It was an attempt to move beyond an object-centred focus on typologies and serialization of artefacts and to study something considered more important, namely humans and cultures, or what is sometimes referred to as 'the Indian behind the artefact' (cf. Olsen 2010:24). It goes without saying that quite a few strategies have been formulated in order to deal with the intricate problem of studying what dwells *behind* things. For instance many archaeologists, inspired by structural linguistics, have tried to see things as texts (cf. Hicks 2010:72ff, or Olsen 2010:46ff).

Similar linguistically-inspired approaches have also been developed for the study of houses and urban space (see for instance Hillier & Hansson 1989, Hansson et al. 2003) and have been used by historical archaeologists as well (for instance Glassie 1975, Johnson 1993, for an overview see Griffiths 2012). And as it is not far-fetched to liken ships to houses, it might appear tempting to approach a ship as a building through 'space syntax' or similar.

In recent years, however, similar approaches have received some criticism for placing things and humans in two separate ontological zones, that of objects and that of subjects. The former is studied in order to understand the latter. Researchers inspired by phenomenology and/or Actor-Network-Theory (ANT) have questioned whether it really is necessary to make a detour via representations and labels such as grammar or syntax? Do things really have to *represent* something else? Is it not possible to be more direct and specific? (For example, see discussions in Dolwick 2009, Hicks 2010, Knappet & Malafouris 2008, Latour 2005, Olsen 2003, 2010, Olsen et al. 2012, Trentmann 2009).

The reaction is sometimes referred to as a 'material turn', in order to highlight that human life is affected by things everywhere and all the time. It is difficult to come up with an act or a routine that does not involve things in one way or the other. Instead of grasping for meaning *behind* things the phenomenology-inspired archaeologist realizes that humans exist *alongside* and *together with* things (Olsen 2010, Olsen et al. 2012).

Most everyday things, the ones that have greatest impact on life, might be difficult to detect. The everyday itself may be regarded as 'being the most obvious and the best hidden' (Lefebvre & Levich 1987:8). Martin Heidegger regarded these everyday things as 'ready-to-hand' and their 'ready-to-hand slumber' makes them almost invisible. They only achieve attention when they for some reason *fail* to be at hand (cf. Olsen 2010:73ff). At the same time these important, but 'hidden', actors are the most difficult to detect, but the search for such relations will be worth the effort as they will reveal some fundamental aspects about being human.

It goes without saying that many 'ready-to-hand' things have been created, existed, been used and vanished without any further thought through the centuries as no one found reason to comment upon them or describe them. *Fluits*, for instance, are such things. Being the most common type of merchant ship, seen every day in the ports of Northern Europe, they consisted of a variety of aspects taken for granted. The berth on board, the privy, the table, the fire-storage, the illuminated spot beneath the window and numerous other aspects guided and directed the routines of the everyday. But as these aspects were so trivial, no one found reason to record a thorough description of them. *Fluits* – as things – have been long lost in the mists of time. Surveying wrecks is a way of bringing these things back to the surface of the present.

A wrecked ship can thus be approached through recognizing that it used to be a physical milieu that guided and directed people's acts and routines. Shipwrecks provide an opportunity to capture a glimpse of where people ate, slept, worked and answered nature's call. The locations of berths, tables, hatches, privies, bulkheads, doorways and similar on board a ship have had a crucial impact on human action. These acts carried out on everyday and ceremonial levels have consequences for interpersonal relations; 'if one could control people's movements and control their interpretation, one could control their identities' (cf. Upton 2002:719, Hacking 1999:161–171).

The ship may have billeted people on board together or separated them into different categories that are upheld through a wide range of small acts and routines. This is why social theorist Henri Lefebvre (1901–1991) thought of buildings as the 'setting' for everyday life (cf. Lefebvre & Levich 1987:7–11). Compared to the events of building, sailing and wrecking a particular ship highlighted from written sources, as described in the previous chapter, a well-preserved and properly recorded wreck can provide an image of what everyday life was like when everything worked as it was supposed to. The dull and ordinary.

It is difficult to pinpoint just exactly what an archaeology of everyday life might consist of, as the everyday itself is difficult to define. One could argue that 'the everyday comprises seemingly unimportant activities.' Or, it is 'a set of functions which connect and join together systems that might appear to be distinct.' Or, 'it is that which is leftover, which falls outside of or runs counter to the scrutiny of power or officialdom. It is an Other of some sort, better defined by what it is not than by what it is' (quotations in Upton 2002:707, see also Goodwin 2002:188–190).

Ships are quite revealing as they contain all features necessary to uphold human life inside a limited container (Peter & Dawson 2009:145ff, Råberg 1998:142–153). This is also why ships are sometimes argued to be 'societies in miniature', 'microcosms' or 'closed communities' (Adams 2003: 31, 33, Einarsson 1997:210, Muckelroy 1978:99, 221ff, Pomey 2011:30, Soop 2001:14ff, see also discussion in chapter 8). But the point I wish to make with this thesis is that rather than being oddities separated from society at large, ships were of course an integral part of it. *Fluits* were integrated and self-evident component parts of any early modern city and they formed the everyday environment for thousands of sailors and passengers. I find it quite unlikely that the dozen or so individuals aboard a given ship, regardless of whether they were at sail or moored in a harbour, saw their ship as a miniature version of the outer world.

Method

In order to reveal and to get at what effect buildings have had on people, archaeologists and researchers of vernacular architecture have added human actions to theoretically populate these environments. That is, to discuss performance, *how* everyday routines were carried out in these settings (Garfinkel 2006). How did people move? Where were they allowed to move? Where did they meet? Where were certain activities carried out? What acts were carried out in privacy and which were not? Such issues may be discussed through shipwrecks.

Buildings archaeologists have applied what is sometimes referred to as an emphatic method. Through discussing the experience of a building or landscape and what kind of emotions the mere confrontations provoked it is possible to get an idea of how built environments have affected contemporary users or visitors. Does the building evoke a sense of familiarity or discomfort? Or does it perhaps induce a feeling of being watched? A direct parallel to such studies is what guru architect Le Corbusier referred to as a *promenade architecturale* – a walk through architecture – which was a way of highlighting that buildings may be understood through the sequence of experiences that emerge through movement (compare Eriksdotter 2005:227–268, 2009:88ff, also Johnson 2002 or Tilley 1994 for similar discussions).

Shipwrecks are 'buildings' located at the seabed, under several metres of water. This of course has an impact on the 'bodily experience' of the ship. Most notably it is difficult to get an overview as the field of vision is distorted by the limited visibility, darkness, the mask and the fact that you are resting horizontal in a diving suit.

For this reason it is necessary to transform the wrecks into a manageable format, into documentation. If the building is properly documented it is possible to grasp some of the lived experience anyway. For instance Danish architect Søren Nagbøl has discussed the impressions from a walk up to Adolf Hitler's work office through pictures and drawings from the long-ago demolished building (Nagbøl 1983). This leads to the second section of this chapter, which concerns how to record large, three-dimensional shipwrecks under water.

Recording shipwrecks

Ships are constructed from a huge quantity of bits and pieces, all adjusted and shaped to fit into specific positions. While Baltic Sea wrecks are sometimes particularly well-preserved, the several hundreds of years below water have still inevitably taken their toll. Erosion grinds the carefully shaped timbers and corrosion deforms bolts, nails of metal beyond recognition. On top of this comes sedimentation and marine growth which further impedes one's view of the wreck and lessens the possibility of perceiving it as it used to be.

When recording, the submerged location is an obstructing factor due to the simple fact that humans are not created for life in an underwater environment. Accessibility as well as the operational time at a wreck are thus always limited. To record a large complicated ship-structure in a restricted timeframe, means that a selection of some specific details must be made. Only a minor part of the information from the wreck can and will end up in the field-report. Quite paradoxically, though ship-archaeologists are usually quite fond of detailed recording:

> The study of ship remains begins with the study of seemingly trivial details: the thickness of a plank, the numbers and sizes of nails, the direction of an adze stroke, the colour and texture of stains in half-rotten bits of wood. In fact, some of those details and

measurements are trivial, but it is often difficult to distinguish the trivial from the significant until long after the recording is finished (Hocker 2004:2).

No doubt it may be relevant to record those things that one does not understand immediately during fieldwork. The quotation however derives from a publication concerning a wreck recorded on land. To record an entire ship under water requires a huge amount of effort and no matter how meticulous you are there is always a matter of selection. Some features will undoubtedly be left out. But perhaps it is not even desirable to record everything? An ambition to record *it all*, is like drawing a map at 1:1 scale. Rather, I would describe wreck-recording under water as a process where those features that are regarded as important are extracted and transformed into a manageable format suitable for analysis.

If the survey itself destroys the site, which is common within for instance contract archaeology, the recording as much as possible (perhaps also things that seem really trivial) may really be worth aiming for. But with coherent ships rising several metres above the seabed and which may be recorded with little or no intervention, it is possible to proceed slightly differently. These ships may be subject to non-intrusive surveys which also mean that one can leave out the aspects that one regards as trivial, those that *might* be of importance, and instead focus on those aspects that certainly *are*. The latter is determined through the research question: what do we want to know about the wreck?

As mentioned above, the focus in this study is on the lived experience of the ship. It is thus such features that may have had an effect on the everyday routines that are considered relevant. For instance the structures that define space such as the location of a bulkhead, a hatch, a window or a deck level, are regarded more relevant than the dimensions and number of nails that hold these constructions together. The location and size of the galley is more relevant than the dimensions of the bricks or the masonry used during its construction.

In the same way it is how life proceeded inside and around the ship, while it was still afloat, that is in focus, rather than how the wreck has eroded at the seabed since wreckage. Of course it may sometimes be relevant to study both nailing patterns and degradation of wood. However, such questions lie beyond the scope of this study.

Figure 3.1: Three steps for producing a side-elevation drawing of a wreck. A: the gathered measurements processed using Nick Rule's Web for Windows; B: a mosaic of sketches drawn in 1:20 scale under water; C: the finished, corrected drawing of the 'Jutholmen Wreck' (Niklas Eriksson).

Figure 3.2: The so-called 'Ghost Ship', which rests at nearly 130 m, was surveyed using a Remotely Operated Vehicle (ROV). Here it peers through the windows of the stern (MMT/Deep Sea productions).

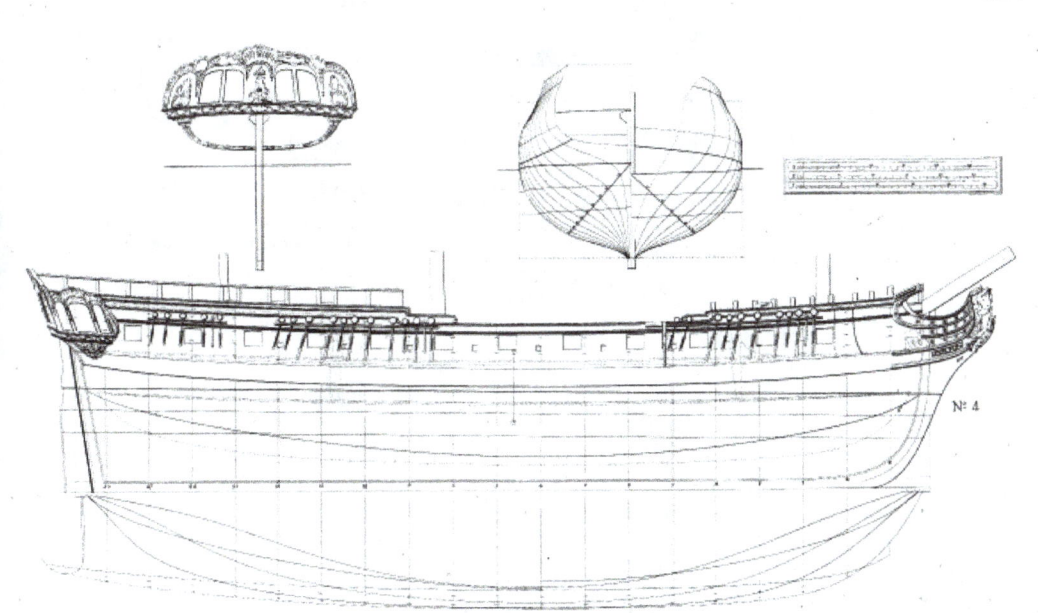

Figure 3.3: Digital 3-D model of the the 'Ghost Ship', created using a multibeam technique (MMT).

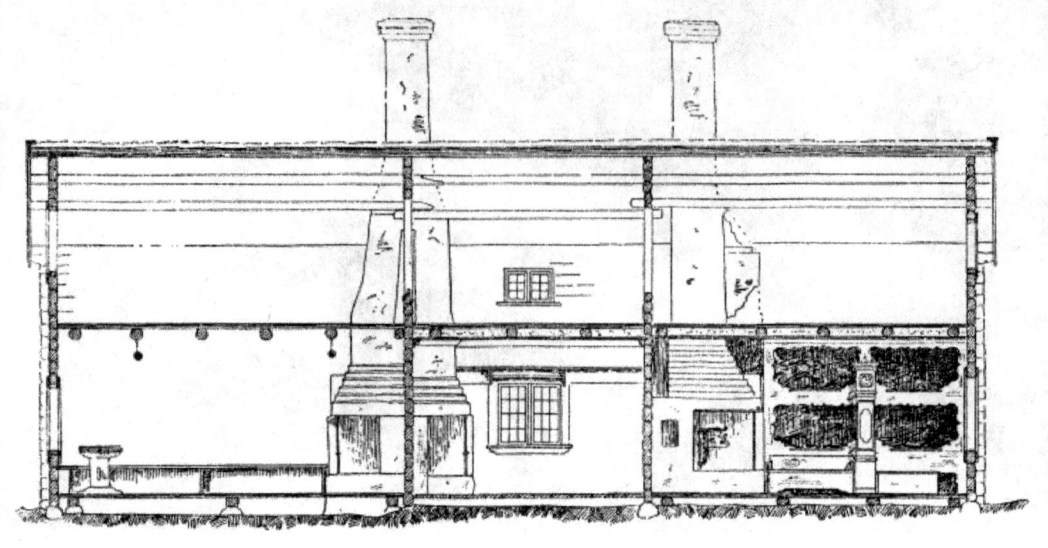
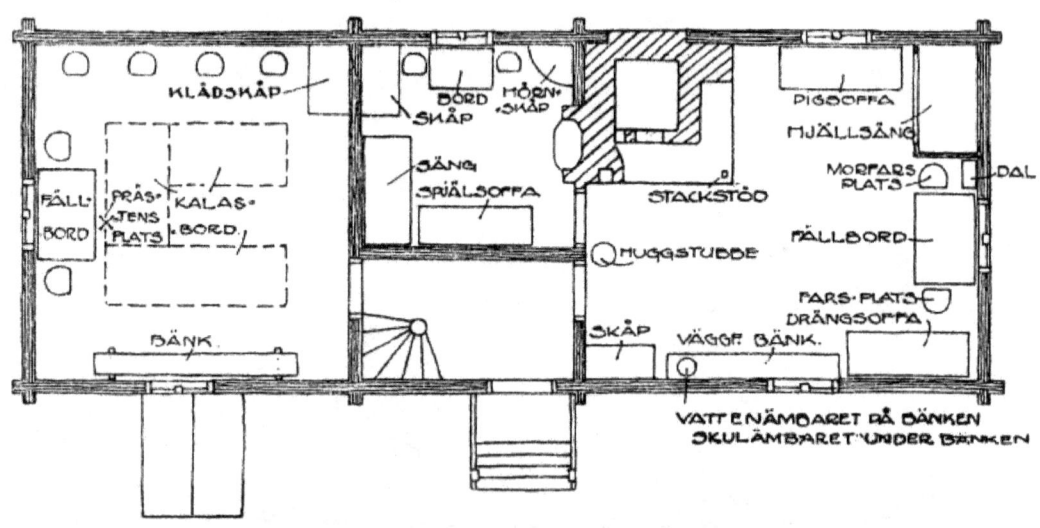

Figure 3.4: Two ways of visualizing large three-dimensional structures, A (previous page): line drawing, including body plan of a ship (after Chapman 1768, Plate 35) and B (this page): a recording of a vernacular house (after Erixon 1947:312).

In dialogue with ship-timbers

Recording can be described as a dialogue with material remains, addressing questions and searching the wreck for answers. This means that the field archaeologist is an active part of the recording process (see also discussions in Eriksdotter 2005:118ff, Hansen 2000:18f and specifically regarding shipwrecks, see Alopaeus 1995:39–46).

Photography is used extensively in underwater archaeology but due to limited visibility in the dusky waters of the Baltic, photos often only show a limited portion of a ship at the time. In order to extend the field of vision, photo-mosaics, where series of photos are pieced together, are used. The method has been used in the Mediterranean as well as in the Baltic since the 1970s (see for instance Cederlund 1982b), and in recent years digital photography has provided new possibilities in linking photos together into mosaics.

A camera does not select which features are to be recorded and depicts everything that happens to be in the field of vision. Needless to say, a camera lens has no idea what is important and what is insignificant. As noted already, the underwater environment deforms wood and the wreck becomes covered with seaweed, molluscs and sediments. These processes reshape the ship into what one may refer to as a 'wreck-based-formation'. Photography thus collects a vast quantity of information regarding marine flora and fauna. When the aim is to understand and to reconstruct wrecks into the ships they used to be, these distorting parameters make gleaning information from photographs somewhat challenging.

In contrast, sketching is a matter of searching the field of vision for forms, components and details needed to form a motif. It is thus an activity that presupposes addressing questions, searching for certain important features like notches in beams that reveal the extension of hatchways and other now missing details (Fig. 3.1). As has been put forth by building antiquarians sketching is a deductive recording method, which *actively* searches for the aspects worth noting. If one should stretch this it may be regarded as a qualitative recording method, whereas a photo resembles a *passive*, quantitative method. The latter will register everything and does not consider whether the object derives from culture or nature (cf. Eriksdotter 2005:120, Sjömar 2000:71, also Sjömar et al. 2000).

Sketching is thus a matter of recording and analysing at the same time. An active way of seeing. With experience from other wrecks it is easier to record and understand subsequent finds as you know what you are looking for. As archaeologist Jon Adams put it, 'if I can draw it I can understand it' (Adams 2013b:88). But as we all have different experiences to draw on, the result is always very personal. Two archaeologists will never end up with exactly the same result even if they were recording the same thing (see discussion in Sjömar 2000:78ff).

Notches or scarfs, which are features that are important when reconstructing a wreck into a ship, may be really tricky to see in photographs due to the presence of molluscs, sea-weed and sediments. Sometimes, the only way is to feel the shape of timbers with your hands, which presupposes that you have the opportunity to dive at the site. The material for the drawings of the 'Jutholmen Wreck' as well as the remains of *Anna Maria*, presented in chapter 4, have been collected through sketching under water (see Eriksson 2010, Eriksson forthcoming).

At deep sites, such as the 'Lion Wreck' that rests at 50 m and the 'Ghost Ship' at nearly 130 m, the wrecks are not accessible through diving with compressed air, which left the author above water. Instead these wrecks were carefully filmed. the 'Ghost Ship' was filmed using a Remotely Operated Vehicle (ROV), which is a small robot equipped with a videocamera (see Fig. 3.2). The 'Lion Wreck' was systematically filmed by the divers who found the wreck. Instead of drawing under water, the sketching was undertaken in front of the TV-screen (Eriksson 2012b:17–25, also Eriksson & Rönnby 2012a:350–361).

The advantage of sketching from film is the unlimited time in front of the screen. The disadvantages are associated with the inability to move around the object, to remove sediments and use fingers to detect cut-away areas and notches in the different ship-timbers. When diving it is always possible to bring a ruler in order to gather all those small additional measurements needed from time to time. At the 'Ghost Ship', this problem was partly solved through mounting parallel oriented laser pointers on the ROV. The red dots of the laser pointers appeared in the picture from the video and functioned as a scale reference (Eriksson & Rönnby 2012a:350–361). At the 'Lion Wreck' some additional measurements were gathered by the divers.

Wreck-sketches, either made under water or in front of a TV-screen, may be fairly accurate when it comes to tracing details and the proportions of smaller objects, whereas the larger proportions are always trickier to grasp. How pronounced is the sheer, the tumble-home, the curvature of stems, the sloop of the bowsprit and similar – all those forms and proportions that reveal the overall impression and the general dimensions of the ship, and which ultimately are crucial for the spatial understanding of it. In order to adjust sketches into position, and to correct eventual distortions in the larger proportions, different positioning systems are used.

The Direct Survey Method (DSM) has been used on the 'Jutholmen Wreck' as well as the *Anna Maria*. In short, it is a method where a number of datum points are usually nailed directly to the hull structure. The distances between these datum points are then measured using tape measures. The relative distance between the datum points is then calculated using specially developed computer software (for a thorough description of the system, see Adams & Rule 1991:145–154, Adams & Rönnby 1996:26–28, Marsden 2003:48) (Fig. 3.1).

At the 'Ghost Ship', information regarding the general proportions of the hull was provided by a multibeam scanner mounted on a ROV which recorded a three-dimensional model of the site, consisting of 6 million depth soundings (for a more thorough account see Dixelius et al. 2011, Erikson & Rönnby 2012a) (Fig. 3.3). This model could then be digitally sliced into desired sections that provided the framework for hand-drawn drawings of the wreck. Several other sites have been surveyed with the multibeam technique, even on sites that lie within the range of conventional diving, as the technique has proved to be both efficient and accurate (Eriksson et al. 2013).

To present ships

Between fieldwork and the finished drawings of a wreck there is a great deal of processing to be done. To have the opportunity to follow a wreck from the seabed into a printed report provides a familiarity with the site and the material, which ultimately leads to addressing further questions and interpretation. Recording, sketching, measuring and drawing are ways to engage with and get to know the material (cf. Almevik 2014:74). Many of the discussions regarding reconstruction and analysis of the hulls presented in the following chapters, in textual form, have arisen through the process of producing drawings.

The finished drawings fulfil the task of mediating the result of this process. Or as Bruno Latour put it: 'You doubt of what I say? I'll show you. And, without moving more than a few inches, I unfold in front of your eyes figures, diagrams, plates, texts, silhouettes, and then present things that are far away and with which some sort of two-way connection has now been established' (Latour 1990:13).

There are however several ways to present three-dimensional objects in two-dimensional drawings. Naval architects, from the mid seventeenth century onwards, have used line-drawings to describe and to define the shape of a ship's hull (Fig. 3.4, A). These are made through slicing the hull like a loaf of bread. The contour of each slice is placed on top of the next. Such drawings may be used for calculating sailing and manoeuvre capabilities for a projected ship as well as its production. An experienced 'reader' of such plans is able to judge many of these aspects simply by looking at them. Line-drawings are not used in the study at hand since sailing performance and hydrodynamics are not of prime concern for the general task.

In archaeology in general site-plans and plan-drawings are very common, and the archaeology of ships and boats is no exception. But archaeologists and naval architects are among the only professionals who depict ships from above. The human vantage point to view a ship is from the side and the sheer-plan to a greater extent corresponds to the lived experience of it. The opportunity to depict side-views is perhaps the most important contribution of a well-preserved Baltic Sea shipwreck. The point is that the visualization strategy should correspond to the analysis. If analysis concerns hull-shape and sailing qualities, then of course line-drawings and body plans are relevant. But if the discussion concerns the ship as a setting for everyday life the information revealed in such presentations does not fulfil the task. I simply assume that the sailing qualities of the 'Ghost Ship' and the other *fluits* described below, lived up to the requirements within contemporary society.

The way wrecks are presented below may have more in common with the drawings made by building antiquarians, ethnologists and archaeologists discussing houses (cf. Eriksdotter 2005, Erixon 1947, Hædersdal 1999a&b, Sjömar et al. 2000) than the body plans and line- drawings produced by naval architects and nautical archaeologists depicting ships (Fig. 3.4, B). Longitudinal sections of a ship are sometimes more informative when discussing division of space than plans are. It is primarily from the vantage point offered by this projection that we may perceive the location of the different deck levels and bulkheads that define space, but also the movement patterns of the persons on board.

But how is it possible to experience space from representations of buildings? Sometimes researchers have tried to overcome two-dimensionality through using 3-D animations. These may provide virtual tours through ancient environments (cf. Eriksdotter 2005, 2009, Westin 2012). However, in this study I have decided not to do so. The main reason being that there are still several blank fields in the documentation that have to be filled with 'something' in order to proceed with a 3-D reconstruction. What one decides to fill these blank fields with will have a crucial impact on the experience of the 3-D reconstruction (for a thorough discussion see Westin 2012). Black and white two-dimensional drawing has the advantage that one may leave some questions open. What is important is to *think* in three dimensions. Two-dimensional drawings have the capacity to mediate inputs for such considerations.

The reading of two-dimensional drawings of ships may be compared with looking for a new home. Skimming through housing advertisements is often a matter of looking at drawings of flats or houses and their floorplans. You populate these with the experience of your own life in order to determine whether the building lives up to your specific demands. Should this house or flat become the 'setting' for your everyday life? Even if the final decision to purchase or not is made after visiting and wandering around the building and its surroundings, the first filter for determining its suitability is through examining two-dimensional representations of three-dimensional buildings.

4. Everyday *fluits*

In this chapter the everyday environment on board *fluits* is reconstructed. The account is given primarily drawing upon the evidence provided by four wrecks: the 'Jutholmen Wreck', the 'Lion Wreck', the 'Ghost Ship' and the large *Anna Maria*. These are not the only known wrecks of *fluits*. The reason for focusing on these is that in each case much of the hull is intact, and also because all have been properly surveyed. The specific focus in the account is on space-defining features, such as the location of decks, bulkheads, hatches, stoves, furniture and similar. Additional information, from other sources as well as other wrecks, will be used along the way. See the Glossary for guidance with the nautical terms in the text.

The 'Jutholmen Wreck'

The 'Jutholmen Wreck' is one of the many wrecks that were discovered as a result of the increased popularity of recreational diving in the 1960s. The wreck is resting at the seabed 15 metres from the surface parallel to the foot of the small island of Jutholmen situated only one hundred metres or so from Dalarö, a municipality strategically located along the sailing route south of Stockholm (Fig. 4.1).

The divers, Sven-Olof Johansson and Erkki Tillman, who found the ship in 1965, reported it to the authorities and started to excavate the site using an airlift. They uncovered parts of the stern and made sketches of the hull-structure, the location of bulkheads and so forth. They did this with great skill and precision, and their unpublished diving log contains important information about the spatial arrangement inside the ship (SMM archive). A major excavation of the site was carried out between the years 1970–1974 by the Swedish National Maritime Museum. The aim was to develop new methods, and several innovative techniques were tried out (see Cederlund 1982b, Ingelman-Sundberg 1976:57–71, Kaijser 1983).

The estimated time of wreckage has been set to around the year 1700, as the most recent coin found was dated to this year (Kaijser 1983:8, 45, Cederlund 1982b:25, Cederlund & Ingelman-Sundberg 1973:325).

Analysis of the clay pipes recovered from the wreck suggest that the ship may have sunk some ten years later (Åkerhagen 2009, also compare Kaijser 1983:39-44). In 2008 a renewed survey of the site was carried out with the aim of producing material for an heritage management plan of the site, but also resulted in drawings of the preserved hull structure (Fig. 4.2) (also Eriksson 2010).

The 'Jutholmen Wreck' is 25 m long between the posts and 6.6 m wide, which makes her proportionally wider but also shallower than many other *fluits*. Another difference is the absence of a lower-deck. Despite the differences in hull-shape and deck arrangement, the location of the crew´s lodging does not seem to differ from the situation of on board the other *fluits* discussed below. An approximate number of 7–14 people would have been required to sail the Jutholmen wreck (compare Unger 1978:45ff, 1994:122).

The cargo in the hold of the 'Jutholmen Wreck' proved to consist of iron ore and tar, which were typical Swedish export products (see for instance Heckscher 1940, Müller 1998, Van Zanden & van Tielhof 2009), suggesting that the ship was on her way from Sweden when she sank (Cederlund 1982b, Kaijser 1983). What caused the sinking is not known and the ship remains unidentified by name. Even if the ship did not reach its destination, the rig and the cargo were not totally lost. Traces of salvage operations are clearly visible in the hull. In a treatise entitled *Konsten at lefwa under Watn* (*The Art of Living Under Water*) published in 1734, Mårten Trievald (1691-1747) describes the practice and different machines used for salvaging goods from sunken ships. Using saws and different breaking devices, powered by capstans on barges, the decks of the sunken vessels were removed in order to gain access to the goods in the hold. Despite the title of his book, the diving bell, which provided the opportunity to 'live under water' was only used in extreme circumstances. The majority of the operations seem to have been carried out from the surface (also described by Westbeck 1829). Cut-off deckbeams and saw-marks in the knees reveal that the deck of the 'Jutholmen Wreck' was removed entirely during salvage.

But even if the deck itself is missing some of the supporting structures are still in place. Alongside accounts from the diver's survey in 1965 and SMM's excavation in the 1970s there is enough information to reconstruct a general account of the configuration of rooms on board the ship, the everyday environment for the persons on board.

Space on board the 'Jutholmen wreck'

Figure 4.2 shows the inside of the starboard side as this half of the ship appears to have kept its original shape (Eriksson 2010:11–15). The location and extension of the upper deck is clearly revealed by a shelf clamp attached to the inside of the hull, which used to form support for the deckbeams. The position of these beams is indicated by notches in the shelf clamp as well as some hanging knees preserved in place.

As the uppermost parts of the stern have disintegrated the orientation of decks further aft is a bit more difficult to determine, but not impossible. *Fluits*, just like other large ships in this period, were steered using a whipstaff, a mechanism that was attached to the quarterdeck-structure (the construction is described in detail by Harland 2011:97–102, Pipping 2003:329–333, Wegener Sleeswyk 2003:45ff). The quarterdeck was thus located above the upper end of the sternpost, allowing the tiller to move freely underneath.

The height of the sternpost thus reveals the level of the quarterdeck. Usually, there was also an inner roof, under the tiller creating a space, called the *hennegat* in Dutch, in which the tiller could move (cf. Hoving 1992:49). The sternpost of the 'Jutholmen Wreck' has fallen to port and is now resting flat on the seabed, but was documented during fieldwork in 2008. Its outline is indicated on the longitudinal section drawing.

When the wreck was rediscovered in the 1960s, the floor of the rooms under the quarterdeck, as well as some remains of bulkheads, were still intact. Unfortunately the stern was damaged by anchorage in the early 1970s. The portside of the hull tilted some 0,95 m outward, the sternpost fell to the side and the preserved floor and bulkhead collapsed down into the hold (Eriksson 2010:11–15). The now collapsed structure was at least partially recorded with notes and sketches by the divers who found the wreck. Together with the still standing starboard-side the original extension of the floor in the stern is possible to determine.

None of the shelf clamps, knees and similar structures, which once supported the floor under the quarterdeck, is preserved in place. A shelf clamp raised in the 1970s (compare Cederlund 1983:99) indicates that the supporting beams were much thinner than those supporting the main deck.

However, there are in fact some traces revealing the level of the floor inside the cabin. When placing a deck-beam into the hull the end is inserted between the frames. If there was not enough room, the space was increased so that the beam would fit. Two such cut-aways have been observed at the starboard side. Their position thus provides an indication of the original location of the floor inside the rooms under the quarterdeck.

According to the sketches made by the divers, remains of a bulkhead running from side to side was still in place in the 1960s and the space underneath the quarterdeck was thus divided in two. The exact location of this bulkhead has not been possible to determine but it is clear that there were two rooms: a galley (Fig. 4.2, B) and a cabin (Fig. 4.2, C). On one of their sketches there is also a bulkhead running lengthwise in the aftermost room. Its approximate location is indicated in Fig. 4.2, G. The purpose of this bulkhead is not known. It may have been some kind of cupboard, or perhaps a small cabin or maybe a berth (see following chapter). On the drawing of *katschip Tamen* the space is referred to as a *Bottelery*, a small room where the cook kept a working stock (cf. Hoving 2012:157).

Fluits often had another room above the two under the quarterdeck, and there are indications that the 'Jutholmen Wreck' had such a room. Three S-shaped stanchions, deriving from a clinker-built outward bulkhead were recovered from the site in the 1970s. The length of these is around 1.3 m (Cederlund 1983:106). Ultimately, there are only two possible position for these stanchions, either they were located at the foremost end of the quarterdeck, or as the enclosing structure of an upper cabin (Fig. 4.2, F). The only argument for an upper cabin on board the 'Jutholmen Wreck', besides the mentioned stanchions, is that such cabins were a common feature in ships of this size, see for instance the 'Ghost Ship' and the 'Lion Wreck' below. But there are also exceptions to this pattern. On a drawing showing the *katschip Nederhorst* of 1690 (Fig. 4.12, A) there is no upper cabin. The absence of this space on this depiction does not necessary imply the total absence of such a space on the real ship. In any case it is difficult to prove that the 'Jutholmen Wreck' had such a room.

Below the two rooms under the quarterdeck was the hold where the load of iron and tar was stowed. The cargo hold stretched from bow to stern. Access to this most likely was through a hatch in the main deck, before of the main mast. The hold could also be accessed through a small port in hull-side amidships. Long objects, such as timbers, would enter the hull through a loading port in the stern. Its lower edge is visible in the hull planking (Fig. 4.2, 1).

The last clearly definable room on the 'Jutholmen Wreck' is the forecastle (Fig. 4.2, A). The deck that once covered this space has disintegrated, as have most of the hull-sides. The height of the forecastle is indicated by the preserved top timbers as well as the end of the apron attached to the surface of the stem facing abaft. The deck covering the forecastle stretches from the bow and abaft to the location of the windlass.

Everyday life on board the 'Jutholmen wreck'

According to historian Richard Unger seven men and a boy could handle a *fluit* of 150 tons in the trade between Norway and the Netherlands (1978:45, 1994: 122). I find no reason to assume that the crew aboard the 'Jutholmen Wreck' would have been much greater than this. The question is: how did the 'Jutholmen Wreck' provide a 'setting for everyday life' for around eight people?

It is difficult to grasp this based on the distributional patterns of the finds recovered from the site in the survey in the 1970s as the methods employed during the excavation in the 1970s were not optimized for an assessment of their spatial provenience. The material was collected from squares, measuring 2.5 x 2.5 m and the location of these squares was made irrespective of the ships 'own' spatial division, by bulkheads and similar. The second complicating factor is that extensive activities over hundreds of years have left countless traces on the seabed in the area where the ship sank (compare Arnshav 2008). Consequently, the material gathered during the excavation in the 1970s, which has also been published in a report (Kaijser 1983), not only derives from the wreck but from the activities on land and the ships moored on the roadstead. Sometimes this is pointed out in the text (ibid. 71), but most of the roof tiles, recent porcelain and similar objects are left without comments.

To determine whether finds belong to the wreck or not and pinpointing their original contexts on board requires a critical reading of the reports. For instance, finds damaged by fire may be rejected as there is no evidence of uncontrolled fire on board. The contexts in which finds are found may also be used to question whether the item should be regarded as part of the ship or not. Personal belongings, eating utensils, bottles and other things located in the cargo-hold, together with the cargo of bar-iron and tar, are likely to be secondary. Why store a sword, or a clay pipe, together with bar-iron and tar?

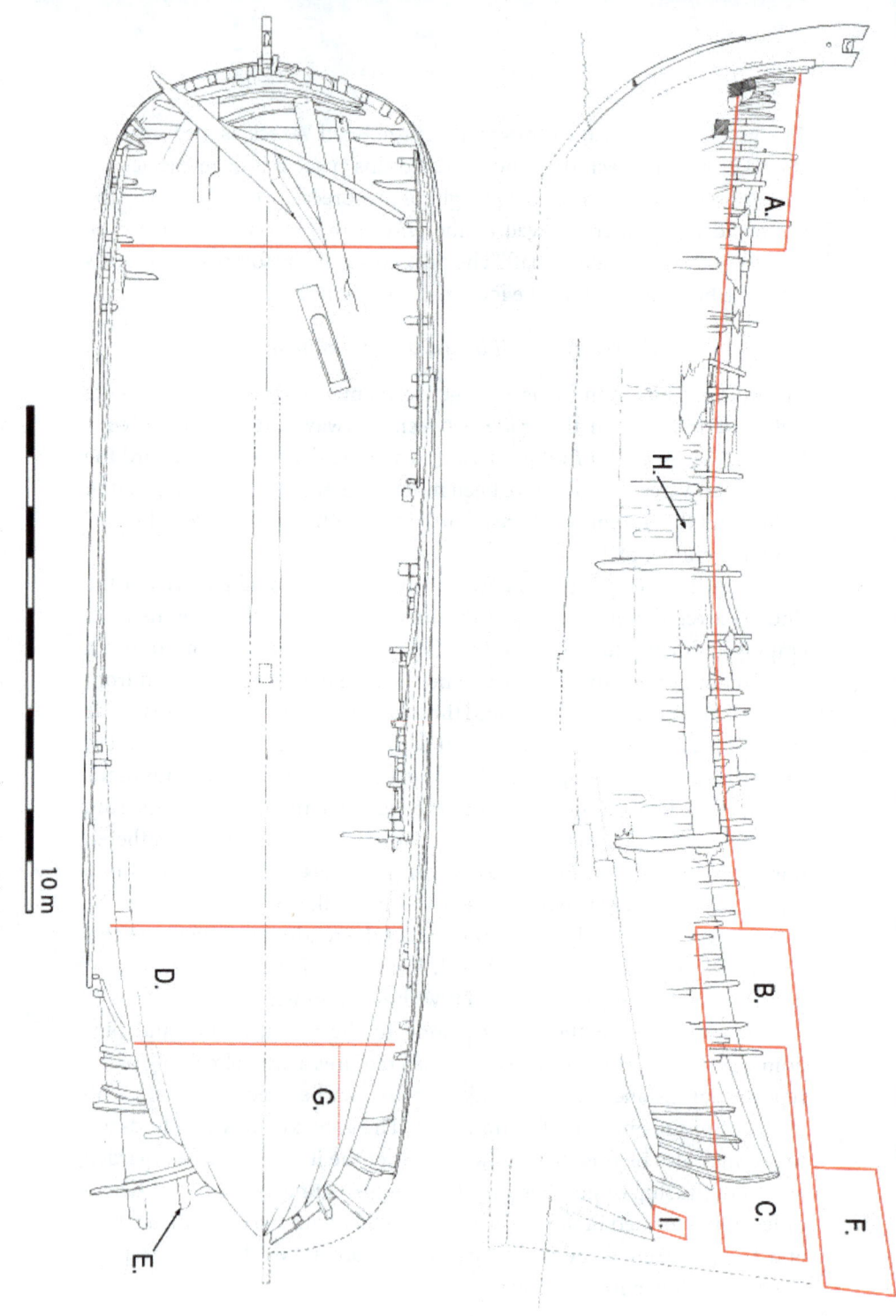

Figure 4.2: Longitudinal section and plan of the 'Jutholmen Wreck'. The section shows the inside of the starboard side with the bow pointing left. A: forecastle, B: galley, C: cabin, D: hearth, E: privy, F: possible extension of upper cabin, G: remains of bulkhead or cupboard, H: loading port, I: loading port (Niklas Eriksson).

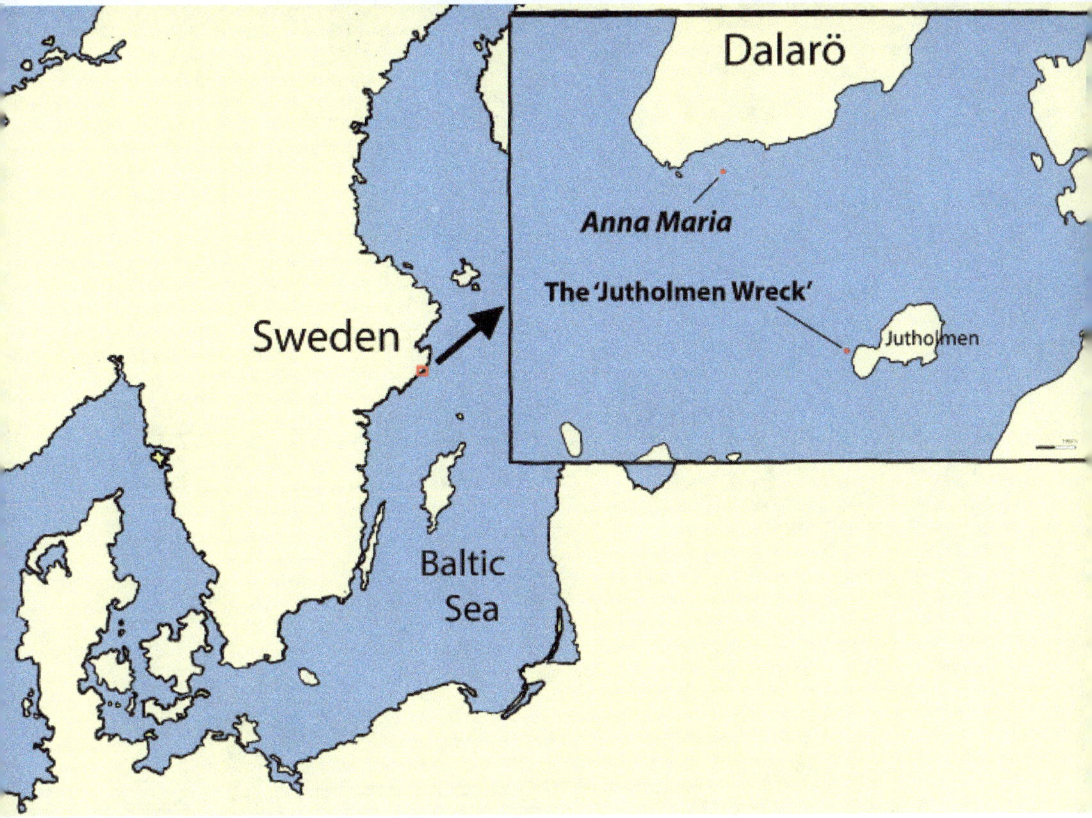

Figure 4.1: Map of the Dalarö roadstead, showing the location of the 'Jutholmen Wreck' and the Anna Maria (Niklas Eriksson).

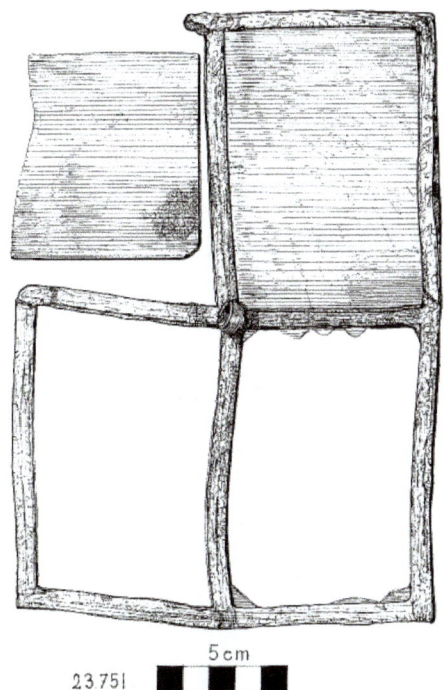

Figure 4.3: Window frame recovered from the 'Jutholmen Wreck', 22.5 cm high (after Kaijser 1983:26, 81).

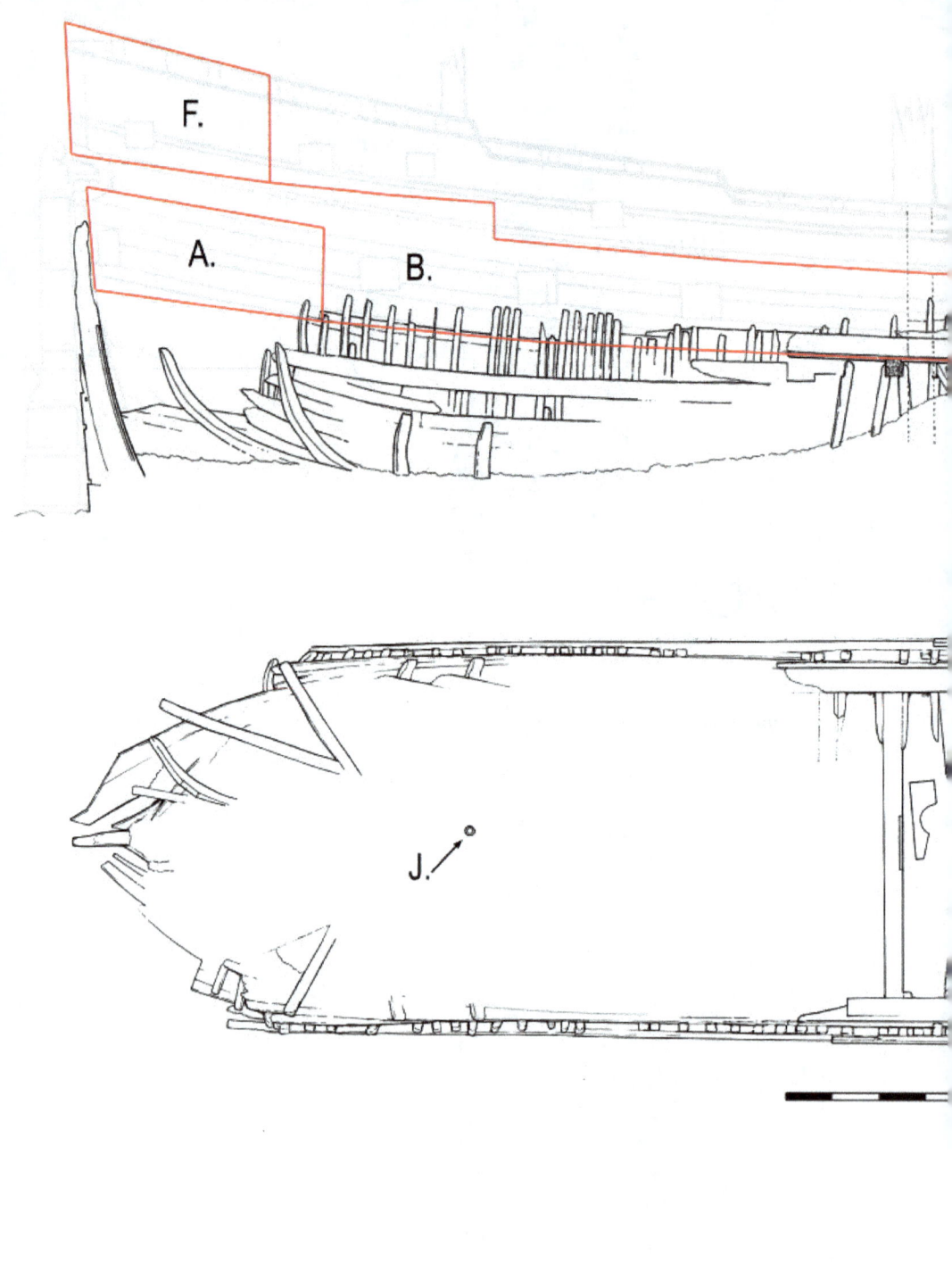

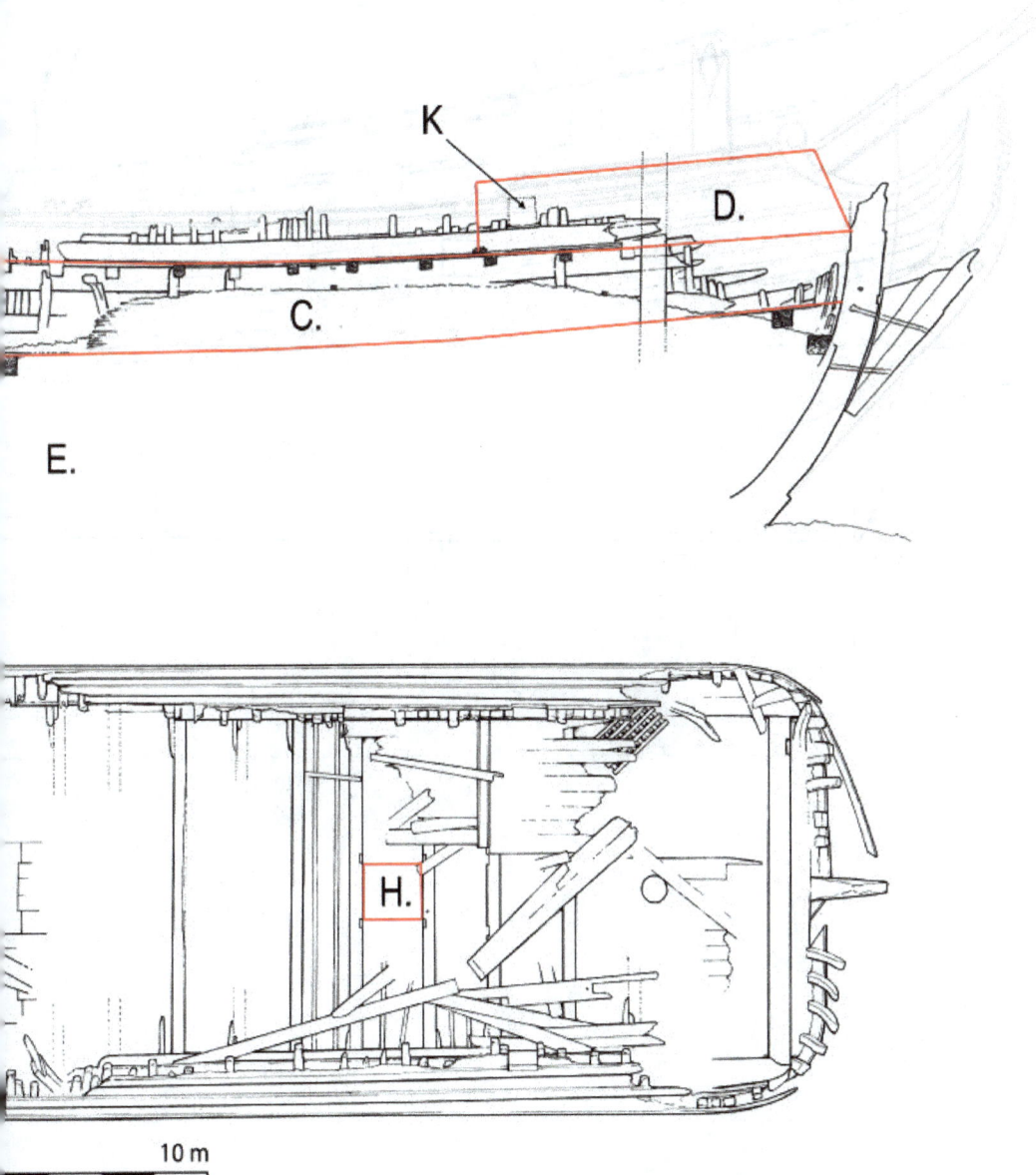

Figure 4.4: Longitudinal section and plan of the Anna Maria, bow pointing right. The contour of the ship is indicated by the shadowed outline of Rålamb's fluit (compare Fig 4.5) A: cabin, B: galley, C: lower deck (loaded with planks), D: forecastle, E: hold (loaded with iron), F: possible location of upper cabin, G: hatchway in lower deck, H: hatch, I: loading port, J: pump, K: gun-port (Niklas Eriksson, P-A Pettersson).

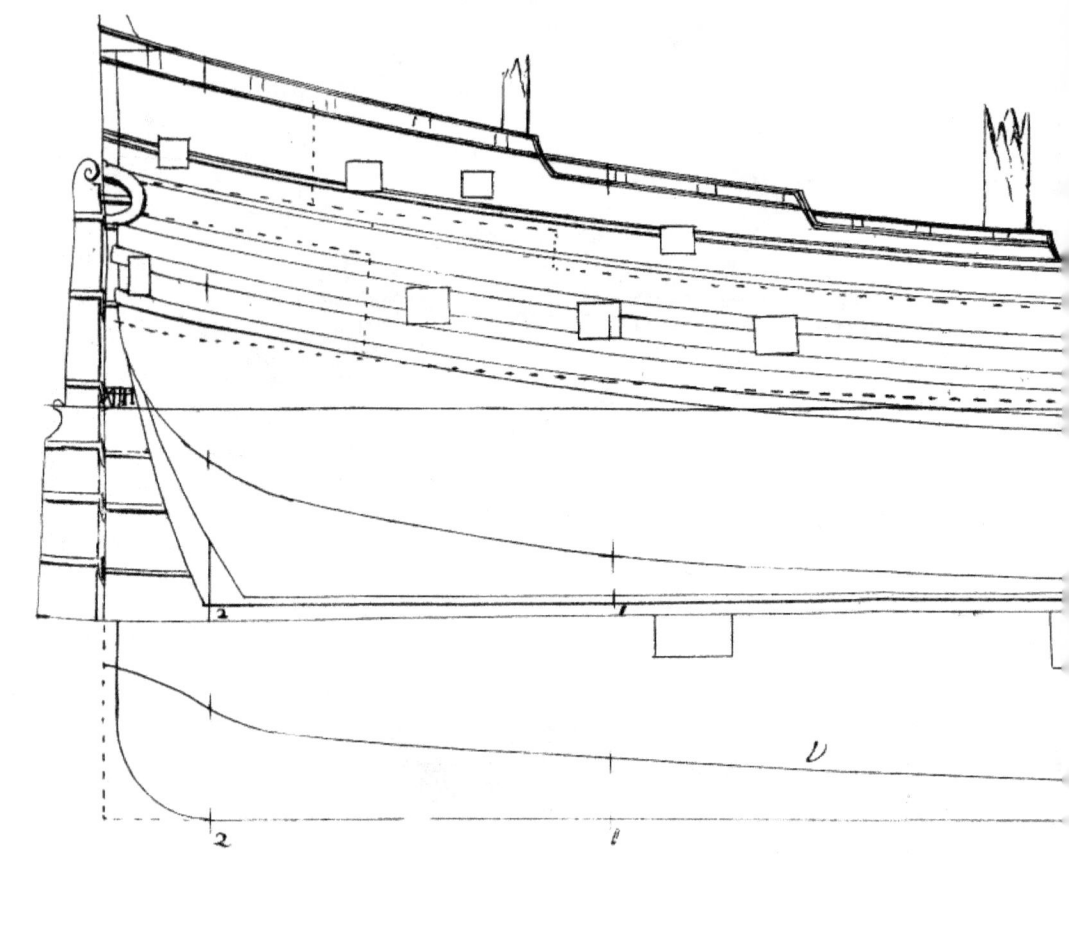

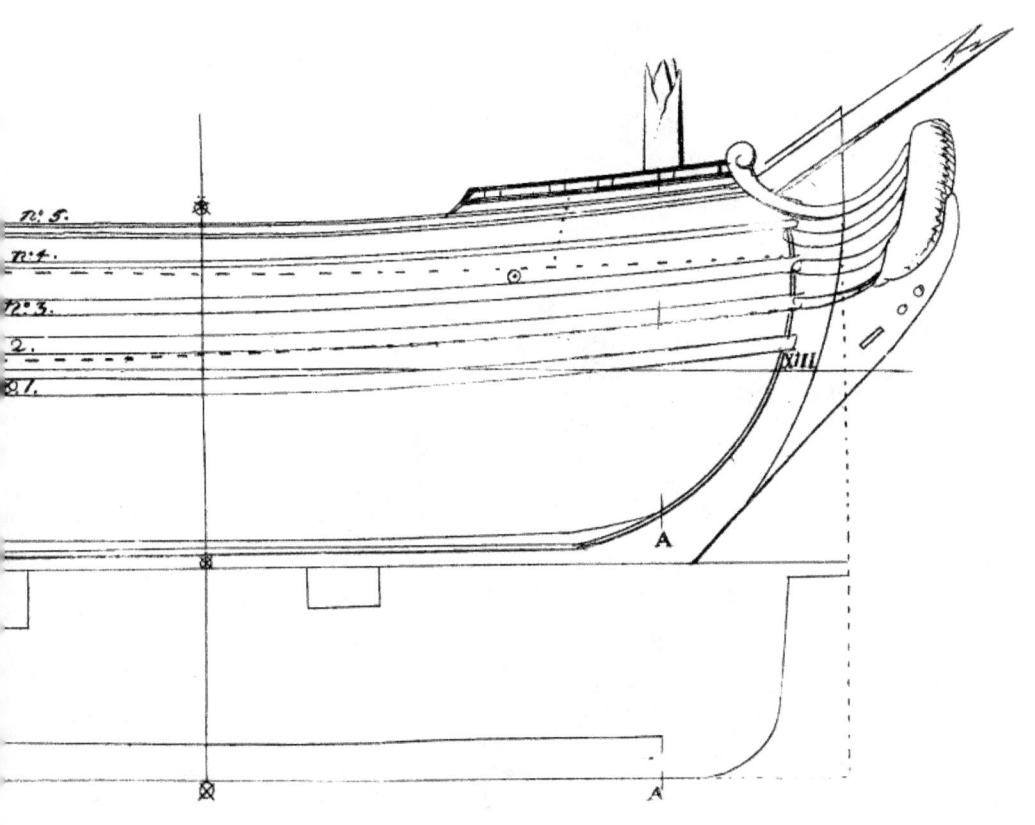

Figure 4.5: Drawing of 'a fluit or cargo carrier of 300 lasts' (Fleit eller Lastdragare aff 300 Läster), published in Åke Rålamb's treatise on shipbuilding, from 1691 (edited after Rålamb 1943:25, plate G.).

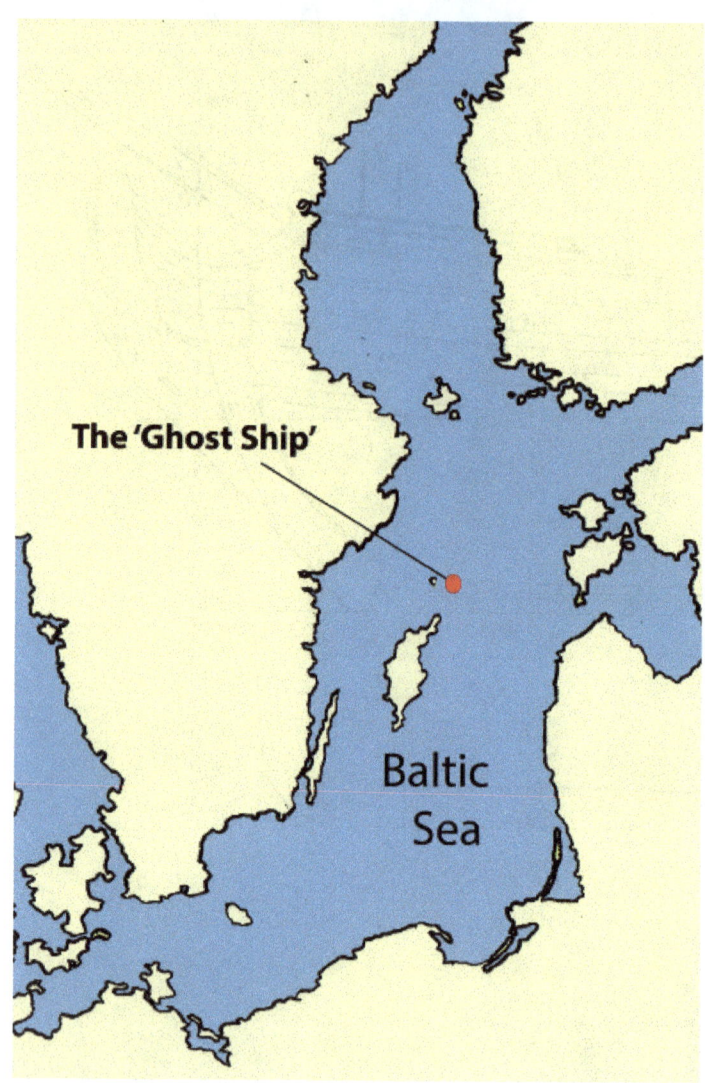

Figure 4.6 : The location of the 'Ghost Ship' (Niklas Eriksson).

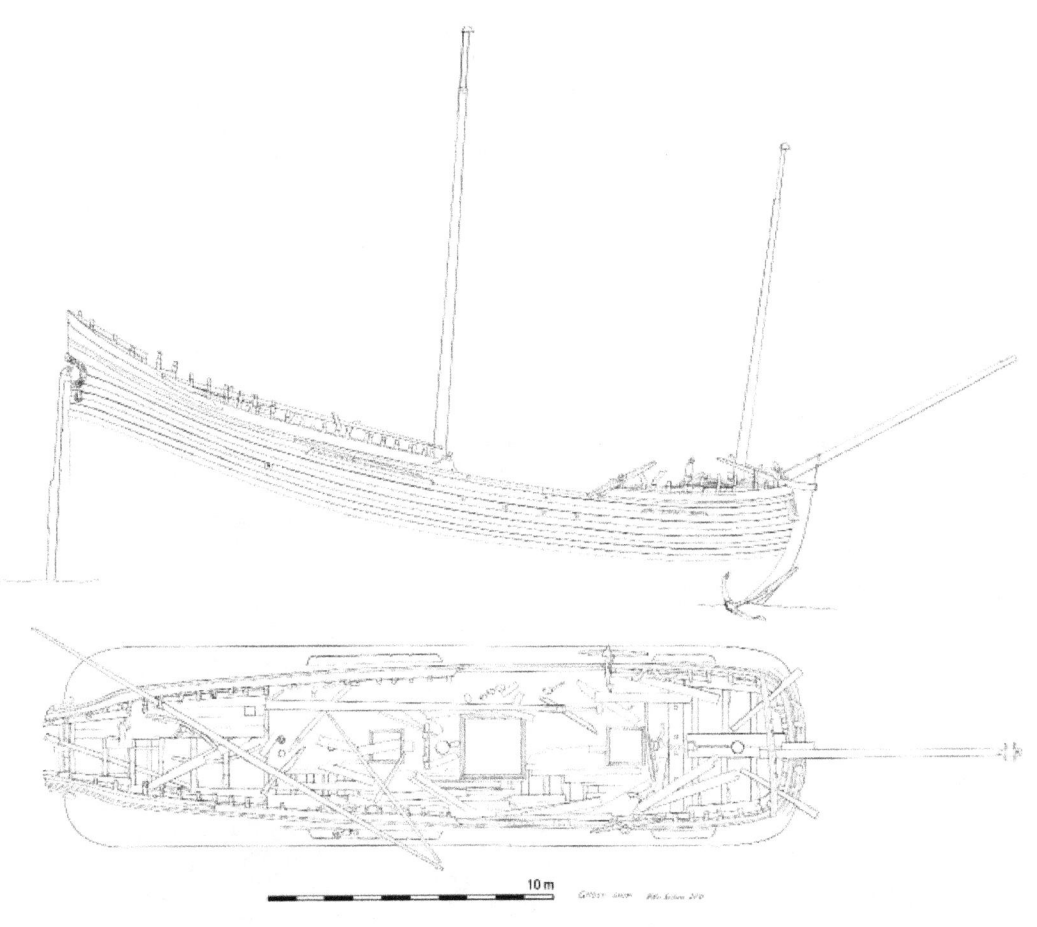

Figure 4.7: Sideview and plan of the 'Ghost Ship'. Note how the bow has sunken down into the seafloor (Niklas Eriksson).

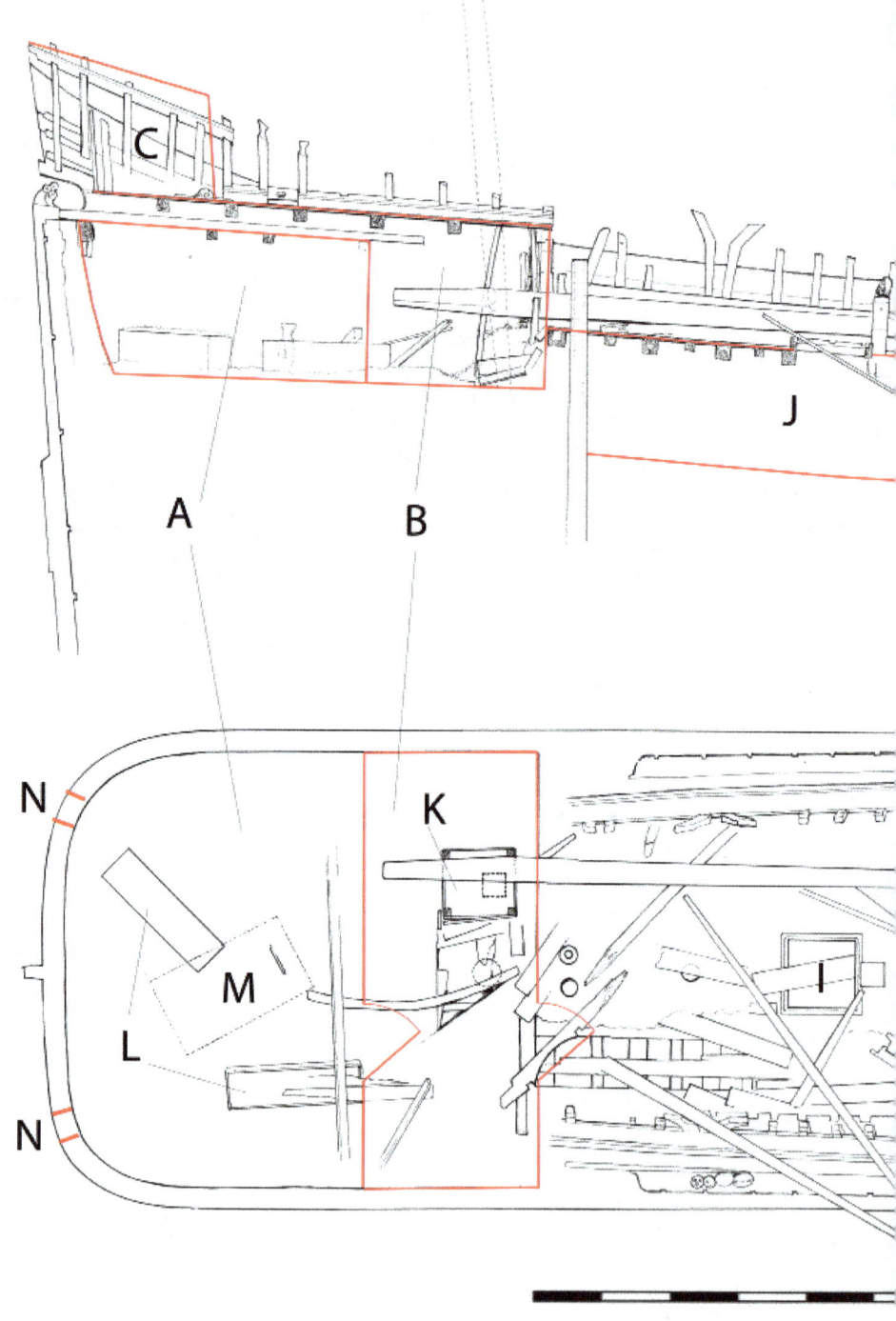

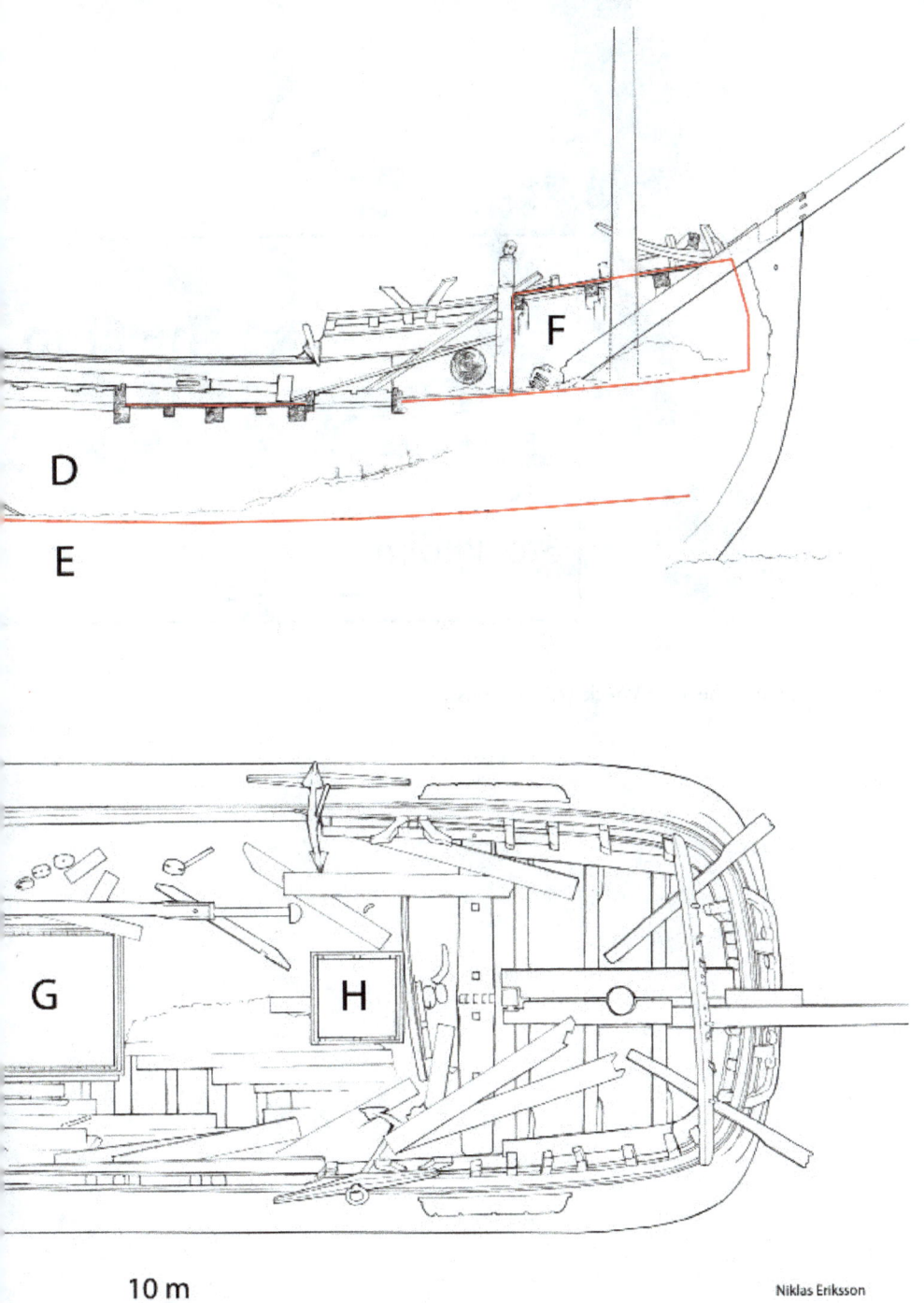

Figure 4.8: Longitudinal section and plan of the 'Ghost Ship', with removed quarterdeck. A: cabin, B: galley, C: upper cabin, D: lower deck, E: hold, F: forecastle, G: main hatch, H: hatch, I: hatch, J: room abaft the mainmast, K: hearth, L: chests/benches, M: table (dotted line indicates estimated shape), N: Windows (Niklas Eriksson).

Figure 4.9: The location of the 'Lion Wreck' (Niklas Eriksson).

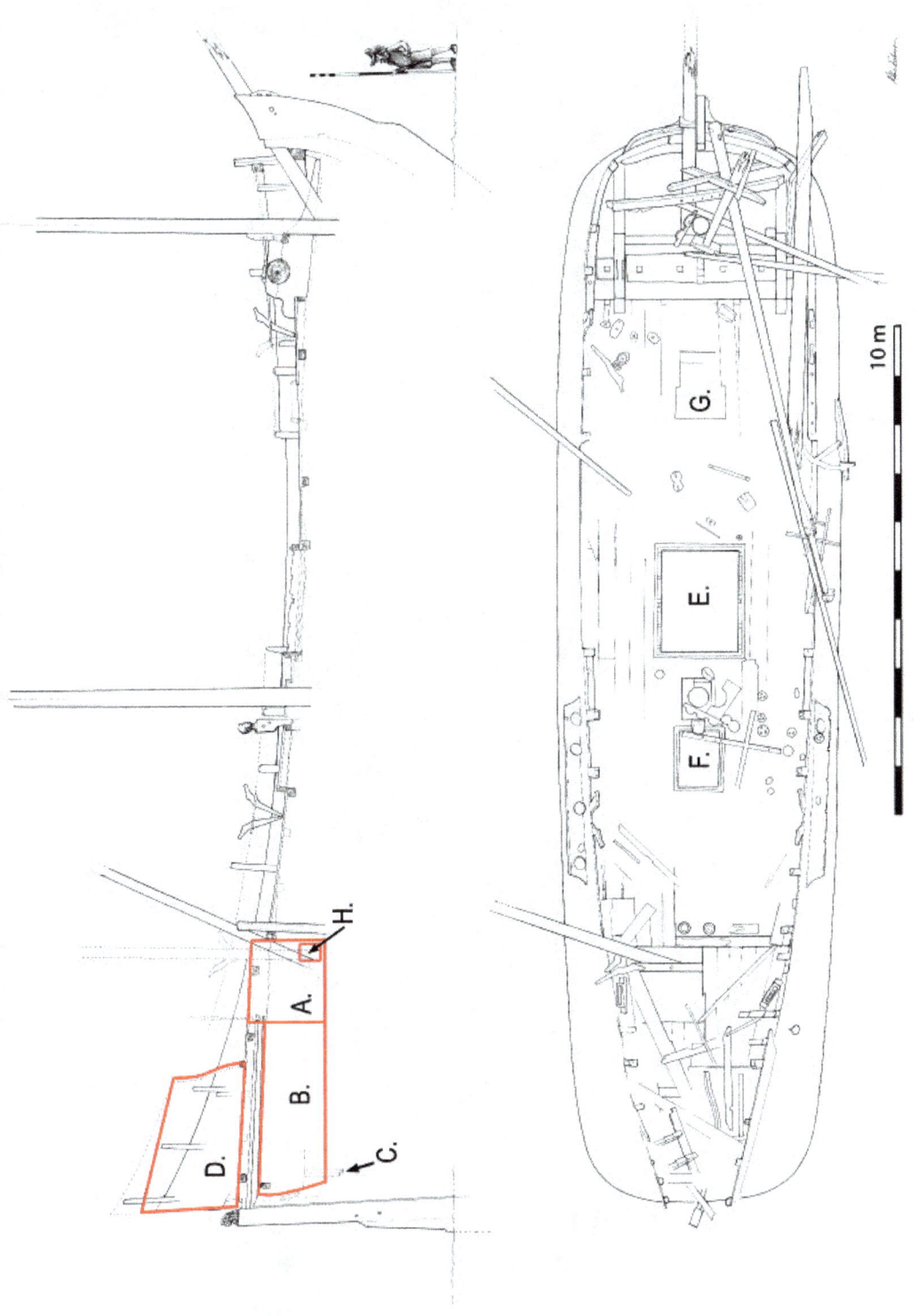

Figure 4.10: Longitudinal section and plan of the 'Lion Wreck'. A: galley, B: cabin, C: privy, D: upper cabin, E: main hatch, F: hatch, G: hatch, H: port in the hull side (Niklas Eriksson).

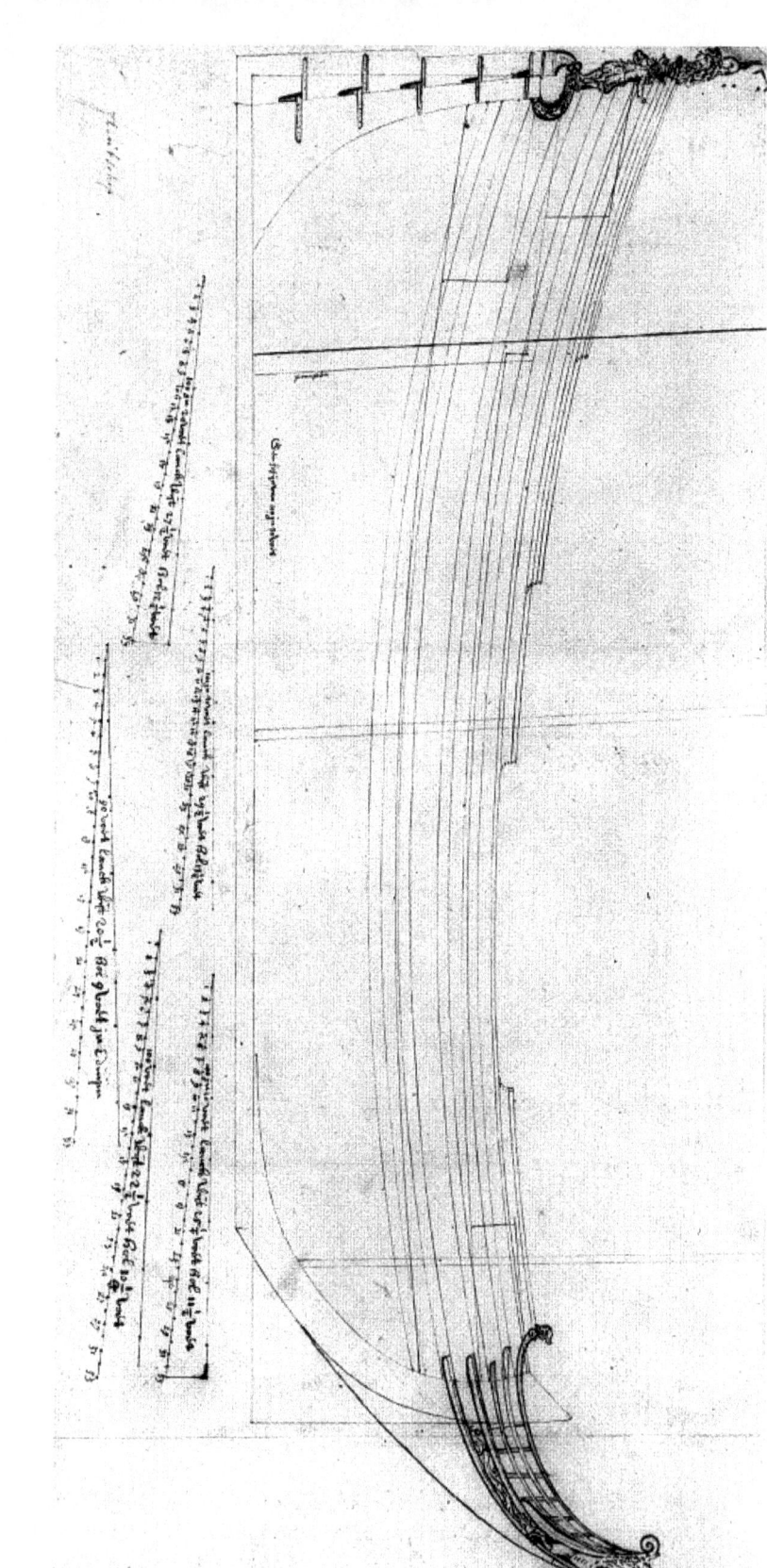

Figure 4.11: A seventeenth-century drawing of a fluit, signed F. C. Keyser. Note that the drawing has five different scale bars. The drawing thus shows a range of fluits of five different sizes, from 90 to 130 feet long (after Hoving 1995:48, original in the Nederland's Scheepvaart Museum, Amsterdam).

A

Plaatsing
Volk
Groote
Groote Luyk
Luyk
Kabel
gat
Fokke Mast
't Ruym
5
10
15
20
25
30
35

B

Bezaans Mast
Luyk
Plaats voor 't Volk
Broot en Zeyl Kamers
Groote Luyk
Kabel Luyk
Kabel
Luyk
Combuys en Slaap plaats voor 't Volk

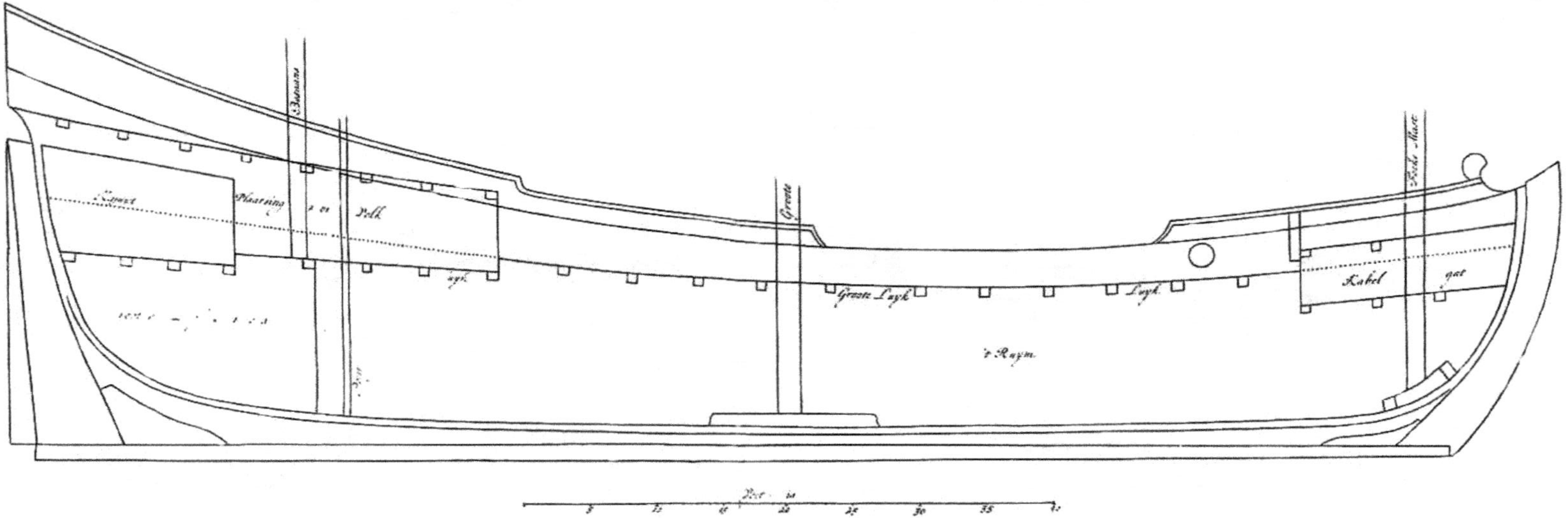

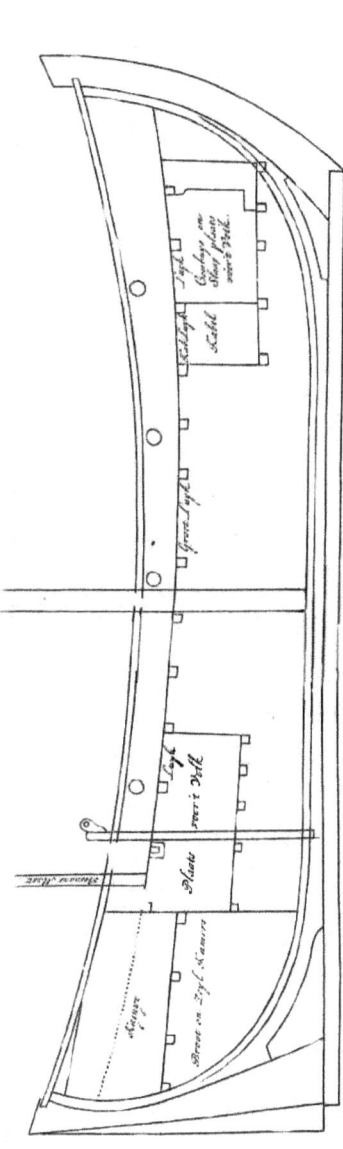

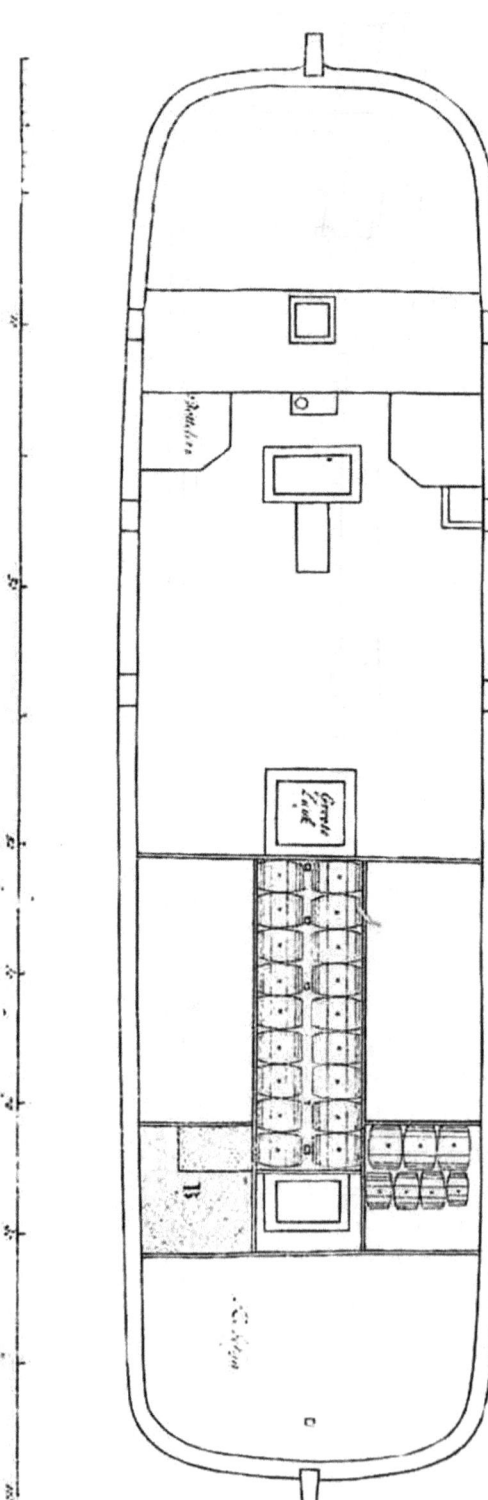

Figure 4.12, A: (previous page): A longitudinal section of the katschip Nederhorst, built for the VOC in 1671. The aftermost part of the hold of the Nederhorst is Broot en Zeyl Kamers, (bread and sail stores). The two rooms under the quarterdeck are mentioned as Kajuyt (cabin) and Plaatsing voor Volk (placement for people). The forecastle is referred to as Kabel gat (cable room). The ship measured 115 Amsterdam feet (32.6 m) between the posts.

Figure 4.12, B: (previous page): a longitudinal section of a Hoeker, measuring 80 feet between the posts (22.6 m). The text reveals that the foremost room under deck contained the galley as well as lodgings for crew, whereas the room in the stern ir referred to as the cabin. The room before the cabin, which is accessible through the small hatchway in the deck, is referred to as Plaats voor't Volk (which should be understood as some form of lodgings).

Figure 4.12, C: Drawing of the lower deck on board katschip Tamen, built for the VOC in 1686. The lodgings are found in the stern of the ship. The room marked Botelery is the storage for bottles, whereas the Combuys is the pantry. Note the shape of the main hatch, marked Groote Luyk. The bulkhead separating the living compartments from the storage appears to run in the middle of the hatchway. Tamen measured 116 Amsterdam feet (32.8 m) between the posts (Nederland's Scheepvaart Museum, Amsterdam).

4. EVERYDAY FLUITS

Two swords have been used as an argument for naval officers being present on board (see Kaijser 1983:13, Cederlund 1982b:27) but the situation in which they were found, in the cargo hold, suggests they are secondary deposits at the site. It should also be pointed out that swords in themselves cannot be used as evidence for officers being present. Swords have been found on other eighteenth-century wrecks that are definitely merchant vessels (for example the so-called 'Mastvraket' outside Oxelösund and 'Fula Gubben' near Huvudskär [SMM archive]).

Some finds were recovered with more distinct contextual information, which reveals distributional patterns to some extent. It has thus been possible to link some of these items to the spatial reconstruction and to determine which room they derive from. The recovered finds may be used to unveil how the different areas were used and how everyday life was spatially arranged.

Distribution of functions and people

As is revealed by numerous pictures of *fluits*, models and wrecks like the 'Ghost Ship', the entrance to the rooms underneath the quarterdeck was usually through a door in the bulkhead at the break of the quarterdeck. It seems likely that that the 'Jutholmen Wreck' was arranged like this as well. After entering through this door one would distinguish the hearth (Fig. 4.2, D). When the wreck was first discovered the floor inside this room was still intact, the remains of the hearth, consisting of bricks, were aggregated towards the portside. The foremost room under the quarterdeck (Fig. 4.2, B.) therefore contained the ship's galley. According to the report from the survey, cooking utensils, like copper cauldrons, tripod pots as well as a cast-iron frying pan were found in the vicinity of the pile of bricks that once formed the galley. Some of the objects deriving from this space have fallen towards the bow, which is explained through the slope of the hull with the bow deeper than the stern (compare Kaijser 1983).

Fluits sometimes carried a few guns but most commonly they were unarmed, hence the expression of being armed 'en flute' when the majority of guns were removed in order to reveal deck space (Lavery 1992:111ff, Unger 1992:122, 2011:257). Several depictions from the period, as well as some models, reveal that *fluits* that carried guns had them located in the foremost room under the quarterdeck. This is the reason why this room is sometimes referred to as the gunroom (see for instance Hoving 1995:49). The only thing that suggests that the 'Jutholmen Wreck' was armed is a chest or bench, containing cannon balls and bar-shot, which was raised from the wreck in the 1970s (Cederlund 1983:58, Kaijser 1983:10, 45). The original context of this chest was not recorded. In the reports it is suggested that the ammunition was intended for the ships guns (ibid.).

That no guns have been found at the wreck may be explained by the likelihood that they were recovered together with the cargo and rig. However, remains such as parts of gun-carriages and wheels are often found on wrecks where guns have been salvaged, such as on the *Vasa* (1628) and *Resande mannen* (1660) (Eriksson et al. 2013:15f).

A just as conceivable explanation is that the cannonballs were a part of the cargo. Together with the tar and bar-irons, cast-iron ammunition was an important export-product. No other items associated with guns, such as carriages, loading equipment or similar, have been found. It appear quite likely that the ship, just like her sister *fluits*, did not carry guns at all.

A large quantity of firewood has been found scattered in the stern area, on both sides of the now collapsed, dividing bulkhead. It is however reasonable to assume that the firewood storage was in the same room as the hearth, for practical reasons. As we shall see below, the written accounts from the foundering of the *Anna Maria*, also state that the firewood storage was between the mizzenmast and the main-cabin-bulkhead on board that ship (Ahlström 1997:97). It is likely that the 'Jutholmen Wreck' had a similar arrangement. After passing the hearth with the cooking utensils and the carefully stacked firewood, one would enter the main cabin (Fig. 4.2, C).

This room was illuminated through windows in the stern (Fig. 4.3). One window frame, with still attached glass, was found during excavation (Kaijser 1983:26, 48, 80–81). The majority of the eating equipment were found astern of the dividing bulkhead. I take this as an indication that the food was consumed in this room. Seven pewter spoons were found at the wreck, the majority of which were in the stern area (compare Kaijser 1983:15). Attempts have been made to interpret artefact assemblages from wrecks through engendering them. Dutch archaeologist André van Holk has for instance discussed whether it is possible to determine the presence of children and woman on board Dutch inland vessels through artefact assemblages. From doing so he could reveal family constellations aboard ships through the evidence from shipwrecks (1997:219–230). Even if we are not dealing with a nuclear family here, van Holk's reasoning on how certain individuals are represented through personal belongings may be of some help. One may start with asking the question: who did these spoons belong to?

In early modern Europe it was common to carry your own spoon and knife (cf. Troels-Lund 1903:170ff) and the seven spoons recovered from the 'Jutholmen Wreck' may thus correspond to the plausible number of crewmembers. The majority of the spoons were found quite far aft in the ship, which indicates that they were located in the cabin when the ship sank. Two spoons were found a few metres forward, in an area which ought to correspond to the foremost part of the galley, at the break of the quarterdeck (Kaijser 1983:96ff). If we regard spoons as personal belongings, the location of these items in the stern would indicate that this was where the crew kept their personal effects.

There are other items that are to be regarded as personal belongings in the ship. No less than 89 parts of clay pipes were found during the excavation, 66 of which consist of parts of the stems and 23 of bowls with stems, more or less well-preserved (Kaijser 1983:49). Many of these pipes should be seen as parts of a cultural layer in the area (see Arnshav 2008) rather than the ship. The dating of the pipes, judging from the manufacturer's marks and typology, span from around 1660 to 1735 (compare Åkerhagen 2009) which further underlines the miscellaneous origin of the pipes. One more homogenous group may be discerned among these pipes. The group consists of eight pipes with similarly shaped bowls (Kaijser 1983:42). According to Åkerhagen this type, fitted with a crowned hammer, was produced by Abraham Reinerz Blom, between 1696 and 1705 (Åkerhagen 2009). The homogenous character of this group, as well as the coherence of the context in which the group appears, suggests to me that the pipes should be seen in context of the ship. Their location in the stern, further underlines the function of this area as the place where the crew stored their personal effects.

In the stern towards the portside, there is a small square opening in the bottom planking (Fig. 4.2, E). The opening was depicted on the early sketches from the site, but without further comments. The reports make no note of it (Cederlund 1982b, Kaijser 1983). It is the discharge hole for the ship's privy. The removal of human waste aboard ships has been an important consideration (for an overview see Simmons 1998, Munday 1978). Evidence for different sanitary accommodations on seventeenth-century vessels derives from various depictions and models. Most of the known arrangements are located outside the hull-planking in beakheads or quarter-galleries, which are very significant structural and stylistic elements and artists and model-makers paid them much attention.

The location of this facility on board the 'Jutholmen Wreck', inside the stern cabin, suggest that it was used by all on board, a condition that contrasts to for instance naval vessels where those of lower rank would have their necessary seating in the beakhead (Simmons 1997, Munday 1978:125–140). The 'Jutholmen Wreck', just like the majority of *fluits*, did not have a beakhead.

In conclusion, the 'Jutholmen Wreck' reveals a spatial configuration suggesting that the crew kept their personal belongings – at least their spoons and pipes – under the quarterdeck in the ship's stern. This is where they would eat, and it seems reasonable to assume that the crew was lodged inside this space as well. This is also the place where the vital seat was located. Whether there was another room in the stern-area, above the quarterdeck, remains uncertain (Fig. 4.2, F). There is no need to get absorbed in hypothetical discussions regarding the presence or use of such a space here as there are other wrecks that are more informative in this respect, namely the the 'Ghost Ship' and the 'Lion Wreck' (see below).

A contrasting picture

It is an exaggeration to assert that living conditions on board *fluits* have been a hot research topic in the past. Books and articles have been written about *fluits*, but not with the ship's interior as main focus. Nevertheless, it is evident that several authors do have ideas on how the *fluit's* interior was arranged. Even if the main focus of the texts has been different, the interior and its arrangement is mentioned in passing. Thus, ideas regarding the internal arrangement of the 'Jutholmen Wreck' have also flourished. For instance it is argued that:

> It was common practice at the end of the seventeenth century, to carry a good deal of wine on board ships. The *captain* would bring out the bottled wine when he entertained guests in *his cabin* (Kaijser 1983:47 my abbreviation, see also Rönnby & Adams 1994:76).

Alas, there is no reference to why this is regarded as 'common practice', nor is the location of the crew's lodgings discussed. The space referred to as the 'captain's cabin' is the main cabin (Fig. 4.2, C).

Contrary to the spatial reconstruction of the 'Jutholmen Wreck' it is apparent that all on board were moving in a shared space in the stern rather than spread all over the hull in accordance to rank. Even if there are indications that the space underneath the quarterdeck was further divided into smaller cabins, as the bulkhead (Fig. 4.2, G) could possibly indicate, the spatial arrangement does not put a huge distance between high and low.

There is reason to return to these and similar observations in the following chapter, and what implications they have for conceptions of shipboard life in general. In any case, it is certain that the spatial arrangement as revealed from this and other wrecks differs from how it has been interpreted before.

The *Anna Maria*

Not far from the 'Jutholmen Wreck' are the remains of a much larger *fluit*. The idea of a shipwreck resting on the seabed at this spot has existed for a long time (Fig. 4.1). According to local tradition, the wreck, called 'The Salt ship' (sw. *Saltskutan*), had sunk in the nineteenth century, and the tradition also mentioned a fire (Ahlström 1995:71, 1997:89). Just as with the 'Jutholmen Wreck', recreational divers raised objects from the wreck. Archaeologists soon realized that the oral tradition must have placed the foundering in the wrong century as the recovered artefacts appeared to be at least one hundred years older (see Cederlund 1997:115, Rönnby & Adams 1994:81).

As described in chapter 2 fieldwork aiming to gather clues that could lead to the original identity of wrecks was common in the 1980s (also Cederlund 1983, 1997). Recreational divers played an important role in this work and a group was formed around the large anonymous ship in Dalarö. Judging from the cross-sectional shape of the hull, which was recorded by the divers in the group, it was assumed that the ship was of Dutch origin, possibly a large *fluit* (Petersén 1987:293-304).

A small excavation in the stern of the ship revealed casks containing bar iron and rolls of copper plate deriving from the cargo (Dahlman et al. 1990). Besides the metals, the cargo consisted of sawn planks, which still rest carefully stacked on the ship's lower deck. Several wood samples taken for dendrochronological analysis were sawn off and revealed that the planks in the cargo came from trees felled in 1707–1708. The conclusion was that the ship most likely would have foundered one or two years after this date (for information regarding the surveys on the *Anna Maria*, see Dahlman et al. 1986, 1990, Petersén 1987:293–304, 1993, also Eriksson forthcoming).

These clues led historian Christian Ahlström to documents describing a large *fluit* named *Anna Maria* that caught fire and sank in Dalarö harbour on the evening of 6 February 1709 (Ahlström 1997:88–110). The *Anna Maria* was owned by a consortium of 15 ship-owners of Stockholm who had ordered the ship to be built in Amsterdam in 1693. The ship was finished the following year. According to the ship-builders the ship's length was 132 feet and the beam 28 ½ feet. Assuming that the information was given in Amsterdam feet that would mean a length of 37.24 m and a beam of 8.04 m (Ahlström 1997:103).

The *Anna Maria* was used in the same way as the majority of her sister *fluits* in this period. Transporting iron, tar and wood out from the Baltic, down to Amsterdam and bringing salt and wine back to Sweden from Portugal. She was a tool in the economic tale of fortune that involved both Sweden and the Netherlands in the seventeenth century – a century known in Sweden as the 'great power period' and as the 'golden age' in the Netherlands (Fahlborg 1923:205–281, Fahlström 1947:73–97, Noldus 2002, 2005 van Zanden & van Tielhof 2009:389–403).

In the fall of 1708 the *Anna Maria* was loaded with sawn pine planks, copper plates, iron and blister steel, packed in casks, intended for Lisbon, Portugal. The combination of both wood and metal-products in the same load was common. If a ship only carried metal-products the hull would be heavy with a lot of unused space, whereas a cargo consisting of wood only was not heavy enough and would result in a filled hull that floated to high (cf. Müller 1998:129).

On her way south from Stockholm, the *Anna Maria*'s crew dropped anchor at Dalarö. It was normal to make stop here waiting for the right weather, taking pilot and similar (Ahlström 1995:77, 1997:107). During their halt in Dalarö the weather changed, the temperature fell, and the ship became icebound. The *Anna Maria*, together with seven other ships, had to overwinter where they lay. The majority of the crew was sent home, but five men stayed on board to keep watch. The winter of 1708–09 was extremely cold and it is easy to imagine that the hearth in the galley was extensively used. It is also easy to imagine just how boring it would be to spend the dark Nordic winter-months on board an ice-bound ship. In order to make the best of the situation the crew invited the crew from another of the trapped ships for dinner on board the *Anna Maria*. After eating, smoking and shaving, they went for a beer at the local inn. The fire in the galley was probably left unattended despite claims to the contrary. In any case, whether from stray embers or sparks, the ship was soon all in flames. Attempts were made to put out the fire but it was futile. The three crewmembers who first left the ship and went ashore were punished with four days on bread and water, whereas the two who later left the ship totally unwatched endured the same punishment for eight days (for more information regarding the written sources regarding the *Anna Maria*, see Ahlström 1995:70–91 or 1997:87–110).

The rooms on board the Anna Maria

Time has passed surprisingly slowly 18 m below the water surface in Dalarö harbour. The traces of the drama that took place here on the evening of 6 February 1709 are still clearly visible. According to the case records, the fire spread from the galley (Fig. 4.4, B), to the firewood storage and then to the rest of the ship (Ahlström 1995:70–91, 1997:87–110). The course of events may be revealed from the drawings as the level of preservation is strikingly better below the lower deck. It was on this deck-level that the hearth was located and the structure above was erased by fire. When the fire reached the waterline the ship sank through the ice.

The hold is the largest room and stretches from stem to stern (Fig. 4.4, E). It is still loaded with bar iron, rolls of copper and similar heavy objects. On top of the hold is the lower deck (Fig. 4.4, C), which is preserved from amidships towards the bow. Before of the now missing mainmast, there has been a hatchway in the lower deck, providing access to the hold. Notches in the deck beams indicate the location of the supporting structure around a hatch and reveal that it was 2.15 m in length and 1.20 m wide (Fig. 4.4, G). A corresponding hatchway would have been placed above, in the main deck to form a shaft all the way down to the lowest part of the ship.

In the planking on both sides of the hull amidships, the lower and forward edges of loading ports are visible (Fig. 4.4, I) which have allowed access to the lower deck. The height of these ports has not been possible to measure, but they are approximately 0.75 m wide. The lower deck provided storage for commodities that were lighter or not supposed to get wet.

The foremost part of the lower deck was used as the cable room, which is indicated by the anchor which still can be observed in here. The anchor cable entered this room through a hatch in the main deck (Fig. 4.4, H.) which is indicated by notches in the preserved deck-beams. The hatch was placed abaft of the now absent windlass, which was raised in the 1960s and placed in the salvor's garden.

The lower deck of a large *fluit* like the *Anna Maria* was built in dimensions that enabled it to also serve other purposes than storage as well. The Swedish customs regulations of 1645 laid down that every merchant vessel made by a Swedish builder and in Swedish ownership was entitled to a one-sixth reduction of the normal customs rates. It was also stated that if such a vessel was carvel-built and could be fitted with 14 guns or more, the reduction of the customs rate could be as much as one-third. The *Anna Maria* was one of these ships (Ahlström 1997:103–104; Glete 2010:434). In wartime the hull of the *Anna Maria* could be converted into a fully-fledged warship (as we will return to in chapter 6). How heavy an armament the *Anna Maria* carried on her last voyage is not known.

The aft extension of the forecastle (Fig. 4.4, D) is revealed by a horizontally-oriented timber, attached directly to the deck. The pawl bitts in which the windlass barrel rotated, have been attached to still visible notches on the preserved deck-beam number 2, counting from the bow. The pawls have been integrated with the forecastle bulkhead. The sides of the forecastle reveal the lower edges of gunports. Wheels from gun carriages as well as iron round shot have been found in the area. If she carried more guns, which seems likely, they were most likely placed abaft the mainmast on the lower deck (compare Fig. 4.5)

The finds observed in the forecastle are of the character that suggests that the forecastle was used as a storage department (compare Petersén 1993) rather than lodgings. This however is an interpretation that runs contrary to existing ideas of how the *Anna Maria* and other *fluits* were spatially organized, as will be stressed in more detail below.

The burnt stern

Even if the *Anna Maria*'s stern to a large extent was destroyed by fire, the sternpost still endures in nearly its original length. This is a lucky coincidence as the height of the quarterdeck can be determined through the length of this timber. As described above concerning the 'Jutholmen

Wreck', the tiller enters the hull just above the end of the sternpost and the quarterdeck is placed just above the tiller.

The length of the quarterdeck can also be determined with some confidence. The break of the quarterdeck is usually located just abaft of the bilge pump. The aftermost beam of the main deck usually serves as the pump dale. The solution was common on *fluits* and many other Dutch ship types, and the outlet of this pump dale is visible on many seventeenth century depictions, as well as on several preserved wrecks (Eriksson 2012:17–25, Eriksson & Rönnby 2012a:350–361). The location of the fragmented bilge pump is located approximately eight metres from the stern (Fig. 4.4, J). The break of the quarterdeck was thus located just abaft of this spot.

Nothing is left of the floor of the rooms under the quarterdeck. Judging from the height of the quarterdeck (as revealed by the height of the sternpost) it seems reasonable that the floor was at the same level as the lower-deck, perhaps diverging slightly from the sheer.

Objects made out of inflammable material, stored high up in the stern of the ship, fell down into the hold as the hull- and deck-structure collapsed. Pottery, a bartmann jug and some bottles derive from the galley and main cabin above (compare Petersén 1993). But the artefacts observed at the site must be handled with care as the contextual situation is complicated. Massive cultural layers on the seafloor in Dalarö harbour through the centuries and the observed artefacts does not necessary derive from the ship. The bricks from the galley are found scattered down in the hold. The location of the loose bricks indicates that the hearth was located immediately abaft of the break of the quarterdeck (Fig. 4.4, B). The location is thus comparable to what we see on many other wrecks of *fluits*, like the 'Jutholmen Wreck' mentioned above, as well as the 'Lion Wreck' and the 'Ghost Ship'. The *fluit Juffrouw Catharina* sunk in Oxelösuds archipelago in 1747 reveals a similar location (Rönnby 1986, 1987, 1988, Rönnby & Adams 1994:90–101).

Clues from other sources

Archaeology in historical periods is sometimes motivated by the fact that everything is not described in the texts. Sometimes it is relevant to turn the argument around and argue that all material culture is not preserved or ancient monuments are rarely complete. So instead of using material remains to fill up the gaps in the written record, texts may be used to reconstruct the materials and artefacts that have been lost through the ravages of time. Instead of providing the explanation to mute material remains, they can offer clues for their reconstruction. The analysis may still be based on the human entanglement with the surrounding world and all the things within it.

There are actually some clues to what the *Anna Maria*'s destroyed stern looked like in the accounts from the trial. According to the case records held after the wrecking of the *Anna Maria*, the 'firewood (was) stored between the cabin and the mizzen mast 3 to 4 feet from the galley' (Ahlström 1997:97). We do not know how big the pile of firewood on board the *Anna Maria* was, so it is not possible to determine the exact location of the bulkhead that separated the galley and the cabin from this written testimony alone. The written account describes that the fireplace was placed approximately 1.2–1.5 m from the mizzenmast. The testimony also mentions another important clue, namely that the space under the quarterdeck was divided into two rooms, the galley (Fig. 4.4, B) and the cabin (Fig. 4.4, A).

A bulkhead separating the space under the quarterdeck implies an arrangement of rooms recognizable on other wrecks of *fluits* as well as on preserved drawings (cf. Ketting 2006:100, Hoving & Emke 2000:42ff Wegener Sleeswyk 2003:141f, 169f). There is one particular drawing which displays many similarities with the *Anna Maria* (Fig. 4.5). It was published by Åke Clason Rålamb (1651–1718), in his *Skeps Byggerij – eller Adelig öfvnings Tionde Tom*, (*Shipbuilding – or the Tenth Volume of Noble Training*) in 1691. According to Rålamb, the depicted ship is 'a *fluit* or cargo carrier of 300 lasts, with a length of 130 feet and a beam of 28 feet' (1943:25, plate G., my translation)'. The dimensions of Rålamb's *fluit*, 300 lasts, 130 feet in length and 28 feet in the beam (ibid.), may be compared to the corresponding dimensions of the *Anna Maria*'s 274 lasts, 132 feet in length and 28 ½ feet in the beam (Ahlström 1997:96,103). The *Anna Maria*'s measurements are given in Amsterdam feet, which are 282.1 mm (ibid. 103) but it is uncertain what standard Rålamb is using. A Swedish foot was 297 mm at this time.

Regardless of the standards, the drawing, published in 1691, and the *Anna Maria*, launched three years later, are not too different. The location of loading ports amidships, the smaller hatch abaft the windlass, the location of the main loading hatch before the main mast and the overall dimensions of the hull suggest that the icebound ship that caught fire and sank in Dalarö harbour would have appeared much like the ship in Rålamb's drawing.

But just as with other preserved drawings of *fluits*, Rålamb provides us with scarce information on how the different rooms were used. He only mentions the rooms under the tiller as *cajutan* ('cabin' in English), the room above the tiller as *Hyttan* (which translated means the 'hut' or 'poop') (1943:25). He gives no information about the location of the galley and similar facilities. Preserved drawings of *fluits* reveal the seemingly standardized pattern when it comes to decks, bulkheads and hatches – the structures that define space (Rålamb 1943:25, Plate G. Chapman 1768, plate LIII, fig.6., Hoving 1992, Hoving & Emke 2000), but are less informative when it comes to describe how these rooms were used. With the information from the *Anna Maria* wreck site and the written sources from the trials held after the loss, we may, with some confidence, identify the functions and use of the rooms revealed by other, mainly iconographic material.

As will be stressed in more detail in the following chapter it is evident that the lodgings on board the *Anna Maria*, were located under the quarterdeck in the stern of the vessel (rooms A and B on Fig. 4.4) rather than in the forecastle (Fig. 4.4, D) in the bow. This is further underlined by the written trials-accounts, which describe how they cooked herring and heated porridge and ate under the quarterdeck (Ahlström 1995:70–91, 1997:87–110). The *Anna Maria* therefore had an internal arrangement which was, at least from what has been possible to reveal archaeologically, more or less similar to the 'Jutholmen Wreck'.

There have been previous attempts to reconstruct the interior of the *Anna Maria*. However, just as with the 'Jutholmen Wreck', the proposed spatial arrangement of the *Anna Maria* differs from the situation revealed above. There is thus reason to have a closer look at the previous reconstruction.

The previous reconstruction

As described in chapter 2, researchers of old ships come from various backgrounds and have different aims and scopes in their ship-interest. An important group here are model-builders, who have their own journals, internet forums and similar, where they share ideas, drawings, pictures and knowledge about old ships, both in full scale and as models. As the discussions within this sphere of ship-research have a tendency to be used in maritime and nautical archaeology, I find it necessary to unpack this reconstruction of the *Anna Maria* with some detail. Not least as we have come to different conclusions.

In an article model builder Cor Emke describes how he has proceeded in producing plans of the *Anna Maria*. His reconstruction is based on Rålamb's drawing (Fig. 4.5) rather than on the physical remains of the old *fluit*. As a result he has come up with an inadequate spatial arrangement on board the ship. He quotes the abovementioned story about the icebound ship and the majority of the crew who were sent home, and claims that:

> The five who remained had to survive the very cold winter with the *galley in the forecastle* as their only source of heating. Because it was impossible to heat this space sufficiently, since the planking was single and with many cracks and openings, they made a fireplace and living accommodation in *the gun room* in the stern part of the ship.
>
> The gun room was a well-protected place inside the ship, and could be heated comfortably. The men would have built a *makeshift* fireplace with some bricks, tiles and sand. (Emke 2001:381, or 2004:6, my abbreviations)

Emke gives no reference to why he think that the crew was lodged in the forecastle, or why the galley was located in this space. One thing is certain, however: there are no traces of a galley in the relatively well-preserved forecastle of the *Anna Maria*. Traces of a fireplace would definitely have been visible at the site. As for the planking, it is doubled inside this space, not single as indicated in the quote.

But there are several other features that do not correspond with the remains of the *Anna Maria* at the seabed in Dalarö harbour. The location of the bilge pump, and the lowered deck in the forecastle. The fact that Emke refers to a space as the 'gun room', or *'konstapels kamer'* in the Dutch version of the article (Emke 2001) in which the 'makeshift' fireplace was made, provides enough clues to establish from which source the spatial arrangement of his reconstruction derives. It is clear that Emke has substituted the arrangement of decks and bulkheads from the *Pinnace* described by Nicolaes Witsen in his *Aeoloude En Hedendaegshe Scheeps-Bouw* from 1671 (compare Hoving 2012: 156, Witsen 1979: 58ff, plate XLII).

At first glimpse it may seem insignificant to borrow the inner workings of a *pinnace*, which were armed and commonly used as warships, and place this inside a *fluit*'s hull. But as spatial arrangements within a building may be argued to reflect the relations between its inhabitants, things become a bit more problematic. A reconstruction where the interior of a naval ship is placed inside a merchant vessel makes assumptions about the relations between officers, commons and gunners. This is a matter of an oversimplistic projection of the social climate of naval ships onto the remains of merchant vessels. There is reason to return to this in the following chapter.

The 'Ghost Ship'

In 2003 the employees of the companies Deep Sea Productions (DSP) and MMT (Marin Mätteknik) discovered a nearly totally intact *fluit* at a water depth of 130 m some 30 nautical miles east of Gotska Sandön, near the very middle of the Baltic Sea (Fig. 4.6 and 4.7). In 2009 MARIS (Maritime Archaeological Research Institute at Södertörn University), together with the companies that made the discovery, formed an international research group around the wreck. As described in chapter 3 all recording and sampling was made using Remotely Operated Vehicles (ROV) (Dixelius et al. 2011, Eriksson & Rönnby 2012a).

Dendrochronological analysis of wood samples has shown that the wood grew in the northeast of current Germany. The felling of the tree has been estimated to between AD 1669 and 1693 (Koehler et al. 2012). The perhaps 300 years that has passed since the ship broke the surface appears to have been remarkably uneventful, and traces of the wrecking process, as well as the ship's last manoeuvre, are still visible at the site.

A coincidence that perhaps does not owe much to the interpretation of everyday life on board, but which illustrates the potential of the wreck as a 'time capsule', is the orientation of the spars and yards of the rig. The yards reveal that the courses of the foresail, as well as the mizzen, were sheeted for starboard tack, while the mainsail was set for port. The manoeuvre is called 'heaving to' and means that one or more sails are backed in order to balance the driving force from the other sails (Eriksson & Rönnby 2012a:359). Through this manoeuvre the ship would stop. We may only speculate as to why the crew decided to heave to and stop. Perhaps the intention was to get into the lifeboat, or maybe they needed all hands at the pumps? The main cause of sinking remains unknown as the hull shows no visible damage.

When the ship broke the surface it healed over to port. A huge amount of air pressure built up inside the sinking hull which pushed up the deck-planks along the starboard-side. Once these were removed and the air evacuated through the gap in the deck, the ship started to sink rapidly. On the journey towards the seabed loose objects drifted away. Most likely the capstan left the ship at this stage and perhaps also the missing starboard side pump.

The ship struck the seabed so hard that the bow sunk into the mud and the mizzenmast fell towards the bow. It broke the foremost deck-beam of the quarterdeck as it fell. The mast was stepped in the floor inside the galley (Fig. 4.8, B). The lower end of the mast kicked out the bulkhead that used to divide the galley from the main cabin. The mizzen mast finally came to rest on the main deck with its lower end in the ship's stove.

After this dramatic episode a more uneventful period followed. The traces visible are just those of the slow ravages of time. Wood gets soft, rope rots away, nails rust and vanish into red stains on the surface of planks, and the disintegration of the ship begins. In stark contrast to the dramatic events when the ship sank, this is a very slow process. The spars and yards of the rig fall down on deck or slide away down to the seafloor. The transom, built out of thin planks and fastened with iron nails, falls apart. So does the clinker planking of the bulwark. The paint on two burghers carved in wood, the *hoekmen* (see chapter 7), with their fancy clothes, starts to fade as these 'lions of fashion' were laid to rest on either side of the stern. The upper compartment in the stern, which is nailed together, collapses and its component parts rest in the vicinity. Sediments build up inside the ship.

Everyday space on board the 'Ghost Ship'

Even if the access to the wreck is limited due to the water depth, it is possible to make some general statements on how the interior of the ship was arranged. The hull of the 'Ghost Ship' measures 27 m in length, and is around 7 m wide. Even if the ship is more than ten metres shorter than for instance the *Anna Maria* and the *fluits* depicted by Rålamb (1943:25. plate G) (see above Fig. 4.5), the 'Ghost Ship' reveals an almost identical arrangement of decks and bulkheads, and thus equivalent comparable set of rooms.

Starting in the bow, the foredeck has partly disintegrated. The waterway, along the ceiling, as well as the two thicker planks oriented on each side of the centreline, functioning as foremast partners, is preserved. The deck does not follow the sheer of the planking as it is more horizontal. The room located underneath the foredeck (Fig. 4.8, F) is low (*c.* 1.4 m.). One standing stanchion is connected to the aftermost of the forecastle's deck beams, suggesting some kind of bulkhead. But one could question how closed this space has been. The construction of the foredeck differs from the quarterdeck as it does not have the laths placed underneath the gaps between the deck planks (see below) and is thus not as watertight as the quarterdeck. This will be considered further below.

A grinding stone and an anchor-buoy have come into view when filming inside the forecastle. A pile of what appears to be some form of soft organic material, possibly sailcloth or rope, has also been found in here, suggesting this room functioned as a storage department. Objects such as this, which were used for the maintenance of the ship, were kept inside the forecastle. Consequently, there would be no need for a totally enclosed space. The fact that the wet anchor cable would have passed through the forecastle would have called for ventilation.

The main deck starts right abaft of the stempost and ends just abaft the pumps, and follows the sheer more or less, perhaps flattening out a bit towards the bow. The aftermost deckbeam of the main deck also serves as the pump-dale. The main loading hatch (Fig. 4.8, G), measuring *c.* 2.1 m in length, is placed amidships. Notches in the longitugal oriented timbers of the coaming indicate that two cross beams could be placed over the hatch, suggesting the opening could be divided into three. The hatch provides access to the lower deck (Fig. 4.8, D).

In between the main hatch and the windlass is a smaller opening in the deck (Fig. 4.8, H) providing access to the cable-tier, which was located in the foremost part of the lower deck. Abaft of the main mast there is another smaller hatch (Fig. 4.8, I). The coamings of these hatches differ from each other. On the main hatchway the hatch itself would fit on the outside of the coaming, and a similar type of coaming is found at the cable-tier hatchway. The coaming of the hatch abaft the mainmast is of a different type as it reveals that the hatch was lowered into the coaming. The so-called 'Lion Wreck' reveals a similar arrangement of the hatches (Eriksson 2012b, also below).

The most likely reason behind this difference in the construction of the hatchway coamings has to do with the required access to the space underneath the deck. The main hatch would not have to be opened during voyage, and the cable tier perhaps did not have to be opened on a daily basis. What was kept in the space between the mainmast and the galley (Fig. 4.8, J) that required more regular access? On board *fluits* that carried guns, for instance the one depicted on Rålambs drawing (Fig. 4.5), the artillery for the ship is located here. On board the 'Ghost Ship' this space was accessible from the galley. It may also be that this was the space where passengers were lodged, as shown on a drawing of a *hoeker* (Fig. 4.12, B). This will be considered further at the end of this chapter.

ROVs have explored those parts of the lower deck, accessible from the main hatch (Fig. 4.8, G) and the smaller hatch (Fig. 4.8, H) abaft the windlass. Amidships the lower deck appears to have been almost empty, apart from the accumulated sediments covering the deck, and most likely a hatch leading to the hold (as seen on the *Anna Maria*, Fig. 4.4, G). When inspecting the space beneath the small hatch abaft the windlass, broken barrels and wooden cases were seen. It appears likely that these objects were pushed forward as the ship hit the seabed.

Quarters

The break of the quarterdeck is located just abaft of the bilge pumps. The bulkhead is not preserved but the location of a door is revealed through notches for a door frame in the foremost quarterdeck beam resting loose on the main deck before its original position.

An unusual feature is the construction of the quarterdeck. Underneath the gaps between the deck planks thin laths have been placed to provide support for caulking. This additional effort must be understood as an attempt to make the quarterdeck, and the space underneath, as watertight as possible. The space underneath the quarterdeck is divided in two by a bulkhead, and the foremost room is the galley. The situation is thus the same as described above concerning both the *Anna Maria* and the 'Jutholmen Wreck'.

The hearth is located towards the portside. The construction of the hearth on board the 'Ghost Ship' is easily to distinguish as it to a large extent still is intact. It consists of four corner pillars, stretching from the floor and up to the underside of the quarterdeck. Short, horizontally-oriented planks were nailed to these pillars to form a box, measuring 0.9 m x 0.9 m.

The preserved corner pillars slope inwards, towards the centre of the fireplace, and the hearth thus narrows towards the roof. The exhaust was through a quadratic opening in the quarterdeck. Inside this wooden construction a fireplace made out of bricks and glazed tiles was built. The bricks and tiles have fallen down and are lying in stacks in connection with the construction. Similar glazed tiles have been found at the *Jouffrouw Catherina* (Rönnby 1989).

Judging from the space around the hearth, the cook stood abaft of the fireplace, while stirring the pots. Originally the hearth would have been fitted with some sort of wrought iron hanging device for the cooking cauldron, like its counterpart on land. Towards the centre of the ship was the mizzenmast. The firewood store should be located in the vicinity, as still visible on the 'Jutholmen Wreck' and as has been described in written sources regarding the *Anna Maria* (Ahlström 1995, 1997). The firewood on board the 'Ghost Ship' is likely to have drifted away as the galley was filled with water.

The bulkhead that separated the galley from the stern cabin is partly preserved. The hull is *c.* 6.5 m wide inside the planking and the length of the galley around 2.5 m, which gives a floor area of around 16.5 m². The tumblehome has reduced the height along the sides which would have reduced the usable area. The space next to the sides of the hull, where standing height is limited, would have been used for different storage purposes, such as sitting benches, berth and so forth. For instance, the triangular space between the hearth and the hull side may have been used for the storage of cooking utensils.

The cabin

The separating bulkhead was placed 4 m from the sternpost (Fig. 4.8). Above the roof is the *hennegat* – the low space housing the tiller. Two of the beams that formed the supporting structure of the inner roof are preserved, while the foremost of these has fallen down. This beam has three notches for standing stanchions. Two of these would also have served as the doorframe. Most likely the door was located towards the starboard side, so that it aligns with the door leading out on deck. This means that one could pass from the cabin and up on deck without interfering with the hearth, and possibly also the cook. Such a location also aligns with the loading port in the stern. Long objects, stowed into the lower area, would enter the ship through a hatch in the stern planking, be carried through the cabin, passing through the door in the bulkhead, and then the galley, before entering the lower deck through an opening that most likely was placed underneath the door leading out on deck. The standing stanchions suggest horizontally-oriented planks for the closing of the bulkhead between the galley and the cabin.

In the middle of the stern cabin is a table. It is now resting upside down with the top embedded under the sediments covering the floor. The table is only revealed through one of the table legs that comes up through the sediments on the floor (Fig. 4.8, M). As the table top, and the corresponding leg at the other end of the table, are missing, it is not possible to determine its size with any certainty.

The ROVs could not go into the cabin, but when filming through the windows in the stern and down in between the beams of the quarterdeck it was possible to distinguish two chests (Fig. 4.8, L). Their dimensions have not been possible to measure with precision, but have been estimated in relation to other constructional elements. It appears likely that these chests were originally placed alongside the table.

The sources that describe interiors of *fluits* are scarce and the situation is quite similar when it comes to the houses of common people on land. Information concerning homes of peasants and burgess, are meagre from the seventeenth century. Through estate inventories from the period it is apparent that there is a conspicuous absence of chairs. Instead, different benches provided seating (cf. Olsson 1957). Similar chests for seating are familiar sights in seventeenth-century vernacular interiors on land (for instance Erixon 1947).

The size of the chest from the 'Ghost Ship' suggest that at least three people could be seated at each chest, and with one person at each end of the table we probably have more or less the entire crew seated around the same table. In this sense the interior of the 'Ghost Ship' provides an entrance to a discussion regarding the social dimensions of eating, as this is an activity that involves bonding or the exclusion of groups (cf. Fahlander 2010:36). On the 'Ghost Ship' one can imagine a crewmember entering the door in the bulkhead at the break of the quarterdeck, jumping down the stairs and landing with his boots on the galley floor. Before passing through the galley he asks the cook what will be served today, perhaps grimacing ironically at the answer before continuing towards the cabin. When passing through the door the fellow crewmembers are already seated, perhaps waiting for the captain to read the prayers. We will return to a discussion regarding foodways and commensality in the following chapter.

Openings in the stern

The cabin of the 'Ghost Ship' reveals the seemingly standardized arrangement of openings in the stern. Two of these are windows, placed in the rounding of the stern (Fig. 4.8, N), enabling a view straight abaft, but also the situation outside the quarter. The frames of these windows are gone but the cases are preserved and reveal their size and shape. Here one may recall the windowframe from the 'Jutholmen Wreck', which originally had a similar location (Fig. 4.3).

On each side of the sternpost there are small hawseholes. Near the floor, towards the starboard side, is a loading port. This hatch would have been of minor consideration during sail as it would only be opened while stowing long objects into the lower deck. A small square opening is visible on the outside of the ship's portside in the stern, and it might be a discharge for a privy, like the one observed on the 'Jutholmen Wreck'. The discharge hole of the 'Ghost Ship' has not been examined in detail, but we shall return to this feature in the discussion regarding the so-called 'Lion Wreck'.

The upper cabin

Just like other *fluits* the 'Ghost Ship' was steered using a whipstaff with the helmsman placed out on the quarterdeck, above the galley and thus abaft of the mizzenmast. The location of the whipstaff is revealed by a notch in one of the quarterdeck planks. Abaft of the helmsman's stand, was a small cabin. The roof as well as the bulkheads forming this space have disintegrated, and the deeply curved beams that used to support the roof reveal the general shape and proportions of this space. The area inside with full height was around 6.5 m². The tumblehome is very articulated here, and the floor area is a couple of square metres more. The height in the front edge of this space was around 140 cm along the centre line.

No clearly identifiable objects indicating how this space was used have been observed in situ. A chest found on the seabed outside the starboard quarter may derive from the upper cabin. This small space was divided further, though. On the inside of the uppermost, clinker-laid planking on the port-side there are remains of a bulkhead made out of vertically oriented planks. In connection to this bulkhead the planking of the quarter-deck ends. The bulkhead is placed *c*. 0.8m before the transom, forming a very small room with no floor. A suggested function for this space was as a toilet. Support for such an interpretation is found as the presence of soil-pipes in iconographical sources (see fig. 6.4, for a comparison see Simmons 1997:40) and thus an alternative to the solution seen on the Jutholmen and 'Lion Wreck' ships.

The 'Lion Wreck'

In 2009 the divers Anders Backström and Marcus Hårde searched the seabed north of Värmdö northeast of Stockholm (Fig. 4.9) with the aim of relocating a sunken steamer named *Alma*. At a water depth of almost 50 m the echo sounder revealed a promising anomaly that might be a shipwreck. But instead of a big rusty steamer, they confronted a seventeenth-century merchant ship, with standing masts and intact wooden carvings – another 'Ghost Ship'! On top of the rudder a small, carved lion grinned at the divers, inspiring its working name, the 'Lion Wreck'. Although extremely fragile, the ship proved to be remarkably intact.

The divers made some initial measurements to record the ship, using measuring tapes, and the site was extensively photographed using both stills and video camera. The material could be processed into rough sketches that formed the starting point for a more thorough investigation of the site, in cooperation with the divers who found the wreck (the fieldwork has been described in Eriksson 2012b).

Down at 50 m the 'Lion Wreck' has remained out of reach for humans since the seventeenth century, and there are no indications of salvage operations. The rigging is complete even if it has disintegrated. The 'Lion Wreck' probably sank due to a collision. The bowsprit is broken and the foremast is cracked right below the chesstres. Whether the ship hit a rock or another vessel remains uncertain. A spar that has no clear function on the ship may indicate the latter.

The lower main- and foremasts are still standing, while the mizzenmast has tilted to port and towards the bow. Its lower end is still resting in its step. The ship has come to rest on its keel with no apparent list, which is quite typical for *fluits* as they are so flat-bottomed. The hull measures 21.8 m between the posts, which makes the 'Lion Wreck' a quite small *fluit*. But, despite her diminutive scale, the ship has all the component parts of the larger sisters.

Embarking

The wreck reveals many interesting details, like the short planks nailed on both hull sides to form a staircase ladder from the waterline up to the deck, used when embarking from a boat. Nicolaes Witsen shows a similar arrangement on a drawing of a *fluit* in 1671 (Witsen, 1979: 174, reproduced in Cederlund, 1982: 37 fig. 17). After climbing up the side of the hull, one would enter the main deck just before the mainmast and the loading hatch (Fig. 4.10, E). The coaming of the hatch is intact. The length of this hatchway is similar to that on the 'Ghost Ship' and that on the *Anna Maria* on the lower deck, just above two metres. Notches in the coaming reveal that it was divided in two using a crossbeam.

Following the examples as revealed by the 'Ghost Ship' and the *Anna Maria* there is another small hatch opening in the main deck, just abaft of the windlass (Fig. 4.10, G). The coaming of this hatch has disintegrated but the surrounding deck-planks reveal its extension. This small hatch allowed access to the cable-tier. The hold is filled with sediment so it is difficult to determine any structural detail below the main deck in the bow. Some kind of bulkhead would have divided the cable-tier from the cargo-hold. While looking between the eroded deck-planks in the bow the divers observed some thick ropes: possibly the anchor cables.

There is also a smaller hatch in the deck abaft the mainmast (Fig. 4.10, F). It is constructed with the hatch cover resting inside the coaming, as described regarding the 'Ghost Ship' (see above). The main deck ends just abaft the windlass. Forward of this point the deck is lowered and slopes down to the hawseholes in the bow, through which the anchor cables used to run. The 'Lion Wreck' differs from the other *fluits* through the absence of a forecastle.

Quarterdeck

Abaft of the pumps and the pumpdale the quarterdeck rises $c.$ 0.65 cm above the upper deck. When the mizzenmast tilted to port it pushed most of the planks of the quarterdeck in this direction. The location of the whipstaff, right abaft the mizzenmast, is visible through a notch in the quarterdeck planks.

As the foremost of the quarterdeck beam is missing as well as the connected bulkhead, the design of the entrance to the rooms below remains uncertain. The hold is filled with sediment which makes it difficult to determine the arrangement of rooms and bulkheads underneath the quarterdeck. However, the location of hatches, ports and windows provide some references to the internal arrangement and makes it is possible to assess the location of unseen structures in the interior.

The rooms under the quarterdeck appear to have been arranged in a similar way to the other *fluits* described above, but with some small variations. On board the previously described *fluits* the galleys were built up of bricks and have been located in the foremost room under the quarterdeck. The 'Lion Wreck' reveals no visible traces of a hearth (Fig. 4.10, A). The room where it should have been located is very small. In length, measured from the pump-dale to the end of the *hennegat* it is 1.6 m long and *c.* 5 m wide inside the planking. This would give an approximate floor area of 8 m². As the shape of the hull sides reduces the ability to make use of the total area the room was even smaller than this. An arrangement like the one on board the 'Ghost Ship' may have been difficult to house inside this limited space.

On the port side there is a port in the hull-planking. It is built up in the same way as a gunport with hinges along its upper edge and could be opened from the inside using a rope. A hole for this rope is clearly visible above the port. Due to the tumblehome the port is slanting upwards. In order to prevent rainwater from getting into the port, it is equipped with a small roof. The port has no counterpart on the starboard side and the location is a bit puzzling. On both the 'Jutholmen Wreck' and the 'Ghost Ship' the hearth is located here. It might be that the hearth on board the 'Lion Wreck' did not have an outlet above the hearth, like the one we have seen at the Ghost ship or the galley funnel described in the written testimony after the foundering of the *Anna Maria* (Ahlström 1994:79, 1997:98). Perhaps the portside port was enough to evacuate the smoke? Unfortunately the explanation for the arrangement of the fireplace and the port are well embedded in sediments 50 m below the water surface.

Main cabin

The main cabin is located abaft of the room that I prefer to call the galley, despite the uncertainties described above (Fig. 4.10, B). Seen from the stern we recognize the compulsory window openings of this room similar to the ones we have seen on the 'Ghost Ship'. That the entire contents of the interior – furniture, personal belongings and other items – everything that was inside this room when the ship sank – are still inside is a frustrating fact when peeping through the windows openings. The room is totally crammed with sediments and loose planks, and thus is impossible to access. The size of this room is around 15 m^2. But, as has been put forth above, the curvature of the hull side reduces the volume to some extent.

The size of the 'Lion Wreck's' crew would not have differed very much from either that of the 'Jutholmen Wreck' or the 'Ghost Ship'. The number and the size of the sails would have been about equal, and the same goes for the number of hands required for handling them. As The 'Lion Wreck' has no forecastle, the option to house the crew in the bow is non-existent. Just as on the ships described above, the crew of the 'Lion Wreck' were lodged in the stern.

The privy on board the 'Lion Wreck' is the best preserved example yet found. It is revealed by a small quadratic hole, 0.14 x 0.14 m, located in the hull's planking on the port side in the stern. It is placed just above the waterline which means that the movement of waves would have cleaned this facility from time to time. Attached to the inside of the discharge hole, there is a tube made up of four planks. The divers probed by sticking a folding ruler into the hole until it could go no further. It showed that the tube is 0.70 m long, which has enabled the seat so be included in the drawing. The seat is placed just underneath the portside window in the main cabin.

Two loading ports are visible in the stern on each side of the sternpost. These were located at level with the floor of the cabin. As on the 'Ghost Ship', long objects stowed in the hold would enter the ship, passing through the accommodation compartments, rather than through the main loading hatch on deck, when entering the hull.

Upper cabin

Astern of the helmsman's stand, up on the quarterdeck, there is a now collapsed upper cabin (Fig. 4.10, D). The framework of the bulkhead is still partly coherent even if it has fallen towards the stern. It consists of a curved beam which reveals the shape of the roof, and attached S-shaped standing stanchions (these are similar to the stanchions found loose at the 'Jutholmen Wreck', see Cederlund, 1982: 106). The room is filled with loose planks. Possible furnishings for this space are difficult to discern without removing loose timbers.

The room is very small. The height would not have exceeded c. 1.5 m. The transom in the stern is only c. 1.4 m. wide. The small hut thus corresponds closely with the one on board the 'Ghost Ship' (Fig. 4.8, C).

Conclusion

As mentioned in the beginning of this thesis *fluits* followed a standard design. The 'same' ship was built repeatedly with adjustments in different sizes. A preserved seventeenth-century drawing in the Amsterdam *Scheepvaartmuseum*, signed Franz Cornelis Keyser, is a revealing example of this as one single side-view is equipped with five different scale bars (reproduced in Hoving 1992:48, Hoving & Emke 2000:45) (Fig. 4.11). Consequently, the depiction shows a ship in five different sizes, from 90 to 130 feet, which mean between 25.4 to 36.7 m in length, depending on which scale you choose (using the Amsterdam foot which measures 0.282 m).

Dynamics in the size may also be read between the lines in Rålamb's description of the drawing entitled '*Fluit* or Spain freighter, for heavy load and convenience' which he mentions can be built '*up to* 114 feet in length' (Rålamb 1943:25, my translation and abbreviation). I read the formulation as an indication that the particular ship could be built smaller than 114 feet in length.

The locations of various bulkheads and hatches are accessible and available from the few drawings that are preserved. For instance dotted lines reveal the locations of decks and bulkheads on both Rålamb and Keyser (Hoving 1992:48, Hoving & Emke 2000:45, Rålamb 1943). The arrangement of decks, bulkheads and rooms is not contradicted by the wrecks described above. All confirm the uniform pattern, from the small 'Lion Wreck', measuring a mere 21.8 m between the posts, to the large *Anna Maria*, which is nearly 40 m.

However, and this is important, the actual wrecks add something that is not possible to determine from drawings, namely how the rooms defined by the decks and bulkheads were used. Without this information, rooms are nothing but empty boxes. As indicated above, regarding the 'Jutholmen Wreck' and the *Anna Maria*, this gap in knowledge has spurred different authors to suggest how they have thought space was arranged.

For instance Ab Hoving suggests that the interior of the *fluit* was arrangement like this:

> The lower deck had a height of no more than 4ft or 5 ft, and was meant as a 'tween deck' for the dry storage of cargo rather than accommodation for crew or passengers. Aft of this koebrugdek (...) but not interconnected, was the gun room, in which there were usually two guns per side. Aft of that was the captain's cabin, with some windows in the stern. (Hoving 1995:48–49, my abbreviations)

He continues, 'The crew were housed in the bow of the vessel abaft of which the ship had a windlass fitted' (ibid., my abbreviation; a similar configuration, this time complete with an illustration, is published in Hoving & Emke 2000:92). No comments are made regarding the location of the hearth and the ship's galley.

According to this version the captain appears to have been rather alone in the stern. The alleged lodgings for the crew in the forecastle are of approximately the same size, or smaller than the one the captain is supposed to have occupied on his own. This is a spatial arrangement that puts distance between high and low, and is what one might expect on board a naval ship, for example. Restricting movement patterns for different categories of people is a way to uphold discipline, and one would have had to behave accordingly. Certain groups were expected to occupy certain areas and have access to different rooms was strictly restricted, through estate and rank (see discussion in chapter 6). Hoving allows for possible variations of the pattern through mentioning that 'the internal arrangement of the smaller examples differed from other ship types' (1994:48).

As shown above, the analysis of the reconstruction and interpretation of the 'Jutholmen Wreck' differs from the previous one, where the captain inhabited the stern cabin on his own, kept his wine, his spoons and so on (see above, or Kaijser 1983:47, Rönnby & Adams 1994:76). A similar situation was apparent regarding the *Anna Maria*, where attempts at reconstructions have automatically installed the crew in the forecastle, together with the galley (Emke 2001 and 2004), regardless of the fact that there are no indications for such an arrangement on the wreck or in the written accounts!

The most important result emerging from the survey of space on board wrecked *fluits* is thus that the crew were accommodated in the stern rather than in the bow. Wrecks provide the possibility to install human actions and routines in spaces which otherwise would remain 'empty boxes' ready for speculation.

As shown in this chapter the fireplace is consequently located in the foremost room under the quarter deck. This is not unique for the four wrecked *fluits* reviewed in some detail above. A similar location for the galley has been observed on an unidentified *fluit* found outside Grässkär in the Stockholm archipelago as well as the wreck after *Juffrouw Catharina* (Maiden Catharina), also known as the 'Högskär Wreck', sunk outside Oxelösund on the east coast of Sweden. Both are examples of large *fluits*. The 'Grässkär Wreck' is 34 m long between the posts. The hull has disintegrated, but it is clear from deck-knees and shelf-clamps, that the ship had a typical *fluit* deck arrangement. A main deck ending at the break of the quarter, located in connection to the bilge-pump and a lower deck below. Clay pipes from the wreck have been dated to 1629 (Åkerhagen 2009), which indicates the time of sinking.

The *Juffrouw Catharina*, sank more than hundred years later, in 1747, but reveals a quite similar spatial arrangement, with a lower deck and the hearth located underneath the quarterdeck. She was some three metres longer between the posts (Rönnby 1986, 1987, 1988, Rönnby & Adams 1994). The wreck thought to be the remains of the German *fluit Engel Rafail* sunk 1724 in the Gulf of Finland also has the galley in this location (Sorokin 2005:42).

But let us also have a brief glimpse at sources other than wrecks that describe the division of space, in addition to the drawings of *fluits* mentioned above. For some reason more information has survived concerning related types rather than the *fluits* themselves in this respect. A manuscript, signed H. Decquer, dated to c. 1690 and kept in *Het Scheepvaartsmuseum* in Amsterdam, is illustrated by two drawings showing *katschips*. Both these drawings reveal spatial organization. The *katschip* is definitely related to the *fluit*. Exactly how they differ from the other *fluits* is a bit uncertain, but generally they are said to be a cheaper version (Hoving 1995:51ff, Wegener 2003:168ff, Ketting 2006:100ff).

One of these drawings shows the *katschip Nederhorst*, built for the Dutch VOC in 1671 (Fig. 4.12, A). This drawing bears many similarities to the division of space on board the 'Jutholmen Wreck', as neither of the two ships has a lower deck. There are also differences between the two, though, such as the aftermost space of *Nederhorst's* hold has been divided into a separate space mentioned as the 'bread and sail-store' (cf. Ketting 2006:100, Wegener Sleswyk 2003:169), whereas the hold on board the 'Jutholmen Wreck' was used for the storage of goods, all the way from stem to stern. The drawing of the *Nederhorst* is interesting as it also informs us that the foremost room under the quarterdeck was a room for the crew, whereas the forecastle was intended for the anchor cable (ibid.). The locations of the hearth and similar facilities are not shown.

The second drawing is slightly more recent than the *Nederhorst* and shows the *katschip Tamen*, built for the VOC in 1686 (Fig. 4.12, C). Apparently the absence of a lower deck was not in itself a feature which defined a hull as a *katschip* as the drawing reveals a plan of this deck level. *Tamen* is another example of where the crew is lodged in the aftermost half of the ship. The bow part of the lower deck is separated from the lodgings by a bulkhead. The main hatch, before the mainmast, is indicated on the drawing. As shown on the other drawings in this chapter, these hatchways are exclusively formed so that they are longer in the ship's lengthwise direction. The peculiar shape of the hatch on the drawing indicates that it provides access to the compartment, before and abaft of the bulkhead. As we saw on both the 'Ghost Ship' and the 'Lion Wreck', the notches in the coamings of the main hatches indicate that the openings could be divided. The foremost portion of the lower deck is occupied by the anchor cable.

The abovementioned *katschips* were built for the VOC and at least the *Tamen* appears to have carried quite heavy armament with a total of six gun-ports on the lower deck. The number of people aboard these ships, during these long voyages, would have been much greater than the *kats* or *fluits* used in the Baltic trade. How the spatial arrangement on board *fluits* was adjusted for these long voyages has been described by Nicolaes Witsen (Witsen 1979:178ff).

From the late eighteenth century, there are drawings of *bootschips* that reveal that the entire crew was lodged in the stern rather than in the bow. A very fine example of such a drawing, dated to 1780, shows the anchor cables in the cable room (MMR Inv nr T2690). The forecastles on *fluits* seem generally to have been used as storage departments. Tools have been found in the forecastle on both 'Jutholmen Wreck', the 'Ghost Ship' and on the *Anna Maria* (Petersén 1993). Of course one should not exclude the possibility that some crewmember, or some occasional passenger, might have chosen to sleep in the forecastle or somewhere else. The general impression is that the lodgings were in the stern.

Why then, do ship archaeologists and historians spontaneously lodge the crew before the mast when they reconstruct *fluits*, when there are no sources that speak in favour of such an arrangement? My short answer is that such an arrangement corresponds to an idea of what shipboard life should have been like. Functions, activities and people are put into the 'empty boxes' corresponding to an already existing idea. I will deal with the longer answer in the following chapter, where the interiors of the *fluit*, as reconstructed based on the evidence of the wrecks, is analysed through theoretically populating it.

5. Embarking *fluits*

In the previous chapter well-preserved wrecks were assembled into more or less complete ships. Even if important components are undoubtedly missing, the assessment of how the different rooms were used can be made with some confidence. The 'great discovery' was that all aboard were lodged in the stern rather than spread all over the hull, with the crew 'before the mast' and the command in the stern.

Even if the aim above has been to describe the *fluits* from what may be referred to as a human vantage point, omitting the descriptions of dimension of individual timbers, joints and trunnels that people most likely did not notice on an everyday basis, focus to a large extent was on the ships alone. In this chapter the objective is to attempt to embark the reconstructions and add human action.

The word *action* does not imply spectacular events but rather the routines and regular doings such as sleeping, cooking, eating and so on. Analysis is grounded in the conviction that life is constantly created through routines and action mediated, governed, encouraged and controlled by the material world – by things! The general question is thus: What kind of everyday life took place on board these ships?

Even if the individuals are long gone, the things involved in these activities are preserved. As noted by archaeologist Bjørnar Olsen, 'if things were invested with the ability to use ordinary language, they would talk to us in ways very banal, but also very imperative and effective; walk here, sit here, eat here, us that entrance, stop, move, turn, bow, lie down, gather, depart and so forth' (2010:60). The specific arrangement of things thus directs human actions. As a crew consists of a number of people the discussion may lead further to reasonings concerning the ship's hull as a mediator for interpersonal relations. Things may force people to do things together with others or in privacy.

Compared to most other buildings ships are special in that they are mobile. They constantly move and exist in different modes or settings. Perhaps the two most obvious modes are 'at sea' or 'in port'. One way to reveal this is to regard the fully working ship as an actor-network that re-orders in different settings. The hull is the same, but it works in different ways and fulfils different tasks whether under sail, moored in an urban centre or stuck in the ice. As will be developed in more detail in chapter 7 the *fluit* more or less becomes an urban house. But let us begin with just being inside the *fluit*.

Being-in-the-*fluit*

Without analysing it one could state that 'the human is in a certain space' or 'the human occupies a certain space'. Like for instance 'the crew on board the *fluit* were lodged in the stern'. This seemingly objectified statement is nothing more than realizing that an object is inside a container. In order to understand the consequences of the spatial reordering of *fluits*, from a human's point of view, it is relevant to try to shift the focus and realize that the lived occupation of space differs from other things in space. Living creatures are not things among other things. A mind may thus be regarded as the ultimate point of departure for the perception of space (compare Bollnow 1994, Eriksdotter 2005:237ff, Tilley 1994:9).

German philosopher Otto Friedrich Bollnow is but one scholar who has considered space from a phenomenological point of view. Drawing on Heidegger, Bollnow argues that dwelling in our own body may be extended to the immediate space that surrounds it. The mind inhabits the body as well as the surrounding space. Thus, the human mind always has some kind of spatial consciousness. The starting point here is what Heidegger refers to as 'thrownness', which is a term to point out that humans are rootless in the world (Bollnow 1994:113). Through experience we will create spaces that are more familiar, spaces in which we dwell. Space therefore has no universal essence, but is a social product and is always centred on human agency and activity (cf. Tilley 1994:10ff).

Being-in-the-world is a matter of being in a certain space and to become affected by the things that define this space. This idea of space is what affects people's behaviour in buildings and, as a consequence, the relationships with other individuals inside it. Entering a space, like when embarking a ship, means submitting to the conditions set by the ship (see discussion with Bollnow 1994, 2011:22 also Eriksdotter 2005:237ff).

The relation to a specific space, it is argued, is partially formed through the opportunity to move through it. Bollnow labels this as *movement space* (German: *Bewegungsraum*). Movement space thus follows the person as he or she moves, but is affected when confronted with other people. The effect is due to the condition that people want to secure their own *movement space* (Bollnow 1994, Eriksdotter 2005:238ff). This protection of one's own movement space, will result in another form of space, namely *possession space* (German: *Beseitzraum*), which is often defined by physical markers. Walls are perhaps the most obvious example of these markers.

The repeated activities of the everyday thus create the relationship towards other individuals. Inclusion or exclusion of a specific group is made through actions, actions that include things and space. Having the authority to structure space means more than just regulating particular events; it is the power to shape society by governing the repetitions that form its component selves. As argued by Henri Lefebvre, 'If one could control people's movements and control their interpretation, one could control their identities' (Upton 2002:719, compare Lefebvre & Levich 1987:7-11).

As will be described in more detail in chapter 6, a naval vessel thus contains several 'possession spaces' that correspond to positions in the hierarchy on board. Think of the 'commons' before the mast, the 'midshipmen' and similar. The boatswain becomes a boatswain by carrying out a boatswain's activities and by dressing as a boatswain; similarly, the designated quarters for the boatswains becomes defined as such by the presence of boatswains (cf. Hacking 1999:161–171, compare also Garfinkel 2006 or Upton 2002).

On board the *fluits* discussed in this study the situation was different as all were lodged under the quarterdeck in the stern. This may be taken as an indication of a relative absence of power relations. I use the phrase 'to an extent' as there are surely other ways to manipulate power over others, not just the use of space.

Even if there is uncertainty about the quantity of personal effects, personal rooms, personal berths and similar it is obvious that most of the routines in everyday life took place and were directed under the quarterdeck. This may partly be taken as an indication for what one may refer to as a familiar social climate. But it actually runs quite well with what has been concluded from written sources relating to *fluits*. The small crews usually consisted of individuals who knew each other fairly well and who had sailed together for quite some time (cf. Van Royen 1992:154ff, also Rönnby 2013:18).

Sleeping

It is possible to assess personal movement space to some degree on the wrecks described above. Even if all were lodged under the quarterdeck it remains uncertain whether there were small huts, if there were personal berths, or if personal effects were reduced to a chest or a sea bag of their own. Information of this character is generally scarce. There are indications in different sources, but I think that one should be a bit cautious with generalizations as there appears to be significant variations between living conditions aboard different categories of ships, and different types of *fluits*.

In 1663, a French valet travelling on board a Swedish-owned armed merchantman, named *Trumbslagaren*, describes that 'all passengers had brought their own beds, whereas the crew sleep, fully dressed in hammocks; (Oscarsson 2013:94, my translation). It is uncertain whether *Trumbslagaren* was a *fluit* or some other kind of ship. She appears to have been quite a large vessel, armed with 24 guns, which means that she could be hired by the navy for war use if required (Börjesson 1932:209). The informant describes how he met 25–30 seamen up on deck (Oscarsson 2013:93). I do not think the situation aboard this ship is applicable to the small *fluits* described here, where the living space was limited to the rooms under the quarterdeck. The conditions on board *Trumbslagaren* appear to be more applicable to the naval ships discussed in the chapter that follows.

Partially enclosed berths have been found on wrecks of smaller seventeenth-century vessels, such as the *beurtschip,* 'Oost Flevoland B 71', excavated in the Netherlands (Hocker 1991:213, PLAN VIII) and the 'Stinesmindes Wreck' in Denmark (Gøthche & Rieck 1990:162). The bulkhead aboard the 'Jutholmen Wreck' (Fig. 4.2, G) might be the remains of a small cubbyhole for a crewmember? A drawing of a *Bootschip*, dated to around 1780 (MMR, Inv Nr T2690), shows some kind of panelling along the sides of the cabin that may derive from bulkheads. Markers defining the 'possession space' are thus not known in detail.

Regardless of whether there were wholly or partially enclosed berths for the crew under the quarterdeck, sleeping makes up only a fraction of all the everyday activities. The places designated for personal things were still in the vicinity of the other crewmembers. Space offering privacy would have been limited and the majority of all the everyday activities were still carried out together with others.

Eating

Among the acts that are recurring, and which are certainly part of 'everyday life', are cooking and eating. As these activities involve many specially designed artefacts they provide an attractive entrance to the archaeological study of everyday life. A commonly used term for discussing food and eating is *foodways*, which has been described as 'the whole interrelated system of food conceptualization, procurement, distribution, preservation, preparation and consumption shared by all members of a particular group' (Deetz 1977:50, see also discussion in Fahlander 2010, Landon 2002:220–221). In archaeology food is often discussed in terms of nutrition, gastronomy and similar, with a focus on the dish or 'mere food' itself. It is the diet, *what* is eaten, that is under study (Fahlander 2010:37ff, also Fischler 2011:531f) rather than *how*. As noted by archaeologist Fredrik Fahlander: 'Eating and drinking require a number of key social elements such as materiality, spatial arrangement and place, bodily experiences, mental expectations, and bonding/exclusion' (Fahlander 2010:36).

The only fireplace on board each of the *fluits* shown above is located in the foremost room under the quarterdeck. The location of the hearth has several repercussions on living conditions and the routines of everyday, not least as it was the only source of heating on board. The trial records from the sinking of the *Anna Maria* clearly demonstrate that the hearth was of central importance for living on board this ice-bound ship. Of course, the situation must have been similar on board all those other ships that had to overwinter in the Baltic.

Another aspect of the location of the hearth is its capacity to illuminate a dusky corner of the ship's interior. As shown in Figure 4.8 the hearth balances the natural light that would enter through the windows in the stern or the door in the break of the quarterdeck.

The location of the hearth, in the middle of living quarters, implies that cooking became everyone's business. Even if there was an appointed chef, the somatic response to the wafting fragrance of food was indeed a concern of all and sundry. The sensual reception in the nose told the crewmember when to gather for a meal.

It is sometimes argued that sharing food brings about a semiconscious sense of intimacy, conveys a sense of belonging and tightens the bond between members of a household. Eating is thus a way to build relations and express confidence. But it can also be described as an arena where hierarchies and social structures are renegotiated (cf. Fahlander 2010:37ff). 'Eating is an endlessly evolving enactment of gender, family, and community relationships' (Counihan & Van Esterik 1997, cited in Fahlander 2010:35). Hence, excluding or including certain groups or individuals from the commensality at the table is a statement of social nature and affects social bonds, roles and behaviour. French sociologist Claude Fischler even argues that:

> ...eating the same food is equated with producing the same flesh and blood, thus making commensals more alike and bringing them closer to each other. The perception that 'you are what you eat' seems universal. It holds that, when absorbing a food, a subject absorbs at the same time salient features of the food (...) If eating the same food makes one become more like that food, then those sharing the same food become more like each other. (Fischler 2011:533)

Needless to say, eating is carried out within the 'Bollnowian movement space'. Aside from space, foodways and commensality include an array of other *actants*. In addition to humans and food – the eater and what gets eaten – foodways include pottery, bottles, knives, spoons and so on, that all affect the way you eat (Fig. 5.1). The procedure also includes chests, chairs, benches, tables that are all parts of, and have effect on, the act and practice of eating. Not necessary *what* is eaten or by who, but rather *how* the food is consumed.

How the meal is performed eventually will effect social bonds, group formation, inclusion or exclusion. Meals can be formal like banquets, they can be creative like lunches together with colleagues, they can be familiar like home dinners, or they can be just sloppy in front of the TV. The different character of the meal is determined by a range of different material components, from white tablecloth to TV-couch. These things cannot be replaced just like that, without affecting the character of commensality (see also discussion with Pollock 2012:2ff).

One component that definitely affects the behaviour at the table is the table itself. The size and shape of this piece of furniture has a crucial impact on commensality. The round-table is often put forth as the ultimate form of equal commensality, whereas tables of other shapes may work in the opposite way. Among these are '(t)he long, rectangular table, with a prominent seat at the high end or, as in pictorial representations of the Last Supper, in the middle of one side, is more adapted to hierarchy and "vertical commensality"' (one in which the attention of the patricians is focused on one leading character, as opposed to "horizontal commensality" with friendly, informal long tables)' (Fischler 2011:534). Thus the arrangement of the participants around the table both reflects and determines relationships between them (ibid. 535).

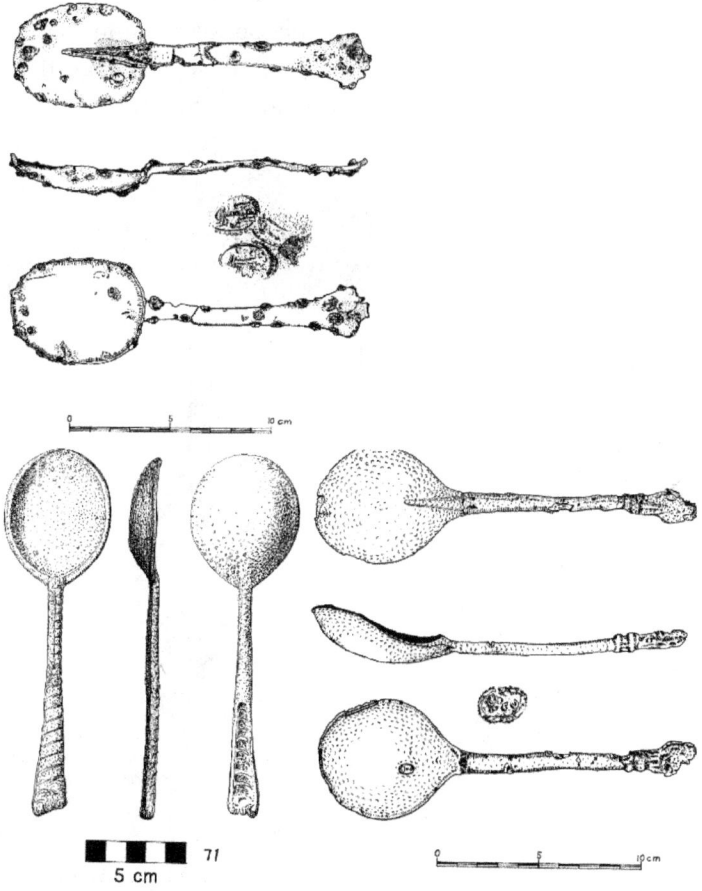

Figure 5.1: Spoons recovered from the 'Jutholmen Wreck' during the excavation in the 1970s (after Kaijser 1983).

What indications do we have about commensality on board *fluits*? The only table that has yet been found aboard a wrecked *fluit* is located in the cabin on board the 'Ghost Ship'. Unfortunately this table is resting upside down with the table-top embedded in the sediments that cover the floor. As mentioned in the previous chapter, the two chests found in the vicinity of the table most likely provided seating at this table. If this assumption is correct, then the shape of the table would likely be rectangular. The furniture of the cabin aboard the 'Ghost Ship' allowed all on board to be seated around the same table (Fig. 4.8, L & M).

Eating utensils, pottery, bottles and all the other objects associated with eating are likely to be still down there inside the 'Ghost Ship'. But as the wreck rests at 129 m deep they are simply out of reach for observation. The 'Jutholmen Wreck', which is only slightly smaller than the 'Ghost Ship', provides us with first class information in this sense.

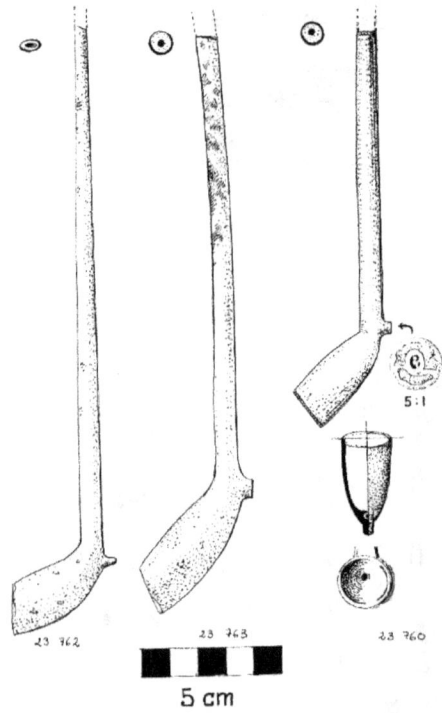

Figure 5.2: Clay pipes recovered from the 'Jutholmen Wreck' during the excavation in the 1970s (Drawing: Lennart Eriksson, after Kaijser 1983).

As reviewed in the previous chapter the 'Jutholmen Wreck' offers a quantity of objects associated with eating. The seven pewter spoons, perhaps the personal spoons of the crewmembers, the three-legged pots and the large number of clay pipes all gathered in the stern (Fig. 5.2, 5.3) clearly reveal the impression of the living quarters in the stern of the vessel. In addition to these, a number of glass bottles (Fig. 5.4) were also found (Kaijser 1983:18ff), suggesting that the storage area for bottled beverages was located in this part of the ship. This seems reasonable considering that food was both cooked and eaten under the quarterdeck. The drawing by H. Decquer, referred to above, showing the *katschip Tamen* of 1686 (Fig. 4.12, C), reveals that the vessel had a '*bottelery*', or pantry, where the cook kept working stock, located in the stern area (Het Sheepvaartsmusem Amsterdam, also reproduced in Wegener Sleeswyk 2003:170).

Figure 5.3: The Smoker, painting by Adriaen Brouwer (1605–1638) (Rijksmusem)

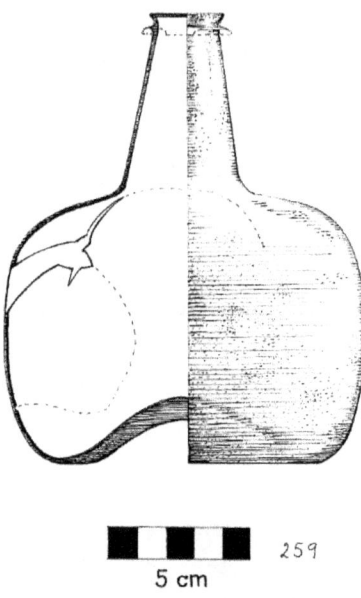

Figure 5.4: Glass bottle recovered from the 'Jutholmen Wreck' (after Kaijser 1983).

The privy

When discard behaviour and privies are discussed within archaeology it is often through studies concerning consumption patterns. The situation is similar to that concerning food in archaeology. It is more common to discuss *what* ends up as deposited material (cf. LeeDecker 1994:345–375) rather than *how* it is deposited. Ships are different in this sense as the refuse was simply thrown overboard. The discarded material may of course be discussed through the cultural layers at the seabed in harbours or roadsteads, but is seldom revealed on board a wreck. Wrecks, however, provide clear evidence for the arrangement of sanitary accommodations. In the same way as the furniture and other objects associated with eating, these facilities reveal movement patterns. It goes without saying that there should be at least one such facility within every space in which humans move. Despite the frequency of its use, or perhaps as a result of this, the sources that describe attitudes surrounding practices as regards privacy, hygiene and similar, are scarce. Did these attitudes differ with estate or gender, on land or at sea, and so forth?

Swedish linguist Professor Gunnar Tilander (1894–1973) has written a both humorous and scholarly book about sanitary conditions and attitudes towards filth and latrines in general (Tilander 1980). Using trial testimonies, travel reports, literature, pictures and several anecdotes he sketches a broad account on the matter from the Late Mediaeval period up to the late nineteenth century, with the primary focus on Europe. From a present day horizon it is perhaps a bit surprising that sanitary accommodations seem to have been quite absent in the past. Tilander refers to a number of decrees, dated to the seventeenth century, where citizens of the large cities of Europe were required to arrange for privies in every house. It is often put forth, albeit in a bit simplistic way, that the 'barbaric people of the past' threw their waste from their windows and directly onto the streets (ibid.). There is some substance in this, but one should of course be a bit careful to state that this is the ultimate expression of being uncivilized (for instance Englund 1991:206–213).

The everyday on the farmsteads in the countryside included the handling of animal dung, and the human bi-products seldom appear to have been handled differently. Devices constructed for this act usually consisted of no more than a rod or a plank to sit on. Privies, offering privacy and the opportunity to do it out of sight, were uncommon (Tilander 1980, Rosén & Wetter 1970).

Ships differ from the general pattern in this respect through having specially designed arrangements. Archaeologist Joe Simmons has written an overview of the development of sanitary accommodations on board ships, from the fifteenth- through the seventeenth centuries (1997). Even though the information regarding these facilities is scarce, he manages to give a thorough account through the use of old pictures, models and similar (see also Lavery 1987, Munday 1978).

There may be several reasons as to why ships tend to have more elaborate sanitary accommodations than houses on land, the most important having to do with hygiene, as it would have been important to let waste leave the hull as quickly as possible. The contents of a jar or a potty that turns over would undoubtedly find its way down to the keelson and mix with the bilge water, breeding fungi and bacteria into a toxic mixture. But it is also a matter of personal safety. It is dangerous to lean out from a rocking ship.

As revealed from the wrecks, the privy on board the merchant *fluits* was located in the portside 'corner' of the stern. Since this facility was archaeologically detected, beginning with the 'Lion Wreck', similar square openings, with a corresponding location, have been revealed from pictures of *fluits*. To locate the vital seat in the same room where all aboard eat and sleep may seem peculiar. Considering the alternative, to have a chamber pot, the tube in the *fluits* stern cabin is both a hygienic and a practical solution as it allowed the waste to leave the ship immediately.

What about privacy? One cannot dismiss that the privy on board these ships was divided from the stern cabin, surrounded by a small room or 'closet'. On the 'Lion Wreck' it is clear that the seat was located just below one of the two windows (Figures 5.5 and 5.6). To permanently enclose the space around the seat with bulkheads would dramatically reduce daylight inside the rest of the cabin. For this reason I find it quite unlikely that the seat was located in a permanently enclosed space. If there was some kind of dividing screen or wall, it is likely to have been of a very temporal character, perhaps some kind of cloth hang in front. It may be, however, that this space was not enclosed at all.

To answer nature's call in privacy should be regarded as a quite recent habit. There are also many anecdotes relating to historical celebrities like Louis XIV, Peter the Great and Anne Boleyn having relieved themselves in public (cf. Englund 1991:208ff). But there is also more concrete evidence. On warships, the 'seats of ease', aimed for the commons, are often found exposed, out in the open air in the ship's beakhead (cf. Munday 1978:125–140, Simmons 1997:41–56).

In conclusion the facilities for cooking, eating, sleeping as well as the privy, were all located in the two rooms under the quarterdeck. These facilities were all within a shared movement space. Thus, the majority of everyday concerns on board were carried out together with other people.

What they were doing inside this shared space under the quarterdeck, besides the most necessary, self-evident acts and routines is difficult to detect from wrecks. This is a bit frustrating considering the vast quantity of time that early modern people spent inside rooms like this. The exception is a gaming piece recovered from the 'Jutholmen Wreck', which provides a glimpse of an activity that is likely have taken place on board this ship during spare time, waiting for cargo, bureaucracy, the right wind or for the ice to break (Kaijser 1983:14, 46).

Figure 5.5: Cabin window frame in the stern of the 'Lion Wreck' (Photo: Jonas Rydin/DSP).

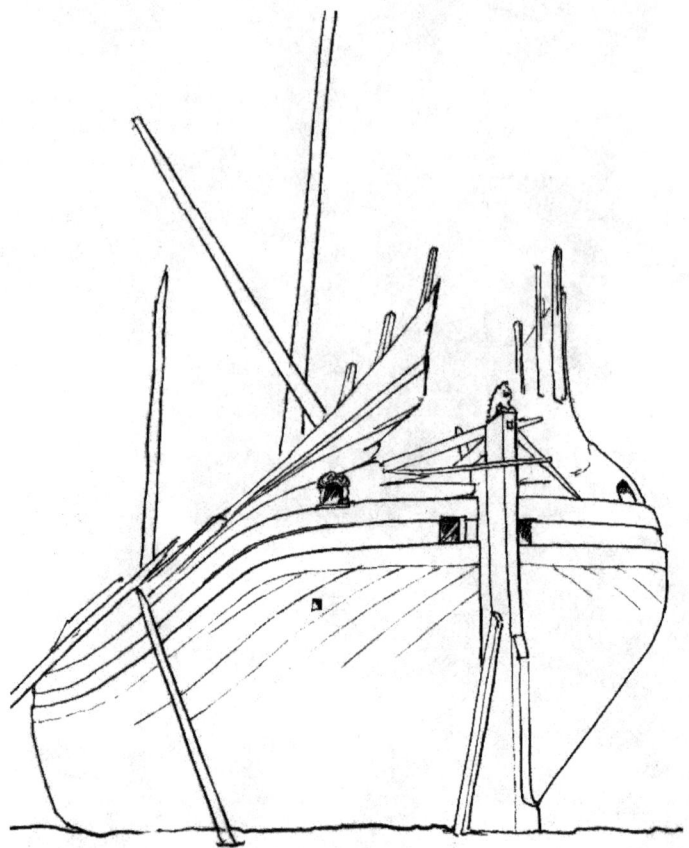

Figure 5.6: Sketch of the 'Lion Wreck' showing the windows and other openings in the stern. Note the location of the cabin window, just above the exhaust hole of the privy (Niklas Eriksson).

Social structure

That all the facilities for everyday life were gathered in the same end of the ship may be used as an argument for an egalitarian power structure on board. But even if the configuration of rooms may be regarded as 'coequal' one should be somewhat cautious to suggest that this was automatically the case. Abstract notions such as hierarchy or other social relations may be expressed through spatiality but still there are a thousand other ways – activities, procedures, routines and acts – carried out continually in order to reproduce and to uphold such relations. Without a doubt, these were present on board even on the smallest and undermanned *fluit*. Several reasons may be put forth for not observing them in the archaeological record. Markers such as where one slept, the clothes and other things people carry around them in order to mark a certain rank, may not have been preserved or they may not have been observed for other reasons.

One aspect that reveals a social differentiation between people is their cash recompense. Needless to say, how this differed between persons on board is quite impossible to detect from the wrecks alone. Written accounts from the large *fluit* the *Anna Maria*, discussed above, reveal that there were indeed considerable differences in compensation between the persons lodged in the shared space abaft of the pumps on board this ship. For instance, the First Mate, Didrich Cornelisen, had a monthly salary of 14 rixdollars, whereas the Second Mate, Sven Nilsson, received 8, the Seaman Philip Bewe received 5, the Seaman Petter Simonsen received 3 and the cabin boy only 2 rixdollars (for a complete list see Ahlström 1995:85f, 1997:108).

The list of wages reveals another important aspect when we are dealing with status in the Early Modern period, namely the marital status of crewmembers. The status of the unmarried man was generally limited and, for instance, you were supposed to be married in order to become a skipper (cf. Stadin 2004:84). We may only speculate as to the effect this had on the attitudes and behaviour among the people lodged on board the *fluits*. Group formation is performed. Whereas the archaeological record provides an opportunity to study the space in which the acts of the everyday took place, and the things involved in and used in these acts, it is more problematic to grasp the acts themselves. As archaeologists we may record a table, but we do not know exactly how people were seated around it, who read the prayers and so forth.

Perhaps it is not so peculiar that high and low, First Mate and cabin boy, lived in close proximity to each other. There are several terrestrial examples where this has been the case. In seventeenth-century Stockholm, the stone houses were often built four storeys high. These buildings were often inhabited by one burgess family, including their servants. Despite the four storeys, both the family and the servants would consume their meals together and sleep in the same room. In part, there is a practical explanation for this as the hearth was inadequate for the large household. The master had to share space with servants in order not to freeze (Olsson 1957:137ff). A similar situation is known from rural contexts in Sweden, where wealthy peasant families were billeted together with servants during the cold months (Erixon 1947, also Almevik 2012:75, 156, 198, 2014:87). But as spring came, high and low could separate into different areas of the farm, or the city estate, being lodged in different rooms, storeys or houses.

A similar situation, where there was no significant spatial distinction between the master's family and servants, is known from the seventeenth-century in the Netherlands. But here, the less pronounced spatial borders between high and low are often explained from an ideological rather than a solely practical argument concerning heating. The servants in the narrow houses of Amsterdam, Lieden, Enkhuisen or other towns, were an integrated part of the household. In most families with one or two servants, the dividing line between dressing, foodways and space were very difficult to distinguish. In several family portraits it is hard to differentiate between the nursemaid and the mother. Just the fact that the nursemaid so naturally was included in the portrait should be noted, and may be used as an argument that the servants were indeed integrated into the family. Older servants, that had withstood the test of time, were just as much confidants and friends as employees (Schama 1988:456f).

Perhaps this sharing of movement space can also be observed on board the *fluits* in the light of the composition of crews during the period. As has been highlighted by Van Royen, using the Danish Sound register, the majority of the men involved in the Dutch merchant service on board the merchant ships often came from approximately the same area in northern Holland. Dutch shipmasters recruited their crews from their immediate geographical and even social environment (Van Royen 1992:154ff). But at the same time Skippers from the larger cities, like for instance Amsterdam, where a large number of ships passed through, tended to recruit crews consisting of people of a variety of nationalities.

Irrespective of the composition of the crew, it is not so easy to draw the line between high and low. Van Royen has argued that even if the ship masters 'held a relatively high position (...) the social stratification of Dutch society was not typified by sharp and insurmountable gulfs and barriers. During the seventeenth century in particular the Dutch social system was rather open and dynamic' (1992:157). If this is correct, perhaps the spatial arrangement, as revealed from wrecks, is not so surprising.

Many researchers have discussed the Dutch *Gouden Eeuw*, in order to understand the rapidly growing economic prosperity, the development of nascent capitalism and what has been referred to as 'The First Modern Economy' (De Fries & Van Der Woude 1997 also Israel 1998, Van Zanden & Van Tielhof 2009, Van Tielhof & Van Zanden 2011). It has been argued that the development should been seen against a background of a mentality that penetrated through society in a profound way. A classic study here is Max Weber's *The Protestant Ethic and the Spirit of Capitalism*, first published in 1905 (1978), where he argues that the idea of salvation affects attitudes towards labour and money. Pre-capitalist man, according to Weber, largely lived on the principle of need satisfaction, as it were, from hand to mouth. Catholic salvation was through confession, indulgences and possibly supported by a donation to the church and its cloister.

The good Lutheran could reach salvation through good deeds and the individual held the responsibility for his/her salvation through actions and thus, to an extent, could control his/her destiny, even if one should accept the social lot one was born into. Calvin, however, asserted that the individual's destiny was already predestined. This idea results in a constant worry and brooding, to constantly ask oneself whether you belong to the selected or the damned. Hard work thus became a way to verify and to confirm your condition for salvation. If business turned out well God may be taken as an acknowledgment of God's benevolent attitude, but if business turned out bad, there may have been a cause for concern.

All the same, riches may be hazardous because of the likelihood of turning to gluttony. The pious capitalist got nothing personal out of their wealth other than the sensation of carrying out his task well. To refrain from success, or to piously relate to it, is a consequence of asceticism, which in Catholicism saw monastic life move out and permeate the masses. This is what historian Simon Schama refers to as an Embarrassment of Riches (1988) in his broad interpretation of Dutch culture in the golden age, a balancing act between God and Mammon.

The nobleman's frivolous delights and the parvenu's vulgar ostentation were equally detestable. The modest burgher, who made his fortune through hard work, was seen as the ideal (Weber 1978:77).

Weber's arguments have received some criticism. For instance De Fries & Van Der Woude argue that: '(i)t makes more sense to argue that the spread of Calvinism drew advantages from the already existing social structure of the Netherlands than to maintain that a capitalist society emerged from the ascetic discipline of Calvinism' (1997:167). However, such an argument hardly seems plausible due to the still very incomplete spread of Calvinism during the Republic's most expansive economic growth (ibid.).

Regardless of whether it was the idea that prosperity, fortune or influence were all predestined by God, or if the attitudes derived from somewhere else, it is obvious that the commander aboard the *fluits* discussed here did not have to distance himself from 'the lesser worth creatures'. There are no clearly visible physical markers between high and low on board the surveyed *fluits* in the way that these are visible on other wrecks (cf. Eriksson 2013:97–109, Eriksson et al. 2013:17–21). There was no use of physical markers or distinctions in space to demarcate hierarchy. Hierarchy was a silent agreement between the persons on board. The wages differed largely among the members of the crew, but their spatial situation did not. There was no point for skippers to claim a specific status, such as through imposing some distance between themselves and the rest of the crew or isolating themselves in a particular space.

At the same time, the captain also lived close to the crew that he commanded, which may have been a way of keeping an eye on them and ensuring good behaviour. Being away from the crew was unwise, as it would offer opportunities for cultivating displeasure with conditions on board.

The *Fluit* as lodging for the town

That there are similarities between burgher's townhouses and *fluits* is perhaps not so surprising. A *fluit* moored in a town more or less became a townhouse. The question is to what extent was life on board a *fluit* formed around the same preferences as life in general? Ships are so commonly referred to as 'maritime', 'nautical' and similar, but they may be regarded all the same as terrestrial or urban. Instead of emphasizing ships as 'societies in miniature' (Einarsson 1997:210, Genrup 1990:104–107, Pomey 2011:30, Soop 2001:14ff) or 'closed communities', (Muckelroy 1978:221ff) it may be relevant to try to see how ships become components of a larger whole.

As mentioned in the beginning of this chapter ships differ from other buildings through being mobile. They thus have to carry with them all the facilities required to uphold human life on board. John Law has discussed ships from an actor-network point of view. Even if he uses a Portuguese Carrack as an example, a ship type that sailed in between the old and the new world in the centuries before the introduction of *fluits*, the discussions are applicable here as well. In order to reveal his case Law describes the ship as an actor-network, consisting of human and non-human actors:

> Hull, spars, sails, stays, stores, rudder, crew, water, winds, all of these (and many others) have to be held in place so to speak functionally, if we are able to point to an object and call it a ship. A properly working ship. One that sails round the globe and trades in spices. All these bits and pieces have to do their jobs. (..) So the ship, to be a properly working ship, has to borrow the force of the wind, the flow of the current, the position of the stars, the energy of the members of the crew, it has to all these and include them (so to speak) within itself (Law 2000:4).

This is why Law also refer to them as 'immutable mobiles' (ibid., also Latour 1990:19–68, 2005:223–228). Mobile, because they move in between different ports, and immutable because they hold their form and structure. As long as the ship holds together as network it will sail, but if there is interference, and movements within the network, then the ship starts to degrade, the crew will starve or the ship will founder (Law 2000:4).

The point of this discussion is that not all actants that are present at a specific time or space, irrespective if they are human or non-human, make a difference. But those that *do* make difference, the actors which make other actors do things, are the important ones. This doesn't mean that the important actors are the known or familiar ones; indeed, quite the contrary (for an overview see for instance Latour 2005, also Dolwick 2009)!

The actor-network, comprising the fully working ships, reshapes as it enters different situations. At sea it consists of one set of human and non-human actors (like the ones mentioned in Law's quote above), whereas the actors involved in the network when moored in a harbour is different (hull, moorings, taverns, relatives, urbanism, customs office, crews from other ships and many others). It is the same hull, but as the network that surrounds them changes form in different situations they work in different ways, fulfilling different purposes and affect the other actors (human and non-human) in the same network (compare Fig. 5.7).

Figure 5.7: Detail from an engraving of Stockholm from Erik Dahlbergh's Suecia antiqua et hodierna (National Library of Sweden).

The moored-state ship affects how the ship is used. The ability to leave the hull, to have contact with people ashore or crews lodged in other moored ships, changes the living conditions inside the hull in a profound way, not least as regards interpersonal relations. As noted by Aubert & Arner '(a) standing piece of advice among seamen is that they should not "take the ship ashore" with them' (1959:203).

Rather than answering the question 'what is a ship?' with arguments that they resemble 'societies in miniature', ships are parts of society. But, and this is important, a ship is what it is at that very moment, depending on the circumstance. Thus, ships participate or contribute to society in different ways, in different situations.

The written accounts relating to the foundering of the *Anna Maria* provide a fascinating snapshot of the situation where the ship becomes a part of the harbour into which it is moored. Even if Dalarö was not an urban metropolis, like Amsterdam or Stockholm, the trial accounts provide us a glimpse at everyday life on board a moored ship during a few winter days in 1709. The *Anna Maria* was a large *fluit*, which is reflected in the size of her crew of 22 people. As the ship got ice-bound in the fall of 1708, the majority of the crew was sent home, including the captain.

Five people stayed on board to keep watch and wait for the spring and ice-break, namely the four seamen: Philip Bewe, Erich Ersson, Carl Sigfridsson, Petter Simonsen, and the cook's Mate, Petter Simonsen (Ahlström 1997:97, 108).

The state which the *Anna Maria* sank in should be regarded as a normal state for a *fluit*. These ships were built to meet the requirements of being moored or icebound as well as being under sail.

Van Royen writes that: 'a voyage to the Baltic (...) may have taken only a couple of weeks (from the Netherlands). Apart from loading and unloading, the crew had time enough to go ashore for a while' (van Royen 1992:158). Whereas a trip between The Netherlands and Sweden took a few weeks, the time that the ship was moored could be much longer. Often it was a matter of months. In the words of the anonymous French valet who visited Sweden during the winter 1663/1664, it was important that the ships leaving Stockholm departed in time, for '...already by the end of November the water will freeze to ice, which means that the passengers will be trapped at sea, and those who are left will have to wait until May when the ice breaks' (Oscarsson 2013:186f).

The *fluit* was designed to be berthed side by side with other *fluits*. This is how they appear in contemporary engravings and other depictions of urban centres (Fig. 5.7). Oriented parallel to each other allowed daylight to enter into the stern cabin, through the small windows in the stern. When looking at *fluits* one could imagine them tightly packed together, side by side with other *fluits*, forming small villages or urban districts.

Dutch archaeologist Jerzy Gawronski has emphasized how the harbour of Amsterdam formed an integrated part of the town plan. The townhouses were situated according to a concentric street and canal system enclosing the outlet of the river Amstel. One sector of the circle was not built up with houses. This corresponds with the harbour, which consisted of a 'continuously changing city block with a mobile set of ships' (Gawronski 2009:17, my translation). The 'buildings' in this sector of the circle consisted of moored merchant ships. I will return to the *fluit* as a parallel to the *halsgevel*-facades in chapter 7.

In Stockholm the harbour for merchant ships was the quay that stretches along the eastern seafront of the island *Gamla Stan* (The Old Town), called *Skeppsbron*, meaning 'The Ships Quay'. The ships thus lay side by side in the very centre of the town. According to French diplomat Charles Ogier, visiting Stockholm during the winter 1634/35 even '(t) he largest most deep-draught vessels are moored so near the town that they almost touch the houses' (Ogier 1914:30, my translation).

During the course of the seventeenth century the iron balance moved to Södermalm, and the merchant ships, the *fluits*, were moored along the shore below as well. Today this part of Stockholm is still characterized by the palaces that were built by migrating Dutch merchants (see for instance Noldus 2005) that in this manner had their ships close by.

Despite the many months that sailors spent on board moored *fluits* not much is known about how life proceeded inside these ships. The accounts from the trials held after the *Anna Maria* foundered in the middle of Dalarö harbour provide an idea. Just like other moored *fluits* in the capital were part of that particular environment the *Anna Maria* was an integrated part of the Dalarö municipality during the winter 1708–09.

In the trials held after foundering, many accounts tend to circulate around the ship's fireplace. This is perhaps not so surprising since it was from this source that the fire caused the ship to sink. The written accounts only reveal the whereabouts of a few of the crew on the day when the fire broke out and the ship sank. The everyday rituals, however, would have centred around this very hearth for other reasons. The winter 1708/09 has been described as extremely cold, hence the reason for the ship being icebound. Only a limited part of the ship was possible to heat at a time, as the ship only had one hearth and the crew had to stay in its vicinity for practical reasons.

The minutes from the trial give us an indication of the events here: 'Seaman Philip Bewe related that on the day the fire broke out in the evening all who were on board held their customary morning prayers and then lit the fire in the galley where they cooked herring and heated porridge, and sat down to eat' (Ahlström 1997:97). But the testimonies also give interesting insights in the bonding between the *Anna Maria*'s crew and the other ships that were stuck in the ice: '…Bewe had been with his ship-mates for a meal on (-board) the ship *Tyghuset* he invited these persons to eat on board the *Anna Maria*…' (Ahlström 1997:97).

As indicated in the case records eating on board the neighbouring ships formed a way of socializing within the temporary communities in the harbours and the ship itself formed the arena for this interaction. The rooms, the table in the cabin, the galley and so on, were the things that set the material limits for these relations.

In Stockholm, and other northerly harbours, rows of *fluits* formed temporary city-blocks during winter. When the sun returned, and the ice let go of the ships, they dispersed. As the anonymous French valet describes: 'In May, when the ice breaks, there are billboards in the ships' masts, where large letters declare the destinations to which the ships are heading' (Oscarsson 2013:186, my translation). It was thus possible to inquire if you could come on board as a passenger or send goods.

Before the mast or abaft the pumps

Above, the aim has been to discuss the kind of everyday life that was revealed through reconstructed ships. What did ships make people do and how the physical ship mediated, manoeuvred and upheld specific human behaviours. The majority of the everyday routines were carried out in a shared space. It was in this shared space that the people on board resided, regardless of whether the ship was at sea or moored in a harbour. The interior of the *fluit* was arranged in a way that did not put a significant spatial distance between high and low ranked individuals. The picture revealed is more of a small familiar group of individuals lodged in a space that did not distinguish between high and low.

After such a conclusion, it is again relevant to recapitulate some previous statements regarding the interior of *fluits*. As mentioned towards the end of the previous chapter, the common way to describe the arrangement of space on board *fluits* is that the persons on board were separated with the crew in the forecastle and the officer in the stern. 'Before the mast' is a commonly cited concept when discussing the distribution of people aboard the ships, not least in literature and songs. The concept should, however, be associated with the ships of the navy, at least during this period, where the common sailors were supposed to have their lodgings before the mainmast, whereas the higher ranks had their quarters in the stern. The higher and further abaft in the hull structure reflected higher up in the hierarchy and organization. This will be discussed in more detail in the next chapter.

To spontaneously install such an arrangement on board *fluits* might be a symptom for what archaeologist Joe Flatman calls 'Hornblower-syndrome', which is used to describe the tendency of maritime archaeologists (and historians) to automatically assume a situation in which the worst excesses of abuse of power and hierarchy prevailed and were always present on board ships. The name stems from the Forester (and O'Brien) novels in which life on board Napoleonic-era warships is described (Flatman 2003:148). In topics that relate to social conditions on board old ships, such as the division of space, the naval and hierarchical stance tends to shine through.

To an extent this may also have to do with the research tradition. The general focus on warships among those interested in ships, from the maritime painters in the seventeenth century (Sigmond & Wouter 2007) to the marine history writings of the twentieth century (cf. Cederlund 1997), and the early wreck salvagers following this path, has contributed to highlighting naval conditions. Another factor is the availability of sources. Whereas models, drawings, treaties and so forth describe the internal arrangement of naval vessels, comparable sources that describe the spatial organization on board merchant vessels do not exist.

As shown above, the study of wrecks provides a different story. It shows that the routines of the everyday were all carried out in a shared space in the stern of the *fluit*.

6. *Fluits* at war

The first sentence in Keith Muckelroy's influential book *Maritime Archaeology* is a frequently quoted one. It states that: 'In any pre-industrial society, from the upper palaeolithic to the nineteenth century A.D., a boat or (later) a ship was the largest and most complex machine produced' (Muckelroy 1978:3). In general there is no reason to question the validity of such a statement, except perhaps for the implication that the technical quality of ships automatically makes them an interesting class of source material.

In propounding his view and motivating his own interest in naval vessels in favour of merchant ships, Anders Franzén sought for arguments within a technical realm. According to him, warships have always represented the cutting edge in technology, whilst merchant ships, primarily consisted of their cargo. Is this alleged technical superiority of warships really a valid observation? Were seventeenth-century warships really that *technically* superior when compared to merchant ships?

Fluits provide an interesting case as to a large extent the hulls of these ships were built using the same methods employed while constructing warships. A *fluit's* rig reveals a more or less equal number of sails and masts as on contemporary warships. A 3-pounder and a 36-pounder cannon work in the same way, even if the size, calibre and effect differs. The difference is a matter of scale. It simply does not stand to reason that a ship with 100 guns is 25-times more *technically* advanced than one carrying four guns!

If an early modern warship is more advanced than a merchant ship, it is in a *social* way. A substantial part of the machinery on board any pre-industrial warship consisted of humans. Sometimes several hundreds of them. The fully working warship thus forms through an interplay between ship, crew, guns, winds, provisions, gunpowder and so on. All these are arranged in a way that form a functioning unit. One can describe this as an actor-network (Law 2000, see also previous chapter). *Fluits* were 'multi-purpose' ships and could be used as anything from merchant ships, whalers or – which is the topic of this chapter – warships.

Turning a *fluit* from merchant to naval ship is a matter of reshaping the actor-network. It has to be rearranged so that it forces the actors involved to behave, think and act in accordance to the specific task. The *fluit's* hull, rig and so on, are all the same, but the vessel itself is used in another way. Also, a fully working warship necessarily entails people carrying out specific acts and behaving in specific ways. In order to more thoroughly understand what is going on when a *fluit* is retasked, one must not only discern what people do with the ship, but also what the ship makes people do.

One may compare this with present day debates between pro-gun and anti-gun lobbies: 'While the anti-gun lobby argues that *guns* kill people, the pro-gun lobby maintains that *people* kill people, with the gun as nothing more than a neutral tool. The dualism here is between materialist and sociological explanations – the former portrays the gun as the responsible agent, the latter puts all responsibility on the human agents' (Knappet 2008:139–156). The answer to the discussion is of course that both guns and humans kill, but through a lethal combination – the 'gun-man' (Riis 2008:287ff, Latour 1999:176ff). Before entering this discussion however it is necessary to provide a brief background as to why merchant ships were turned into naval vessels.

The armed merchantman

In October 1644, the Swedish Navy won a great victory against the Danish north of the island of Femern in Denmark. No less than 10 Danish ships were taken as prizes by the Swedes. The victory to a large extent was due to an auxiliary fleet consisting of 21 ships with crews hired in the Dutch Republic. The ships were hired by Louis De Geer, a finance man who had immigrated to Sweden from the Republic. De Geer is sometimes described as the 'father of Swedish industry' and earned a great fortune and societal influence through iron works and cannon manufacturing. His contribution to the Swedish fleet is sometimes regarded as having been a demonstration of gratitude towards his new country, but just as importantly it guaranteed protection of his business interests (cf. Noldus 2005:58, Glete 2010:439).

The success of the auxiliary Dutch fleet in the autumn of 1644 immediately inspired the Swedish Chancellor Axel Oxenstierna to launch the idea of promoting Swedish long-distance shipping with reduced custom rates for Swedish-built ships that could be armed with guns. At a meeting in 1645 he remarked that such ships might be hired by the navy when required. It was decided that ships that were built in Sweden or the provinces were eligible for a one-third tax reduction if the ship was built in oak, heavily framed and could carry 14 guns or more (Glete 2010:434–448).

The large *fluit* the *Anna Maria*, described above, was one of the ships that achieved tax reduction. When she sailed as a merchant ship between Lisbon, Stockholm and Amsterdam, her voluminous hull housed a crew of 22 persons in addition to her cargo. When the ship sank she formed a stationary housing for five frozen crewmembers that had to overwinter on board the ice-bound ship. It is known that the crew on board the *Anna Maria* were able to defend the ship against pirates in 1698 (Ahlström 1997:108). It is unknown how many guns she carried. Parts of burnt gun carriages have been observed in the forecastle of the wreck. However, if the ship had been drafted by the navy, to be used exclusively as a warship, her hull would have been adjusted and altered to function as an artillery platform.

Important here is also that armament requires an increased number of people on board. The merchant *fluits* were renowned for their small crews, a condition which is commonly explained through the fact that they usually sailed totally unarmed (Kirby & Hinkkanen 2000:189, Lucassen & Unger 2011:3–44, Van Tielhof & Van Zanden 2011:49, Van Zanden & Van Tielhof 2009:289–403). The armed *fluits* hired by the navy were however just as crammed as any other naval ship.

The *Constantia*

To date, only one wreck of a *fluit* transformed for Swedish war service has been found, the *Constantia*. The ship was hired in connection with the so-called Scanian war (1675–1679). Through an alliance with France, Sweden had indirectly become in conflict with the Dutch Republic. In this situation Denmark, which was now allied with the Dutch, saw a chance of re-conquering territories which had been lost to Sweden in 1658.

In April 1676, the Swedes sent two reconnaissance patrols to the southern Baltic with orders to attack enemy merchant vessels. One of the patrols consisted of the armed *fluit* the *Constantia* and the *pinnace* the *Caritas*, both under the command of Pål Rumpf.

The Danish navy, consisting of 14 naval ships under the command of Admiral Niels Juel was anchored at Bornholm in the southern Baltic. As the news about the Swedish vessels cruising the waters reached the Danes, they set out with the objective of attacking them. After a few days they saw the Swedish ships and started following them. The Swedes aimed to escape into the Blekinge archipelago and warped the ships into shallow water between the islands. On the evening the 23 April they opened fire but stopped as the night fell. The Swedish commander, Pål Rumpf, realized that the situation was hopeless. In the cover of darkness, the crews of both the *Caritas* and the *Constantia* left the ships and escaped to land. Both ships were set on fire by their own crews. The *Constantia* blew up and sank, while the *Caritas* was rescued from the flames by the Danes. She was later brought to Copenhagen as a prize. In a letter to the Danish king, Admiral Juel describes the *Caritas* as a fine, well-equipped ship with good sailing capabilities. In passing, he also mentions the wrecked remains of the *Constantia*. As the ship sank at a depth of only five metres, most of the hull must have protruded above water. Juel estimates her to have carried 40 iron guns (Lisberg-Jensen 1972:42), but as all had been annealed by the fire he saw no use in salvaging them from the shallowly resting wreck (Fig. 6.1).

According to Swedish records made at the beginning of 1676, the armed merchant The *Constantia* carried 30 guns (Tornquist 1788:144) whereas the list of armed merchant ships says 36.[1] A compilation of the navy's losses during 1676 and 1677 mentions 32 which is perhaps the most likely number to have been taken on board the ship.

The *Constantia* was built in 1672 and was thus relatively new when she was hired by the navy. Her displacement was 200 Swedish lasts (Tornquist 1788:144, Wetterholm 1994:146), which may be compared to the 274 lasts of the *Anna Maria* (Ahlström 1997:104). Thus, the *Constantia* would have been slightly smaller than the *Anna Maria's* 38 m between the posts. According to preserved documents the *Constantia* was planned to have seven officers, 96 seamen and 34 soldiers on board (Tornqvist 1788:144), in all 137 people (Lisberg-Jensen1972:34 only mentions the 90 seamen, as does Wetterholm 1994:146). Compared to the crew of 22 people that were on board the *Anna Maria* the situation on board the armed *Constantia* was far more crowded and cramped.

Transforming a *fluit* from merchant to naval ship was not only a matter of adding more guns or people to the hull. The process also involved convincing everyone to act and behave in specific ways to form

---

[1] Krigsarkivet (KrA). Amiralitetskollegiet. Nya nummerserien, avd II nr 12a. Skeppslistor m.m. 1600-talet.

the fully working warship. To an extent this also involves forcing people to do things they may not wish to. The ship's hull (frames, planking, keel and so on) is the same but the interior of the vessel is rearranged to fit and to form the new roles and tasks of both ship and persons. Most importantly the rearrangement permeated the everyday routines on board to be carried out in accordance with the ship's new naval role. On board the *fluits* discussed in the previous chapters, the everyday routines were carried out in a shared space in the stern. The situation inside a naval ships hull is more complicated, not least as it has people all over it.

Not only was the ship transformed into a warship, peasants, Taylor, blacksmiths and so on were all the same transformed into 'commons' put under the command of officers. This transformation was made with the ship as a mediator. The new roles of both ship and people, was created through an interplay between both, through being lodged in a specific spaces on board, through fulfilling specific tasks and through regulating everyday routines in accordance to rank. Discipline and hierarchy, may be executed through punishment. But there are several other more subtle ways to maintain power. These are created through the individuals in themselves and through the everyday practices on board.

The wreck

The *Constantia* was set on fire by her own crew and blew up when she sank. The shallow water depth at the site, with great water- and ice-movements, have had further impact on the remains of the old *fluit*. Just as with most other known wrecks of warships, several salvage operations, aiming to recover black oak, have been carried out at the sites. The first was known in the 1930s (Cederlund 1983:47, 56, Spens 1942:374), but the site seems to have been forgotten quite rapidly after these events. In 1970, the remains of the *Constantia* were relocated by a group of recreational divers. What they found was a huge pile of stones, most likely deriving from the ballast (Fig. 6.2). The divers carried out a survey and removed many of these stones. Several objects were recovered and were sent for conservation at the SMM. During the excavation it became apparent that a substantial portion of *Constantia's* lower hull survives underneath the pile of stones.

Figure 6.1: Location map (Niklas Eriksson).

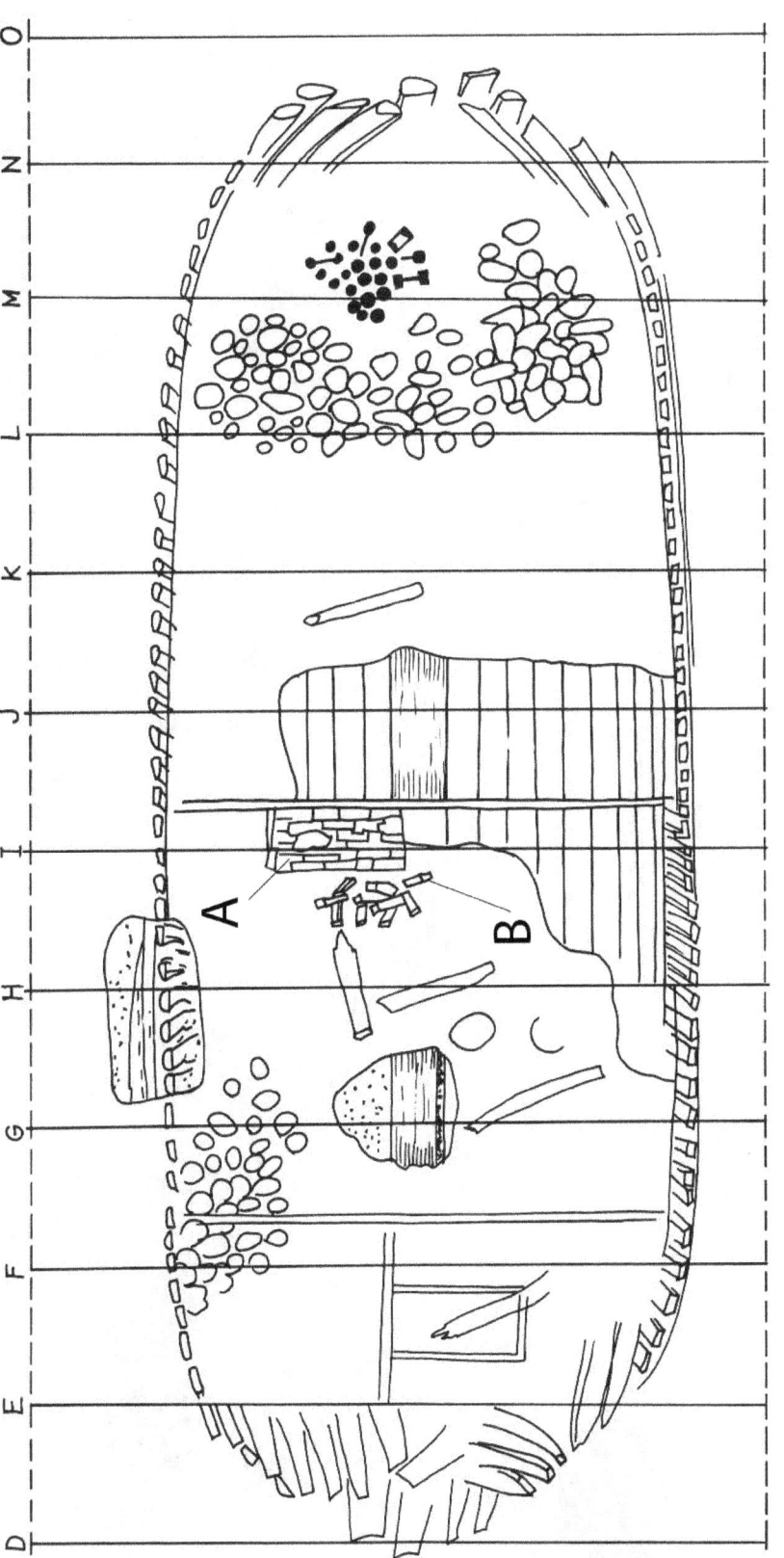

Figure 6.2: Site plan of the wrecksite for the Constantia. A: Galley; B: Firewood (after Åke Jahnsson).

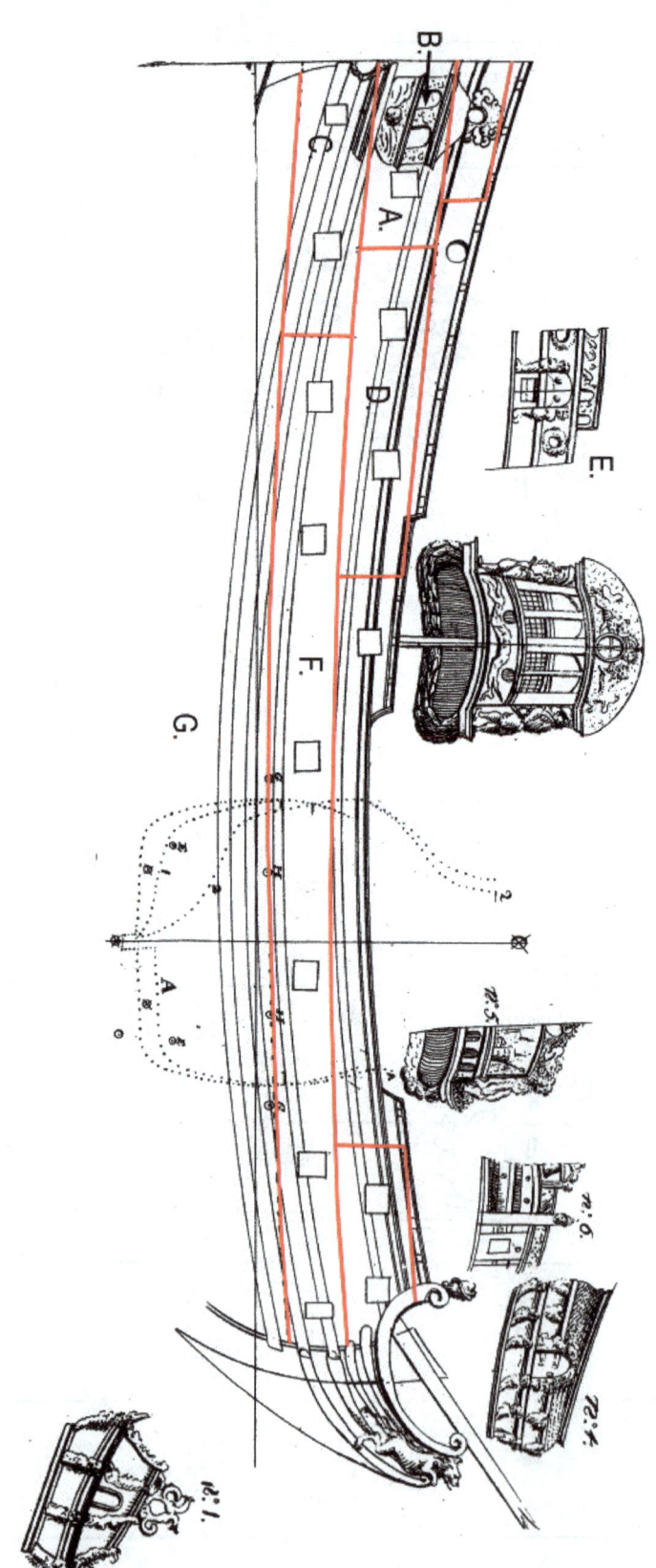

Figure 6.3: Åke Rålamb's drawing of a Spaniefarare 'that can be built for a heavy load and great comfort for crew.' The spatial arrangement on board this fluit differs from the ones shown in the previous chapter. A: great cabin, B: quarter gallery, C: artillery store, D: helmsman's stand, E: bulkhead before helmsman's stand, F: gun deck, G: location of galley (after Rålamb 1691:26, Tafl. G., edited by the author).

Due to the relatively fragmentary state of preservation of the *Constantia*, the information concerning the internal arrangement of the hull is limited to the lowest parts. Perhaps the most conspicuous feature here is the hearth and, in direct connection to this, a storage area for firewood. Tripod pipkins, bartmann jugs and eating utensils were found in the vicinity of the hearth (Jahnson 1971). The hearth, built out of bricks, is of considerable size and is located near amidships. This is one of the most obvious differences between the armed *fluit Constantia* aimed for war-use, and the merchant *fluits* discussed in the previous chapters. Those wrecks clearly reveal that it was a standard feature to house the galley in the foremost room under the quarterdeck.

Why then is this relocation of the galley so important? The logistical difference between preparing food for 22 people, as on board the *Anna Maria*, or 137 people as on board the *Constantia*, should not be neglected or underestimated. But as will be stressed more in detail below, the (re-)location of the galley is important for understanding what makes a warship as it is also an important ingredient in the process of making people carry out their required tasks and duties.

The location of the hearth on board the *Constantia*, near amidships, is similar to the hearths on board the purpose-built warships from the period. Archaeological examples include for instance *Vasa* (1628) (cf. Cederlund & Hocker 2006:372–376 also Söderlind 2006:204–210). A recent archaeological discovery, which is very illustrative in this sense, is the great two-decker of 86 guns, *Svärdet*, launched in 1662 and sunk only one and a half months after the *Constantia* in the infamous battle of southern Öland (Eriksson & Rönnby 2012b). To locate the galley below the waterline meant that it was protected from gunfire (Hoving 2012:157f). But in contrast to all warships the galley was located in the hold. Within the English Royal Navy, the location of the galley was under intense debate (Lavery 1987: 195) and they preferred a different solution. As a consequence several smaller and larger English ships from the late seventeenth century have the galley located in the forecastle (for instance Goodwin 1987: 160; Lavery, 1987: 195–201, also Eriksson 2014a:103–114). Statements in written sources, as well as evidence from shipwrecks, confirm that the Swedish Admiralty preferred to have the galley located down in the hold (Jakobsson 1999:36) before the mainmast.

In his treatise on shipbuilding from 1671, Nicolaes Witsen mentions the different locations of the galley on Dutch ships depending on whether a ship is used for trade or naval purposes. Even if he is referring to the situation on board a *pinnace*, he mentions that 'The galley is on the level with the stores for bottles' (Witsen 1979:59, my translation). The location, on either side of the mainmast on the lower deck, is revealed by a plan of this deck-level. He also mention that on warships the galley is located in the hold (ibid. also Hoving 2012:157f).

A similar situation, where a vessel's transformation for war-use included the relocation of the hearth, is known from the Netherlands. It is a wreck of what is described as a '*Tjalck*-like vessel'. *Tjalcks* are much smaller than *fluits* and were usually rigged with one single mast. The wreck, which is believed to have been converted for service in the Dutch Navy in the late seventeenth century, is long and narrow, with leeboards compensating for the shallow draught when sailing. The wreck, called 'K25', was probably armed with a small number of guns; only three were recorded at the site. The conversion of 'K25' consisted of complementing the hull with an additional hearth amidships. The hearth in the bow remained intact. Archaeologist Karel Vlierman has suggested that the secondary hearth may have been used for casting led-shot for muskets and similar. However, the eating and cooking utensils found at the site correspond to a larger crew than what is usual for this type of vessel (Vlierman 1997b:157–166).

Thus, the transformation of a vessel for naval use included a movement of the hearth to a new central location in the space that used to be the cargo hold on board the merchant *fluit*. To install a warships galley into a merchant ship did not necessary mean that the deck- and hull structure had to be adjusted. The main loading hatch would have provided a shaft from the upper deck, through the lower (which has now become a gun deck) and down into the hold (compare the drawing of the *Anna Maria* Fig. 4.4, G).

That the greater number of mouths to feed on board required a galley of greater capacity is part of the explanation to why it was moved. But I find it relevant to stress that the relocation also had a crucial impact on the everyday practices concerning foodways and commensality. As argued already in the previous chapter food-related practices are crucial in creating specific social relations, and thus also to create order, hierarchy and discipline on board. That is, to make people perform their specific roles as commons, gunners, officers and so on.

6. FLUITS AT WAR

The *Spanienfararen*

Only the lower part of the *Constantia* is preserved and the wreck thus primarily reveals how the hold was arranged. But just as was discussed regarding the *Anna Maria* in chapter 4 information from different kinds of sources, the wreck, written accounts but also pictures and drawings, can together form a fuller picture of how the interior of *fluits* were arranged. The situation is the same regarding the naval version.

As mentioned above the *Constantia* most likely carried 32 guns. But the written record does not reveal how these guns were distributed in the hull. Pictures of armed *fluits* are more revealing in this sense and provide indications of how guns were distributed on board. Hence, there is reason to return to the drawings in Åke Clason Rålamb's book about 'Skeps Byggerij' from 1691. On the same plate as the *Fleit eller Lastdragare*, shown in chapter 4 (Fig. 4.5), Rålamb provide us with a drawing of another ship (Fig. 6.3). He mentions this ship as a *Spaniefarare* (literary meaning Spain trader) which was a popular denomination for those ships used for the salt trade with Spain and Portugal (compare Magalotti 1912:42). These ships were often synonymous with the ships which received tax-reduction, such as the *Constantia*.

The shape of the two hulls on Rålamb's drawing are obviously identical as the attached body plan is said to depict both ships. The orientation of deck-levels and bulkheads are shown through dotted lines and reveal that the interior of *Spanienfararen* not only differs from the other *fluit* shown by Rålamb, but also from the wrecks discussed in the previous chapters. The differences between the two *fluits* are found in the arrangement of decks, bulkheads and gunports, the structures that enclose space.

The *Spanienfararen* has two complete decks, running from stem to stern. The forecastle and the rooms under the quarterdeck are oriented above the upperdeck level. What is important here is that the two divergent arrangements of space shown by Rålamb have to do with the different purposes of the ships. The diverging arrangements make the persons on board act in different ways.

The origin and provenience of all drawings in Rålamb's book is uncertain and this particular one is no exception. Rålamb tells us that *Spanienfararen* could be built 'up to 114 feet long, (about 34 m) and carry 16 guns' (Rålamb 1943:26, my translation). The last statement concerning the guns is a bit peculiar. The drawing shows 16 gun ports at each side, which means that the total number should be (at least) 32! Half of the gunports are located on the lower deck. Most notably they are distributed along the entire length of the hull, which contrasts to the merchant *fluit* in Rålamb's book, where the guns under deck are placed abaft the mainmast (compare Fig. 4.5).

If one reads the text carefully, Rålamb provides some information regarding the denomination of the different rooms, which eventually reveals something on how they were used and the kinds of people that were lodged in them. There is a drawing of a transom (close up in Fig. 7.8, A) which he writes is a *fluit*, where the main cabin (*kaiutan*) is located above the tiller, which explains the windows on the transom. Thus *Spanienfararen* has its cabin above the tiller (Fig. 6.3, A). This contrasts with the version of transom dubbed 'N:0 5', which is the version aimed for the first ship (see Fig. 4.5), where the cabin is located below the tiller, as on the merchant *fluits* discussed in chapters 4 and 5.

The drawing of *Spanienfararen* reveals another feature which is seldom seen on *fluits*, namely quarter galleries. These are decorated balconies on the sternmost part of the hullside. None of the ships discussed in chapters 4 or 5 have these. Access to the quarter galleries was from the cabin. The galleries serve several purposes, one of which was to house sanitary accommodations. This we have reason to return to below.

Rålamb mentioned that the tiller on board the *Spanienfararen* is housed in the room below the cabin, which he refers to as *arkliet* (artillery store) (Fig. 6.3, C). The location of the tiller and whipstaff was thus the same as on the merchant *fluits* described in the previous chapters. But on board the merchant *fluits* there was an inner roof, underneath the tiller, which formed the *hennegat*.

On the *Spanienfararen* the quarterdeck was lengthened towards the bow and ends a few metres abaft the mainmast. The room underneath formed an enclosed helmsman's stand (Fig. 6.3, D), which contrasts to other *fluits* where the helmsman stood out on deck. Rålamb provided us with a drawing of the bulkhead that enclosed the helmsman's stand (Fig. 6.3, E). The upper part of this bulkhead has apertures through which the helmsman could glimpse the sails and the situation out on deck.

The arrangement reminds us of what Nicolaes Witsen describes in his treatise from 1671 regarding the particularities with '*fluits* that go more distant, as for instance India'. According to him the helmsman's stand, 'which otherwise is open, is covered with an apron' (Witsen 1979:178, also

Sténuit 1974:213–256). Witsen also mentions that the huts on board these *fluits* were divided into three separate rooms and the room underneath the cabin is divided into three or four rooms underneath the artillery store (*Konstapels Kamer* in Dutch or *Arkliet* in Swedish), bread, spare rigging details as well as gunpowder was stored (ibid.).

There are also a few detailed sketches of armed *fluits*. Just like it is possible to get an idea of the interior of a house through looking at the location of windows, ends of beams and similar, sketches of ships also reveal clues as to how the interior was arranged, even if they depict the exterior. Gunports, scuppers, pumpdales and similar provide a lot of clues. There is one particularly detailed sketch of an armed *fluit* in the National Maritime Museum in London (Inventory nr PY1712), which is commonly regarded as the work of Willem Velde the Elder (1611–1693) (others suggest it is the work of the younger (1633–1707), see Hoving & Emke 2000:41). It depicts a large *fluit* viewed from the port quarter (Fig. 6.4).

Figure 6.4: Drawing of a fluit made by Willem van der Velde, the Elder. Note the windows on the transom and the exhaust pipe from the privy (NMM, Greenwich, Inv nr PY1712).

The ship has eight gunports on the lower deck, which should now be referred to as the gundeck, two in the forecastle, two under the quarterdeck and two in the poop, the small room highest up in the stern, which gives a total of 28 guns. The gunports reveal the arrangement of the decks. The five foremost ports on gundeck follow the sheer of the wales, whereas the three aftermost are more or less horizontal. In the bow the gundeck is not armed at all as the lowered floor in the forecastle was made at the expense of standing height on the gundeck. The location of the bilge pump is revealed by the muzzle of a pump dale, which is similar to the *fluits* described in previous chapters.

The main cabin is placed as the aftermost room on the main deck and is revealed by two windows on the transom facing and one on the quarter. The main cabin was thus placed above the tiller just as on Rålamb's *Spanienfarare* (fig. 6.3). Below the portside window a soil-pipe reveals the location of a privy. This facility was only accessible from the main cabin and would have been used exclusively by the officer's, rather than the crew. Rålamb is less informative concerning this facility, but very likely this was housed in the quarter gallery (Fig. 6.3, E).

The remains of the *Constantia*, and the depictions and Rålamb's drawing, provide a concordant impression of the spatial arrangement on board an armed *fluit*. The wreck of the *Constantia* reveals where the food was prepared but not where it was consumed. The drawings reveal where the different ranks were lodged, but not where their food was prepared. The point is that it is necessary to use the different sources *together* in order to understand how the armed *fluit* or *Spanienfarare* formed a setting for everyday life. Thus, the sum is greater than its component parts.

The spatial arrangement on board these *fluits*, which could be used either as trading vessels or fighting artillery platforms, thus differs from the merchant versions in quite profound ways. On the contrary, the *Spanienfarare* reveals many similarities to the arrangement on board another ship-type, namely the *pinnace*. These ships were also used either as armed trading vessels or as warships. The interior of the *pinnace* has already been described with some detail by Nicolaes Witsen. In his treatise of 1671, he shows a *pinnace* with two deck-levels that stretch to the entire length of the hull a cabin and *stuerplecht* (helmsman's stand) under the quarterdeck (Witsen 1979:58, plate XLII, Hoving 2012:156). He also mention that the galley was relocated if the *pinnace* was used as a warship (Hoving 2012:157f).

6. FLUITS AT WAR

Manning the naval *fluit*

When the *fluit* was transformed to a warship the number of persons aboard increased dramatically. Instead of being a small group lodged together, within a shared space in the stern, the entire ship became crammed with people. How did the relocation and the increase in numbers affect the experience of being on board?

A warship is a complex organization with a lot of people and chains of command. The arrangement of space ensured that everyone stayed in their predefined place in accordance to rank in this chain. In the previous chapter movement space on board merchant *fluits* was revealed from the location of facilities used on an everyday basis, things associated with sleeping, eating and answering nature's call. The *fluit* transformed for war may be studied in a similar way, but with the difference that the groups of people on board were more clearly demarcated. The ship itself helped to define and separate people into different groups.

Depending on the amount of information available it should be possible to pinpoint many different categories or groups of people on board a vessel. In the following, however, the focus is on two distinctt groups installed within separate movement spaces on board, namely the officers and the crew. The analysis thus revolves around the way these two groups inhabited their defined space.

Already the documents describing armament and manning of the naval vessels distinguish between different categories. As mentioned above the *Constantia* was designed to have seven officers, 96 seamen and 34 soldiers on board (Tornqvist 1788:144). In order to create a fully functioning warship out of the hull of a merchant ship, these people were distributed in a specific order that made them perform together.

Space for officers

The size and the spatial relation between huts on board naval ships were strictly regulated and is revealed through preserved drawings and treaties. Differences in rank were expressed through the size and location of private space. The majority of the sources that describe this are from the eighteenth century (Sutherland 1717, Harris 1989:67, 178), but some information also exists regarding conditions in the seventeenth century (Witsen 1979, Lavery 1981, 1987:151–185).

The relationship between one's position in the hierarchy on board and inhabiting a specific space is reflected in the habit in Sweden of batching all officers together under the term *kajutfolk* (literary meaning 'cabin-people') (cf. Glete 2010:609, Hammar 2014:102ff). The most separate and private room inside the transformed *fluit* was the stern cabin (Fig. 6.3, A) in which the highest in command were lodged. Most likely, Pål Rumpf, the highest in command on board the *Constantia*, was lodged in this room.

Lower ranking officers could be lodged in the artillery store (*Arkliet* in Swedish, *Konstapels Kamer* in Dutch; see Witsen 1979:58). On Rålamb's *Spanienfarare* a bulkhead separates the artillery store (Fig. 6.3, C) from the rest of the gun deck. The seven officers, *kajutfolket*, on board the *Constantia* were thus lodged in the cabin or, regarding the lower officers, in the artillery store, below the cabin.

In contrast to the merchant *fluit*, where all on board were lodged together within a shared space in the stern, movement patterns on board the naval *fluit* were more regulated. The vast quantity of individuals on board, the 90 seamen and 34 soldiers, were lodged before the cabin and the artillery store, out on the gun deck (Fig. 6.3,F), or perhaps also in the hold (Fig. 6.3, G).

As mentioned in the previous chapter the crew on board the armed merchantman *Trumslagaren* slept in hammocks during a voyage from the Netherlands to the Baltic in 1663 (Oscarsson 2013:94). Perhaps the *Constantia* had a similar arrangement.

The regulation of space on board the armed *fluit* was a matter of keeping up appearances and reinforcing a hierarchical structure between those in command and the commanded. This was often regulated already through the fact that often officers were recruited within the nobility, or as became more common in Sweden during the late seventeenth century, they became ennobled (Englund 1989, Stadin 2009).

But being a nobleman was not simply to possess a certain societal position, but implied a certain mentality as well, including how one acted on everyday basis. It was a matter of keeping up appearances. Becoming a member of a social group may be described as participating in astaged performance, not least in relation to other groups. Thus essentially social groups do not simply exist, but are constantly renegotiated and created (see also discussion with Latour 2005:27-42). A nobleman was created through the rituals and routines of the everyday: 'Through where they sat in church, who they doffed their hat to, how they behaved at festivities. A failure to act the part could lead to a loss of social status. Social identities are to some extent the result of performance at an everyday and ceremonial level' (Johnson 2002:11ff).

Foodways

As discussed in the previous chapter, foodways and commensality are crucial ingredients in bonding and group formation. The mechanisms involved may also be used the other way around, to separate and to exclude. Preparation and consumption of food, and, in particular, the separation of these activities, are perfect exponents on the daily practices that constitute peoples' identities. This is why the (re-) location of the galley is important. It should be seen as a way of creating and upholding the officers as a group, separate and distinct from the others on board.

On board the merchant *fluits*, food was prepared in the galley, in the foremost room under the quarterdeck, and was consumed in the main cabin immediately astern of the galley. Even if it is difficult to prove that they actually did, it was *possible* for all on board to eat together, and I find it very likely that they did; not least as the only heating source was located under the quarterdeck. All on board thus had to stay in the vicinity of this feature.

The naval *fluit* is different in this sense. On board the *Constantia* food was prepared in the centre of the ship, but most importantly, it was consumed in spaces specific to groups with explicit roles. Officers ate among officers and seamen among seamen. But not only did they eat in separate corners of the ship, they also ate different things.

As shown with some detail by economic-historian Ulrica Söderlind, there is a considerable difference between the officer's diet and that of the crew, both regarding quantity and nutrition. There was also a difference in quality. For instance, during the unfortunate year 1676, when the *Constantia* sank, the ration of beer within the Swedish Navy was four litres per person per day (Söderlind 2006:52), but there were several different kinds of beer. Officer's beer, commonly referred to as *kajutöl*, literary meaning 'cabin beer' as it was aimed for those in the cabin, was of higher quality and also had a higher percentage of alcohol compared to *skeppsöl*, which literally means 'ship's beer' and was offered to the commons (Söderlind 2006:50–69).

In the Dutch Navy, which was renowned for having a good supply of food for all on board, the rations for officers differed in that they were doubled (Schama 1988:184).

The separation of preparation and consumption of food brings with it other performative consequences. It distinguished categories of people, the most obvious being those who retrieved the food and those who had it served to them. As discussed by Söderlind, using *Vasa* (1628) as an example, the food was prepared in the galley located down in the hold, before the mainmast. The officer's food was transported to the cabin and served. The commons ate in groups of 6–8 people and had one designated person who went down to the galley to fetch the food. Officers (*kajutfolk*) thus became officers through being lodged in the cabin, behaving as officers, eating in the cabin, eating like officers and eating the dishes, drinking the beverages, only served in the cabin.

As argued by historian AnnaSara Hammar higher officers seem to have considered the cabin as an extension of their own estate or sphere of power. It was a space for formal representation but also personal dwelling in which the officer could invite friends and family, store personal belongings and utilize after own ideas (Hammar 2014:104f).

Before the mast

The vast quantity of the persons on board the transformed *fluit* were lodged at the gun deck where they also ate. It is uncertain whether tables were on board such a relatively small warship as the *Constantia*. It is possible that the men ate sitting directly on the deck. The 'commons' space on board the ship was thus the foremost part of the ship, which included the beakhead. Most *fluits* did not have beakheads at all, whereas it was a standard feature on warships, quite irrespective of their size. Only the really large merchant ships were equipped with this feature, such as the *Anna Maria* described in chapter 4. She was a ship that achieved reduced tax following the condition that she could be hired by the crown and converted into a warship.

The beakhead should be regarded as the crew's area before others as it contained the 'seat-of-ease'. The word 'head' is still a term used for toilets on board ships, boats and airplanes (Landström 1980:89). The 'seats-of-ease' located in beakheads usually consist of a vertically oriented tube made of four planks nailed together. A frequently referred to example of such a facility are the seats-of-ease in the beakhead of the royal ship *Vasa* (1628) (Simmons 1997:44ff, Landström 1980:89).

Movement patterns and behaviour on board were mediated by the location of these facilities used regularly by all, on an everyday basis. To be assigned to a specific seat of ease would thus define your role on board the warship. To visit the accommodation in the beakhead was an act (among numerous others) where for instance the seamen became seamen. But it also meant subordination in relation to officers.

There are some archaeological examples which further highlight the difference between the officers and the commons on board ships. During the *Vasa* excavation two pewter potties were found. These were of first class craftsmanship and as such were high status items, and were likely stored in one of the quarter galleries (Soop 2001:65ff) or the disintegrated upper- or the great cabin (cf. Hocker & Wendel 2006). The situation was likely to have been quite similar on board the naval *fluit* where the officers would answer nature's call either in the quarter galleries (compare Fig. 6.3, B) or with the means of a privy inside the cabin.

In that case the waste would leave the ship through a round soil-pipe made of metal as shown in Figure 6.4. What is interesting is that the pipes, located in the quarter galleries or the main cabins of naval vessels, differ in the sense that they are made out of lead or copper (cf. Eriksson et al. 2013:17ff, also Hoving 2012:153f, Witsen 1979:56 Plate XXXI) whereas the seats-of-ease, aimed for the crew were usually made of wood. As shown in the previous chapter, the preserved soil-pipes on merchant *fluits* are also of wood.

There is thus a difference in the materiality of soil-pipes, which cannot be understood as anything other than exclusivity. I would like to see these metal tubes as a parallel to the metal chamber pot placed in the night stools used by the nobility (Skeri 1992:15–34). The difference is that the tube on board a ship lacks the bottom of the pot and is thus automatically emptied overboard. Ordinary people though were used to answering nature's call with less sophisticated devices (Granlund 1992:9).

A seamen's experience of the stern

In the previous chapter it was argued that the mind is the ultimate vantage point when discussing the perception of space (compare Bollnow 1994, 2011 or Tilley 1994:9). Important for the perception of space is the ability to move through it. Following Bollnow, people want to secure their *movement space*. Through this protection of space another form of space is rendered, namely *possession space* (German: *Beseitzraum*). In its most obvious form *possession space* is often defined by walls and similar physical markers. The transformation of a merchant *fluit* into a naval ship was a matter of restricting *movement space* in order to create *possession space* (cf. Bollnow 1994, Eriksdotter 2005:237ff).

As shown above the ranks, tasks and places in the hierarchy and chains of command, correspond to and emerge out of their location inside the hull. This means that there were particular areas where one felt more 'at home' than in other locations. On board the *fluit* transformed for war, just as on any warship for that matter, there were several clearly defined movement spaces, most notably: the space for seamen and soldiers and the space for officers. How is the experience of the ship affected through such a changed vantage point? How did those lodged 'before the mast' experience the space in the stern?

The relation to the object, area or similar, is to some extent determined by your vantage point. In attempts to get at such relations, architects, archaeologists and others have undertaken simulated walks through buildings, an embodied way of seeing (Giles 2007:108). A 'promenade architecturale', may thus provide a step towards understanding (Eriksdotter 2005:227–268, 2009:85–96, Nagbøl 1983:39–52).

If one of the 'commons' were standing amidships and gazing aft, towards the stern, he would have perceived that the deck slants upwards and the hullsides slopes inwards. The first bulkhead visible from this vantage point encloses the helmsman's stand. The second bulkhead is placed above and beyond, further aft. It is both narrower and lower than the bulkhead enclosing the helmsman's stand. The difference in the size of the bulkheads, the deck that becomes narrower towards the stern, the incline of the bulkheads and the tumble-home of the sides, all function as a manipulations of the geometrical perspective. Seen all together, the stern appears more distant than it really is (cf. Borgersen & Ellingsen 1993:40). It is uncertain whether the seventeenth-century naval architects were aware of this visual effect. The principles of the geometrical perspective had been widely appreciated among artists and architects for several hundred years at this point (cf. Kleiner 2009:425ff), as were manipulations of these principles, making things look larger, more distant or similar as well.

What effect would this have on the seamen's experience? A person placed on the quarterdeck would, thanks to this illusion involving perspective, appear larger than he or she really was. This geometrical trick may of course be a coincidence, but the person placed in this spot just happens to be a commanding officer. Was it actually a matter of manipulating the crew to feel small?

To communicate power may be done through punishment or threat of punishment. The process of imposing discipline does not always consist of direct messages to the consciousness or rational thinking. Possibly the most effective way is through suggestive manipulation of emotions. On the one side the centre of power remains closed for every attempt to orient in relation to it, and on the other hand the power can be perceived everywhere (Nagbøl 1983: 40).

As argued, not least among psychoanalysts, the mechanisms of power are already present within the individual. This is what Sigmund Freud calls 'the Uncanny' (*Unheimlich*), the unconscious relieving of suppressed emotions (2003). The architecture of power works through bringing up such emotions from our unconscious. So what physical aspects inspired the uncanny emotions in the chest of our seaman as he stood out on deck, besides perhaps feeling small?

Bringing forth an uncanny emotion may be done by evoking a feeling of constant visibility, and there are several architectonical ways to accomplish this. In the discussion of surveillance, the term 'panopticon' or 'panopticism' tends to pop up. The origin of the term is the ideal prison invented by the English philosopher and social theorist Jeremy Bentham in 1785. Many buildings have been inspired by his ideas on surveillance and power since then. The ships discussed here are of course older than Bentham's prison, but his ideas are useful when investigating surveillance from a more general point of view (see Lundgren 2002: 9–45).

The Panopticon was circular, with the prisoners located in cells radiating from the centre. The guard, or rather the observer, could observe (-opticon) all (pan-) prisoners at the same time, but the latter could never tell when they were being watched (Bentham 1995).

If the inmates are convicts, there is no danger of a plot, an attempt at collective escape, the planning of new crimes for the future, bad reciprocal influences; if they are patients, there is no danger of contagion; if they are madmen there is no risk of their committing violence upon one another; if they are schoolchildren, there is no copying, no noise, no chatter, no waste of time; if they are workers, there are no disorders, no theft, no coalitions, none of those distractions that slow down the rate of work, make it less perfect or cause accidents (Foucault 1995:200–201).

On a ship the inmates would consist of its crew and the ships architectonical structure had to adapt to various principles of surveillance. The arrangement of naval ships, with the officers in the stern and the commons before the mast meant that surveillance was permanent in its effects even if it was discontinuous in its action. The ship thus was an architectonical apparatus for creating and sustaining a power relation independent of the person who exercises it. According to Bentham's original idea, the principle of power should be visible but unverifiable. The inmate should see the built structure that covers the observer, but he should not be able to verify if being watched (Foucault 1995:195ff).

Even though the ship does not have the physical form of a panoptic prison, some of the mechanisms are all the same present and perfectly implemented into the ship-structure. It is the implementation of discipline, power structure into the individual minds of the people on board, which could effectively be built into a ship's hull (for a similar discussion see Hammar 2014:167ff).

The stern as a consequence of the ship's sheer, but also from the quarterdeck rising above the main deck, provided as perfect vantage point in several aspects. From this position it was not only possible to see all the sails and which direction the ship was heading; it was also a vantage point suitable to watch over the crew. This vantage point was placed so that the crew would work below the monitoring officer who would have his eyes on the crew in a quite discrete way. In Bentham's own words '(T)he essence of (The Panoptoicon) consists, then, in the *centrality* of the inspector's situation, combined with the well-known and most effectual contrivances of *seeing without being seen*' (Bentham 2002:72, my abbreviation).

Idling, laziness, or conspiring activities were easy to spot by an officer at this location just by turning the eye a couple of degrees. The crew-member, on the other hand, had to turn around, let his eyes off the task at hand, turn his head and search the structures on the quarterdeck for a surveillance officer, or officers. But even if the crewmember's eye cannot spot the observer, he is never certain if he is being observed.

What about the visible but unverifiable observer? Was it possible to 'see without being seen' on board a *fluit*? On a merchant *fluit* the helmsman stood out on deck abaft the mizzen mast, steering the ship with a whipstaff coming up from its bearing in the quarterdeck. This is the arrangement that meets us on the 'Ghost Ship', and the 'Lion Wreck' (see chapter 4) as well as many other *fluits*.

Interesting here is that the covered location of the helmsman calls for a bulkhead before the whipstaff (Fig. 6.3, E) and equivalents are shown in Witsen (1979:58, even if they depict *pinnace*). Witsen also mention that the helmsman's stand was covered on board the '*fluits* that go (...) to India' (ibid. 178). Sketches of the van der Veldes as well as *Vasa* (1628) reveal a covered helmsman's stand, as doEnglish naval vessels from the seventeenth century. In the upper part of the bulkheads enclosing the helmsman's stand there are small apertures which make it possible to see through the bulkhead. Obviously these openings enabled the helmsman to see out on deck. Aside from this, the openings enabled observations of the activities out on deck.

On many warships, the foremost room under the quarterdeck, which is equal to the helmsman's stand (*stuerplecht* in Dutch, *styrplikt* in Swedish), were equal to the gunroom (compare Winfield 2010:123). There was thus the possibility of hidden, unobservable officers behind the bulkhead.

Approaching the stern

As pointed out above, from the position down on deck, the quarters in the aft part of the ship appeared far more distant than they really were. This is due to the narrowing of the stern and the height of the different bulkheads which emphasize the perspective. Seeing is one thing, but the embodied experience of moving from amidships towards the stern further underlined the subordinate position of the person approaching the stern. Due to the sheer of the deck the crewmember, walking towards the stern, would have been walking uphill. This meant that a person approaching the quarters did so in a posture almost bowing forward, a condition which further acts to subordinate person.

The uphill climb of the main deck ends with the bulkhead before the helmsman's stand was equipped with openings enabling the helmsman to look at the sails and to communicate with the crew up on deck. But, all the same, it meant that you did not know if you were being watched when you were out on deck.

The very passage through the bulkhead is interesting. Rålamb and Witsen offer only limited information about the content and message in the decorations on this bulkhead. Were they part of a specific message to the persons moving through the structure?

The only more or less complete setting of a bulkhead separating the helmsman's stand from the upper deck is found on board the *Vasa*. Here it is evident that the structure is supposed to be experienced through approaching it from the upper deck and moving through the bulkhead. The bulkhead is decorated by pilasters in the form of sculptured devils who are holding their hands over their ears. The explanation for the devils, depicted as an orchestra of angels, becomes clear upon entering the helmsman's stand (Landström 1980:108, Soop 1992:227–230).

The devils are directed towards an observer out on deck, either the crew or a visitor. Their postures and the way they behave – covering their ears – is a constant reminder that there is something else on the other side of the bulkhead. One way to see it is that on the short walk from amidships on the *Vasa* to the officers in the stern, one had to pass through hell and finally reach the divine superiors in the stern. The seamen, visitor or someone else who for some reason was approaching this area would have felt with their entire body that they were in the wrong space. The slope of the deck helped the person to almost roll downhill, back to the allotted place before the mast.

The order in which the rooms appear when walking from amidships and to the officer's cabin in the stern is similar on Rålamb's *Spanienfarare* and on board the *Vasa*. The experience of approaching the officer's cabin actively created subordinate groups and privileged people. The mutual spatial relation between cabin and hearth in this sense worked as a way to uphold an order as the built structures forced the ship's inhabitants to perform this social structure on a daily basis. It was a way of making the commons exercise power over themselves.

Conclusion

To conclude, the transformation of a *fluit* from a merchant to a fighting ship was not just a matter of installing more guns or persons. It was also a matter of arranging and positioning all these human and non-human actors in a specific way to form a fully working warship. In order to renegotiate an already existing ship to do new things, all on board had to agree that from now on the peaceful merchant ship would become a warship.

In the previous chapters we saw that *fluits* could do different things, in different modes, whether under sail or moored in an urban harbour. The naval *fluit* may be regarded as a third mode. The hull or rig alone did not make the *Constantia* a warship. It was the situation. Rather than pointing at a specific hull or rig and claiming they were either merchant or naval, these things, together with cannons, people and a whole lot of other things may be described in terms of an actor-network.

With this said, we shall disembark the converted *fluit* and try to assess what the *fluit* does in a wider context. It has been touched upon briefly already, although not commented upon in any detail. However, the fact that merchant ships were now sailing and fighting alongside the king's own men-of-war should be seen in the context of the societal influence of the *fluit*-owners. As mentioned in the beginning of this chapter, the initiative to give privileges to armed merchant ships was taken after the victory at Femern in 1644. The auxiliary fleet that facilitated this triumph was funded by Louis De Geer, a finance man of Dutch origin. In a way this is symptomatic of the development of Swedish society during the seventeenth century, from a strictly feudal society that was based on the estates and where the king and nobility had the power. By the mid seventeenth century the burghers, of which many had migrated from the Dutch Republic, achieved an increased societal influence in Sweden. In many cases, these persons were equal to those who owned shares in *fluits*. Their ships were now sailing side by side with the Royal Warships.

7. Urbanism under sail – the exterior of the *fluit*

The printing press, resulting in the mass-production of texts, is often put forth as one of the most important innovations for distribution of information in the Early Modern period (Braudel 1981:397–402). The content of a text, and the complex relationship between the letters and the words, are the same in every copy. With the printed text undistorted messages could be distributed like never before. These texts can move through space and are distributed over large areas to be read in different corners of the world. The content is immutable, but the printed texts are mobile. With their ability to deliver undistorted messages, 'immutable mobiles' are necessary for domination on a large scale (cf. Latour 1990:12, also Law 2000:3ff, compare discussion with Moreland 2001).

But 'immutable mobiles' do not necessary have to be texts like books, letters or e-mails. For instance, in archaeological research we use information from different sites in the form of plans, drawings, tables, written reports and so forth in our analysis, all of which are essentially forms of 'immutable mobiles' (compare Latour 1990:19–68, 2005:223, 227, Olsen et al. 2013:88, Westin 2012). We have already become acquainted with John Law's discussion on the topic (Law 2000:4).

As mentioned several times already, *fluits* are surprisingly uniform when it comes to hull-shape, deck-arrangements and rig. But the standardization also includes the sculptures on the exteriors of these ships. This uniform pattern may be likened to printed books in the sense that they contain a message, which is fairly equally presented in every 'copy' of the ship. The composition of sculptures is always the same – it is immutable – while the ship itself is mobile. The message expressed through the sculptures on these ships is composed and manufactured at one place and sent out and distributed over large areas. This chapter deals with the external sculptural decoration of *fluits*, the visual appearance of such a ship. What does the appearance of *fluits* signal to the surrounding world?

The discussion below, thus considers the different associations that the appearance of a *fluit* might have evoked depending on its destination.

Figure 7.1: Wolfgang Hartmann's engraving of Stockholm from 1650. Three categories of ships are clearly distinguishable. In the foreground are the ships of the Royal Navy, at the left hand are the small undecked clinker-built vessels, used by the peasants to transport firewood, fish and similar products to town. Along Skeppsbron are the merchant ships, and among these several fluits (Stockholm City Museum).

A view of Stockholm

Wolfgang Hartmann's often reproduced engraving of Stockholm, made to commemorate the coronation of Christina in 1650, provides an indication of how *fluits* appeared in the middle of the capital (Fig. 7.1). The viewer hovers somewhere over the island of Djurgården and looks out over Stockholm from the east. Even if the houses have changed character through the centuries that have passed, one may discern many familiar buildings fairly quickly. The churches, the Admiralties House, and the old Castle *Tre Kronor* (Three Crowns) are only a few of these structures that are still standing or partly included in existing buildings. But the ships, which are just as prominent as the other buildings on Hartmann's picture, vanished from the scene long ago.

Looking a bit closer at the vessels one is able to detect that they may be divided into three clearly distinguishable categories. The first is found along Skeppsholmen's eastern shore in the foreground. These are the naval vessels. The rigs are dismantled, which indicates that the navy is not prepared for conflict. Despite this, they are an important feature where they are moored at the entrance to the capital. The exteriors of warships were an excellent medium for communicating ideas and symbolic messages from a centralized monarchy (Cederlund 1994:47–86). A ship's appearance was discussed extensively within the Admiralty during the 1600s (Jakobsson 2000:225–243).

To regard warships as 'floating palaces' (cf. Soop 2007) is perhaps particularly felicitous in this context, when they were moored at Skeppsholmen in the middle of the capital. As long as they were at the dock both domestic and foreign observers could view these ships up close, and observe the sculptural message they brought, something that is glimpsed, for example, in the portrayal of Lorenzo Magalotti's visit to Stockholm in 1674 (Magalotti 1912:22f), and noted by the anonymous French valet that visited the capital in 1663 (Oscarsson 2013:169f). The sculptures on the warships' transoms, galleries and beakheads communicated royal ambitions and claims to power. In their seemingly idle moored state these ships were still on active duty through declaring an explicit royal ideology.

At Södermalm, at the left hand of the engraving, in the water below *ryssbodarna* (the Russian huts), are the second category of vessel. These are the small undecked craft, with one mast, used by peasants to transport firewood, fish and other goods to the capital. Tightly packed along Skeppsbron in the middle of Hartmann's picture, we find the third category, which comprises a number of large ships. Of the fourteen ships anchored stern to the viewer, there are nine which undoubtedly exhibit the characteristic pear-shaped stern of the *fluit*. The exception is a warship moored right below the castle, which must be one of the Royal transports.

The anonymous French valet provides an interesting snapshot of the port:

> For strolls in the city, the best place is the port that has a long quay built on stilts along the seafront and which extends from the southern city gate to the north, covering the whole of one side of the city. [...] the quay has no guardrail because all vessels moor directly to it (Oscarsson 2013:186, my translation).

Unfortunately he gives no description of what the ships look like, what kinds of sculptures they were carrying and what messages these proclaimed.

Hartmann's engraving does not provide us with so much additional information here either. Even if it is remarkably detailed and reflects everything from kite flyers to pipe smokers and mongrels, he too fails to reveal how the stern of the *fluits* moored along the quay were decorated. He does not let us know how the carvings on the moored *fluits* differ from the of warships at Skeppsholmen. What was the unique contribution of the *fluits* to the urban landscape? As we shall see, wrecks of *fluits* provide first-class information on these matters.

Name

Most of the sculptures on seventeenth-century ships are placed in the stern, on the flat transom above the rudder. The transom may be likened to a facade of a house that reveals to the outside what kind of activities and people that dwells behind it. In a time when those who could read or write were a minority, painted or sculptured depictions worked as the prime tools for communicating the ship's name, its home-port and a lot of other information. Having the ship's name spelled with letters on a small sign in the stern started to occur in the seventeenth century, mostly on naval vessels (for instance Laughton 2001:155) but there are examples on seventeenth-century depictions of *fluits*, as we shall see.

Figureheads were almost exclusively found on ships with beakheads. As mentioned in the previous chapters these are more or less synonymous with warships, East Indiamen and similar in the seventeenth- and early eighteenth centuries, although important exceptions do exist. Some large *fluit*s, like the armed versions, had beakheads (Hoving 1994:49f, Unger 1978:45). Both the *Anna Maria* and *Constantia* discussed in the previous chapters had this feature. In the seventeenth century the figurehead usually consisted of a lion and seldom had anything to do with the ship's name, which is a custom that appears later on, in the eighteenth- and nineteenth centuries. The sculpture that revealed the ship's name was exclusively found on the transom in the stern.

Fluits thus often had names that could be expressed with a painted or sculptured picture. When reading names of *fluits* one may try to imagine the kinds of sculptures that were placed on the upper part of the pear-shaped stern. Common names were: *The Sun, The Wine Cask, The Pearl, The Golden Phoenix, The Iron Balance* and so on. The practical aspects of having the name expressed in pictures rather than in letters should not be underestimated as the sculptural 'language' may be considered to have been a fairly universal one. When '*The Rose*' entered a Swedish port it changed name to '*Rosen*' and when it entered a Dutch port it would be called '*Roos*'.

Needless to say, the interpretation of the name figure came to vary. For instance, a ship named *Gotlandia*, is sometimes mentioned as *Lammet* (the Lamb) (cf. Zettersten 1903:569), which is explained by the fact that the province of Gotland had a lamb in its coat of arms.

There are also a few archaeological examples of name figures from *fluits*. While surveying the seabed astern of the 'Ghost Ship', the sculptured body of a bird came into view. The size as well as the location in which it was found, abaft of the stern, suggests that the original location of this sculpture was the transom. This means that it is very likely that the original name of the 'Ghost Ship' included a bird. Judging from the shape of the bird's body, it is likely to have depicted a Swan. Several ships are known to have had names like *Gilded Swan* and *White Swan*. Presumably, the 'Ghost Ship' had a similar name (Fig. 7.11).

To express a ship's name with symbols presupposes that the symbol is recognized and well understood. Those who see the ship may reasonably agree on what is being imaged. Besides the rather obvious *Crescents*, *Brown Horses* and the like, the names of *fluits* often alluded to familiar episodes from the Bible: *David and Goliath, Noah's Ark* and so forth (see Fahlborg 1923:222 for more examples). Besides the more earthly '*Guilded Swans*' and similar, names associated with Christianity were common, such as the armed *fluit*, likely named *The Good Shepherd* as shown in the previous chapter (Fig. 6.4). A parallel to such semiotic representations is the iconography on the walls of Catholic churches. Pictures here revealed the Christian message as the Latin words of the priests were incomprehensible to the vast majority of 'common people' (see Moreland 2001:33–55).

There is one quite unique example preserved which reveals the habit of depicting motifs from the Bible on ship's sterns. It consists of a nearly complete transom from a *fluit* and is kept in Harritslev church in Denmark (Fig 7.2). According to tradition it derives from a ship that foundered at the nearby coast. The 1.75 m high and 0.93 m wide transom is built up of horizontally oriented planks. Naturalistically painted carved figures are attached to these planks (cf. Hoving & Emke 2000:9). These consist of a man in Roman-inspired clothing, which is a seventeenth-century way of emphasizing that the event being depicted took place long ago. The man wields a sword and is clearly in the process of decapitating the young man who kneels at his feet. An angel hovers over both of them and keeps one hand on the swinging sword to prevent the brutal execution from taking place. The motif derives from the Old Testament, and the seventeenth-century observer would soon recognize that the scene depicts Abraham who is about to sacrifice his son Isaac as ordered by God. As he raises his sword God's angel stops him. He was put to the test and had fulfilled it to God's satisfaction. Thus the name of the *fluit* was *Abraham, Abraham's sacrifice* or similar.

Not only was it a common feature to have the ship's *name* signalled through sculptures, but the rest of the decorational programme follows an equally predictable, and at the same time informative, pattern. Many *fluits* have their home port represented through depicting the coat-of-arms of that city. The transom in Harritslev church is not an exception to this rule. Above the angel and Abraham's sword we find the arms of the town Hindelopen, in Friesland (Hoving & Emke 2000:9). The curtain that flanks the motifs on the transom is a very common feature on *fluits* and other contemporary ships. In the lowest part of the transom we find the year of construction, a feature that is also detected on various engravings and other depictions of *fluits*. For example, *Abraham's sacrifice*, from Hindelopen, was built in 1639.

In a similar way the stern of *The Good Shepherd* described above (Fig. 6.4) has a coat-of-arms on the top of the stern. It is a shield with a castle, held up by two lions, which probably represents the arms of Dutch town Middelburg. The transom also reveals the building year, 1642 (NMM, Inv nr PY 1712).

During the archaeological excavation on the 'Jutholmen Wreck' (see chapter 4) a sculpture depicting the body of a Roman warrior was raised (Fig. 7.3). It has been suggested that it was placed aside of the transom with an identical, but mirror-image sculpture on the other side (Cederlund 1983: 55–56). The preserved portion of the sculpture is just 64 cm, which means that the overall length of the sculpture is not likely to have been more than one metre.

Judging from the size and orientation it is perhaps more likely that it was placed on the flat part of the transom, as a component in a scene revealing the ship's name. It is also possible that the lion, which, it has been suggested, would have been placed on top of the transom (see Cederlund 1982b:56), were a part of this motif as well. The Roman style may be used to signal something archaic, just like '*Abraham's sacrifice*' on the transom in Harritslev church.

Another example of how a biblical name has been expressed through pictures is revealed by a votive ship from Täby church, north of Stockholm (Fig. 7.4) (Berg 1968a:18, 1968b:39–44). As is common for this kind of model, the ship is very accurate in details even though the proportions are incorrect. The rig has been modernized but the hull seems to be fairly original. At the transom the model reveals the text: 'D KONINC SALOMON' (King Solomon). As has been mentioned above the habit of writing the ship's name in letters becomes common later on (see also Laughton 2001:155). However, the inhabitants of Täby parish did not need to be able to read in order to grasp the name. The praying King Solomon is depicted on the ship's stern. Above his head, flanked by two fish, is the coat-of-arms of Amsterdam (Berg 1968b).

Figure 7.2: The transom from a fluit, probably named Abraham's Sacrifice which is preserved in Søndre Harritslevs church in Denmark (Niklas Eriksson).

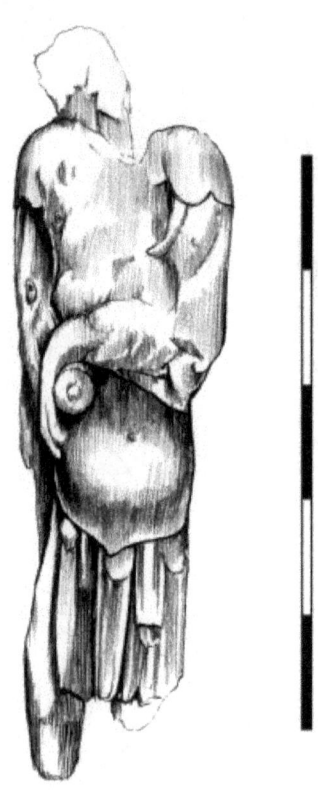

Figure 7.3 (left): The sculpture from the 'Jutholmen Wreck'. Most of the head and the lower parts of the legs are missing, but it is clear that it depicts a figure in armour, ready to draw a sword (Niklas Eriksson).

Figure 7.4 (below): The transom from the votive ship King Solomon from Amsterdam in Täby church in Sweden. Note the city of Amsterdam's coat-of-arms, the name text and the two hoekmen that flank the iconographic representation of the ship's name (Niklas Eriksson).

Figure 7.5 (right): The raised hoekman from the 'Ghost Ship', a mid-seventeenth-century 'lion of fashion' (Niklas Eriksson).

Figure 7.6 (below): The Batavian Senior Merchant Pieter Cnoll and his Family, painted by Jacob Coeman in 1665. As pointed out by Koehler et al. (2012) his outfit closely resembles that of the hoekman from the 'Ghost Ship' (Rijksmuseum/Amsterdam).

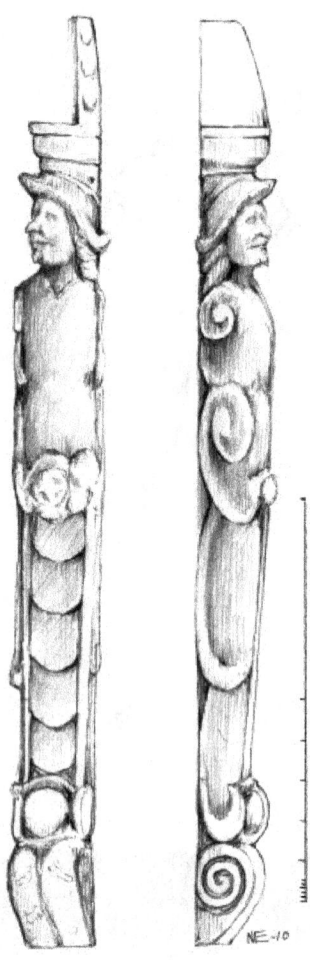

Figure 7.7 (left): The hoekman from the 'Lion Wreck' (Niklas Eriksson).

Figure 7.8 (below): The two transoms from Åke Rålamb's book on shipbuilding from 1691: a) A transom of a fluit where the cabin is located above the tiller; b) A half transom where the cabin is placed below the tiller. Note that both versions are flanked with hoekmen (after Rålamb 1691:26, plate G).

A.

B.

Figure 7.9: Three bearded men are carved onto the knightheads astern of the mainmast on board the 'Ghost Ship' (DSP).

Figure 7.10: Abraham Storck's (1644-1708) painting, 'The whaling grounds', oil on canvas. Judging from the motifs on the transoms the fluit in the middle appears to be named 'Polar bear' or similar, whereas the one on the right reveals the moralizing name 'Jonah and the Whale'. Note the wrecked fluit on the far right (Rijksmuseum, Amsterdam).

Who is the Hoekman?

The ship's name, its home-port and year of construction were thus found on the flat transom in the stern. The transom itself was usually flanked by two near life-size statues known as the *hoekmen*, which is Dutch and directly translated means 'corner man'. This derives from the fact that they are placed in the corner of the transom. The most common English equivalent appears to be 'Strongman' (cf. Peters 2013:69). One of the finest examples of a *hoekman* has been raised from the 'Ghost Ship' (Fig. 7.5). Originally it was positioned on the ship's portside while a mirrored example would have been placed on the starboard side.

These two *hoekmen* were standing with their backs against the aftermost quarter of the hull side, turning their heads as if gazing abaft. Unfortunately, the lifted '*hoekman*' has lost most of his face due to erosion and we thus have no details of the nose and a possible moustache and beard. His long curly hair is of the fashion that became popular in the Dutch Republic in the 1640s and which upset the Calvinist church as personal abomination (Schama 1988:62). The *hoekman*'s left hand is behind his back while his right hand holds his mantle in a tight grip over his chest, as to protect himself from high seas and the cold wind of the Baltic. The posture is identical to corner-sculptures, in the shape of Roman warriors on warships. The model of the warship *Hollandia* of 1664 (shown in Laughton 2001, Plate 35, Peters 2013:69) is an example. Important to note is the fact that although the posture is the same, the characters are totally different, a fact we will return to below.

The woodcarver who made the *hoekman* on the 'Ghost Ship' was highly skilled in terms of technique, and managed to shape and model the hair and clothing very naturally. Despite this, the proportions of the *hoekman* are a bit naive. The head is carved in more or less life size whereas the body, and in particular the legs, are very short. Whether this was made in order to achieve a specific visual effect when the sculpture was placed in position at the stern, or if the sculpturing process just happened to end up this way, is difficult to tell.

Besides perhaps his short legs, the *hoekman* from the 'Ghost Ship' depicts a person whose appearance would not have differed from the prosperous merchants in Amsterdam at the time, an urban fashionista with slinky stockings, puff pants, shoes with heels and cravat. The *hoekman* is thus a clear parallel to the 'Burghers' depicted by Jan Steen,

Frans Hals, Rembrandt and other 'Golden Age' painters (Fig. 7.6). Originally the sculpture was naturalistically painted. The preliminary results from analysis of the paint remains on the sculpture reveal that the clothes were mostly black, while the hat was red (Koehler et al. 2012). There are other examples of *hoekmen* aside from the ones on from the 'Ghost Ship'.

The 'Lion Wreck', was also equipped with such sculptures (Fig. 7.7). One of these has been found loose on the seabed. It is an alternative version in the form of a hermpilaster. It is thus only the head of the merchant that has been naturalistically sculptured, whereas the body is replaced by ornaments (Eriksson 2012:17–25). He has long hair and wears a triangular hat on top of it. Underneath the articulated nose he has a moustache, and on the tip of his chin there is a small beard. Not least, his chubby cheeks reveal his prosperity.

The composition of the stern of the *fluit* is also shown on several paintings, engravings and sketches from the period and the characteristics are easy to distinguish when one has learned what to look for. After looking at finds such as the 'Lion Wreck' and the 'Ghost Ship' these sculptures appear more distinct in various depictions. The skilled hand of Villem van der Velde, the younger has depicted a *Buis* (a smaller type of vessel, which had a scaled down *fluit's* stern) with *hoekmen* of quite similar fashion to those on the 'Lion Wreck'. At the location of the ship's date of building, we read '1640', and the name is expressed through what appears to be a sculptured version of Sandro Botticelli's *The Birth of Venus*, hence the *Buis* was likely named *Venus* (NMM, Inv nr PAH 1719, also in Unger 1994:128).

Åke Clason Rålamb shows two transoms of *fluit*s in his book on shipbuilding from 1691. The first transom (Fig. 7.8, A) belongs to the drawing of *Spanienfararen* (see previous chapter) and has windows on the field that usually contained the ship's name. The name is here spelled with letters (Rålamb 1943:26). Unfortunately the name is illegible in every edition of the book that I have managed to trace. In any case, the transom with the windows is flanked by the *hoekmen* (ibid. plate G., fig. 3). Only half of the second of Rålamb's transoms (Fig. 7.8, B) is visible. Judging from the motif on the transom the ship was named after a city. A chubby *hoekman* is standing on the starboard quarter (ibid. plate G., fig. 5). Even if the carvings are schematic, there are two *hoekmen* present on the stern of the votive ship in Täby church as well (Fig. 7.4).

The *hoekman* may be regarded as depicting the appearance of a ship's owner. Not necessary a particular person, which would be complicated as *fluits* often were used by a group of ship-owners, but rather a representative for a specific social group, the burghers. Through their presence on the ship's exterior, there would be no doubt as to what echelon in society the ship belonged to.

In analogy with this we may briefly consider the contemporary Swedish warships which belonged to the crown. A well-known archaeological example is the warship *Vasa* (1628). In the exterior of *Vasa* there are various allusions to the owner himself, Gustavus Adolphus, as well as his alias 'Lion from the North' and his father, King Charles IX (cf. Soop 1992: 57–70).

From the wreck of the large ship *Kronan* (1676), which was built and also sunk during the reign of Karl XI, a sculpture that bears a suspicious likeness to his father, Karl X Gustav, has been raised (Einarsson 1997:216–217). Just as the great warships of the seventeenth century formed a kind of floating *alter ego* of the king and the nation (cf. Cederlund 1994:47–86), *fluits* may be regarded as portraits and symbols of merchants, who achieved an ever increasing wealth and societal influence in Sweden during the seventeenth century.

Whereas Roman warriors were almost compulsory on naval vessels in the seventeenth century, their appearance on the exterior of *fluits* is scarcer. As described above, the 'Romans' that are components in the embellishment on *fluits* are parts of allegoric expressions of the vessel's name. They do not necessary refer to the ship's owner, which for instance is the case on the *Vasa* (Soop 1992:57–70) or *Kronan*, where the former King Karl X Gustav is depicted in a Roman-style outfit (cf. Einarsson 1997:216–217).

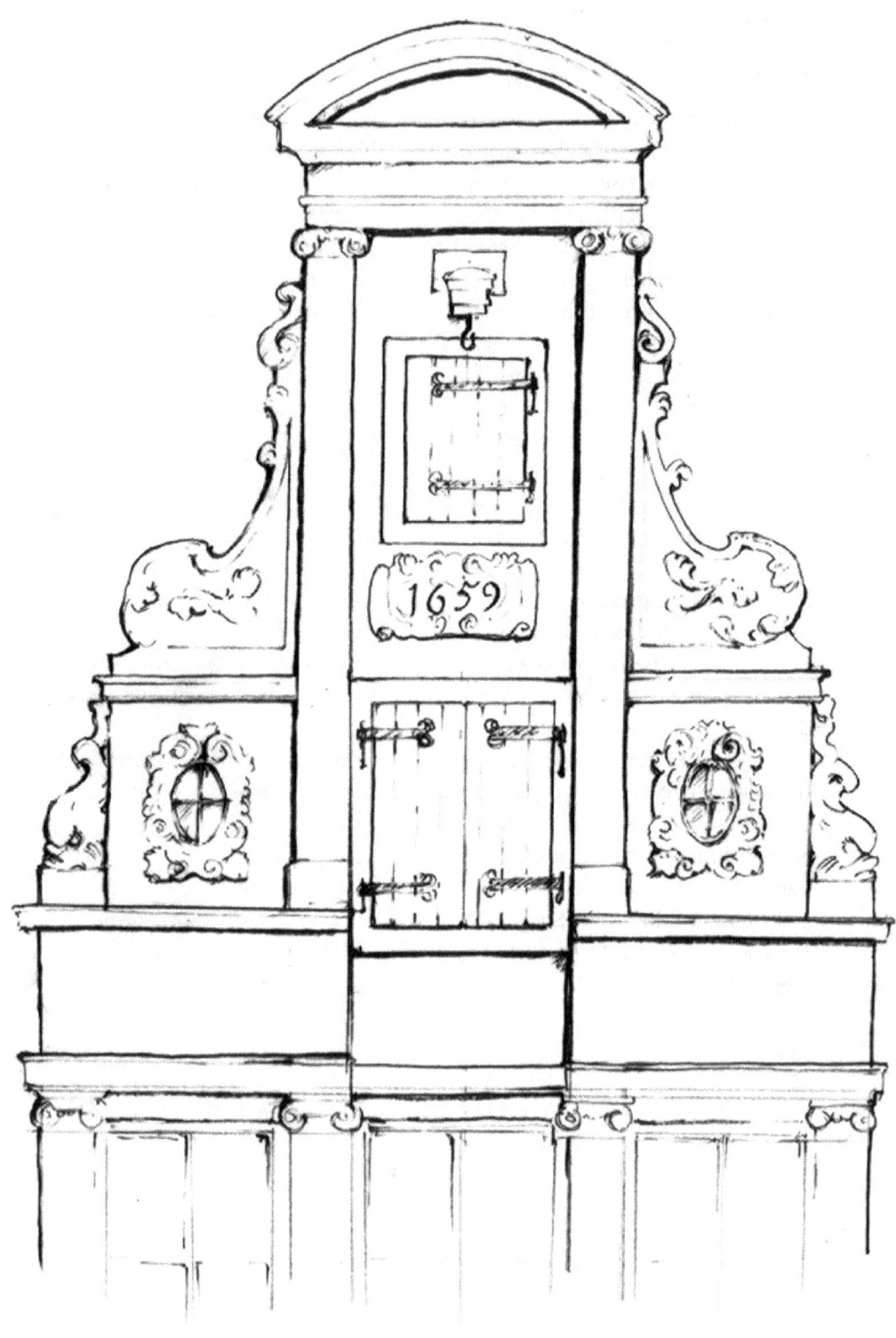

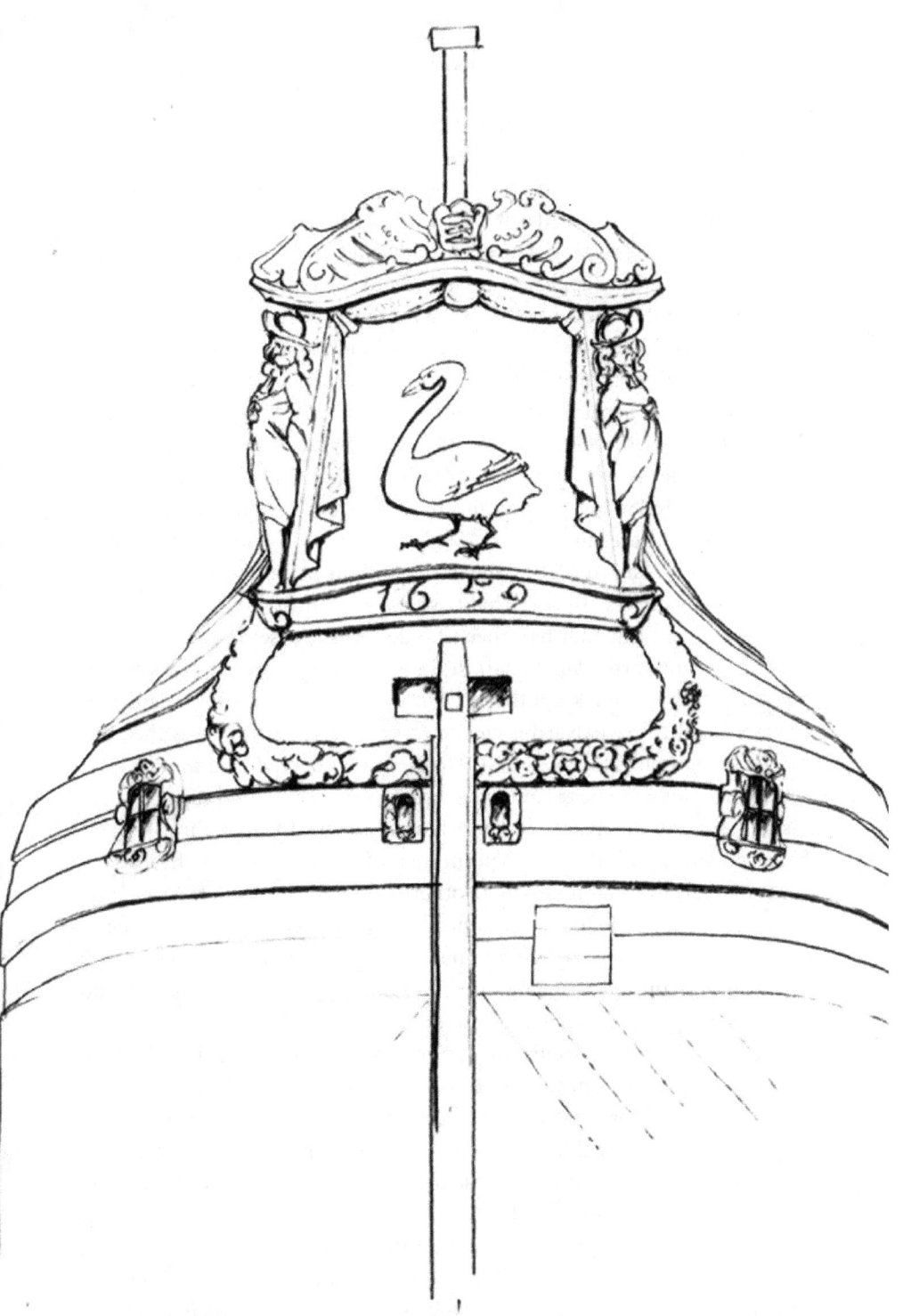

Figure 7.11: The facade of a halsgevelhuis beside the reconstructed stern of the 'Ghost Ship'. Note the corresponding silhouettes, and the location of the rounded windows. The year of construction on the stern is just hypothetical and used for illustration (Niklas Eriksson).

Knightheads

Sculptured Roman warriors are commonly found on board naval ships on the knightheads, timbers that stand on deck, with sheaves for the halyards and other running rigging. The decorations of the *fluit* also differ through having motifs, which appear to be specific to the type.

In the seventeenth century it was common for these timbers to have carved heads. When it comes to carved knightheads there are several detailed models that reveal the motifs on these (Franklin 1989, Laughton 2001), as well as archaeological finds. The Swedish warship *Solen*, sunk during battle in the Gdansk bay in 1627, reveals a knighthead with a military helmet (Cederlund 1983:24ff, Smolarek 1985:421–436, Wallace 2010). *Vasa* (1628) had seven sculptured knightheads on the main deck. At least two of these knights have 'Turks' heads', with turbans or so-called 'muffin hats' (Wallace 2010). One of the knights has a female head.

When it comes to merchant ships we must rely on the few archaeological finds that have been made. In this case there is the 'Lion Wreck', but in particular the Ghost Ship' has a prominent position as it has no less than four knightheads. On the 'Ghost Ship' the knighthead that served the fore halyard is carved out of the same timber as the pawl bit for the windlass (see Fig. 4.8). The figure is covered by a thin layer of sediments, but a full beard and what appears to be a knitted cap are is still visible. Abaft of the mainmast there is a group consisting of three knightheads standing with their faces pointing aft (Fig. 7.9). The knighthead for the main halyard is larger than the others, and depicts a man with a nearly overgrown beard. He has peculiar headwear, the origins of whichhave not been established. Two knights joined together with a cross piece stand before the main halyard knighthead. They both have full beards and knitted caps similar to the one from the fore-halyard.

Bearded faces are recurrent features on the 'Ghost Ship'. A small sculpture of a man's head, and whose original location and purpose is unknown, rests loose on the quarterdeck and the brackets that supported the catheads, used for lifting the anchors, are shaped like a bearded man with a flower on his chest. All these bearded men must mean something, but it is a bit uncertain just what.

The knight for the main halyard on the 'Lion Wreck' is similar to all those bearded men on board the 'Ghost Ship', and an almost identical knighthead is present on board the wreck of the *St Michael* (1747)

(Nurmio-Lahdenmäki & Hökkä 2006). It has been suggested that the knight from the 'Lion Wreck' wears a Roman helmet (Wallace 2010:106), but I find such an association quite vague.

That the king as well as the Swedish nobility were associated with the Romans in the seventeenth century is well known (for a discussion see Bedoire 2001), but it may be questioned whether the owners of the *fluits*, their crew and all those other people involved would have found reason to do so.

Quite certainly the persons depicted on knightheads were well-known characters within contemporary frames of reference and association. As stated in 'The Seaman's Dictionary' of 1644, the knight-heads 'are commonly carved with the picture of some head upon them, by which they are easily knowe' (cited in Wallace 2010: vii). However, through the mists of time we have lost the key for unlocking what associations these sculptures inspired. They appear alien for the moment, even if it seems quite likely that someone will come up with a well built, and well-argued interpretation in the future. What may be concluded, however, is that the carved heads on board *fluits* differed from the sculptures on board the men-of-war. The 'Lion Wreck' and the 'Ghost Ship' did not have the Turkish heads or Roman warriors that are so common on contemporary warships (compare Laughton 2001:249–251, Soop 1978:144f, Wallace 2010).

Apart from the name, the *hoekman*, the coat-of-arms of the home ports, the year of construction and the carved knightheads, *fluits* were decorated with ornamental flowers, leaves, buds, grapes and the like. It is a kind of cornucopia symbolism that recurs not least in the Dutch paintings of everyday life, moralizing motifs with references to the delicate balance between opulence and Reformed Christian morality.

Abraham Storck's (1644–1708) painting 'The whaling grounds' is an example of this fondness of everyday motifs accompanied by various symbolic connotations, not least the split relationship between economic growth and success (Fig. 7.10). In the water a whale is harpooned and two boats are approaching the animal. In the foreground a polar bear is shot by a musket while another is stabbed. Standing to one side, a person aims to hit the bear in the head with an oar. The whalers depicted on this painting are shown in the process of turning the bodies of the beasts that inhabit this hostile place into richness and wealth, and money. The fortune is brought back to the civilization with their prime tool, the *fluits*.

Storck has put much effort into making the ships appear as accurately as possible. The details on the hulls and the rigs are correct, as are the representations of the sculptural details. One of the ships is depicted from astern. We recognize the three flowers on top of the rudder, just like the ones on the 'Ghost Ship', as well as the two *hoekmen* flanking the transom. The custom of having the ship's name ichnographically reproduced in the stern is visible on this ship as well. Looking carefully on the ship to the right we find a whale and a male figure, either painted or sculpted onto the stern. It is quite likely that the motif shows Jonah and the whale, a very popular story during this period not only among whalers and seamen, but also within Dutch society as a whole (cf. Schama 1988:142ff).

Jonah, who had offended God through his greed, tried to escape by boat. A huge storm then arose and the crew began to throw their earthly belongings overboard. But still, the storm gets even worse. Through casting lots, it was concluded that it was Jonah who caused the storm. When they throw Jonah into the sea, he is swallowed by a whale and the storm calms down. Jonah spends three days and three nights inside the whale and then begs for mercy. The whale then swam to the shore and spat out the repentant Jonah.

Wealth thus poses a great danger as the temptations would never end. This is why Simon Schama characterizes the Dutch Golden Age, as a moral tightrope between abundance leading to ruin and Christian virtues – between God and Mammon (1988). The entire composition of Storck's painting, just as the story about Jonah, is that if God wants it, you may earn great prosperity, but if you go too far and you succumb to gluttony, you will be punished. A sinking *fluit* in the right edge of the canvas reminds us that success should not end up in gluttony. The modest burgher, who emerged, became an ideal (Weber 1978:77). Perhaps it is against such a background that we shall see the more or less mandatory sculpted *hoekman* merchants on the sterns of *fluits*?

Halsgevelhuis and fluits

Below the *fluit's* transom there is an opening for the tiller to enter the hull. There is often an ornament that surrounds and forms a garland around this opening. On the 'Ghost Ship' this ornament, formed with leaves, flowers and grapes, is preserved intact. The rudder head also reveals flowers, which are placed so that they form a trefoil, a very common ornament on Dutch rudder heads (compare Laughton 2001:157). The trefoil may be argued to represent the Trinity, which thus helps to steer the ship (for a discussion on sculptures on rudders, see Soop 1978:68f, 2007:89).

The flowers, and grapes and several other more or less abstract ornaments in the embellishment of *fluits* are recognizable on contemporary townhouses. As indicated above, the royal warships from the seventeenth century, with their abundance of sculptures, are sometimes described as floating castles (Soop 1978:55, 2007). The relationship between the nobleman's position within society and the size of the castle was both well-known and thoroughly discussed in the seventeenth century. In Sherring Rosenhane's (1609–63) manuscript *Oeconomia* the relationship between the nobleman himself and his castle is stressed, and he argues that one should not build over your rank, but he is also warning his reader to build below it (Bedoire 2001:133, Rosenhane 1944). The properties of the castle would spill over to its owner. A great castle would make a great man, and vice versa (Englund 1989:79).

The Swedish nobility were not alone in showing their power and influence through sculptures. One of the most important and effective stages for displaying personal wealthutilized by Dutch patricians were their houses. And, just like the *fluit*, these followed a set pattern. The Dutch townhouses lay at right angles, with the gable towards the street, or canal. Constraints in space in rapidly crowded cities like Lieden and Amsterdam were partly responsible for the convention that depth should be greater than breadth (Schama 1988:311).

The gable facades were ornamented with a heraldic blazon of the mercantile burgher, and whose owners commissioned all kinds of self-promoting devices to sprout from their roofs. Coat of arms, allusions of trade or even emblems from astrological bestiaries might appear, especially as the earlier *trapgevel* (step gable) became transformed into the more elaborate and profuse *halsgevel* ('neck' gable) of the mid-century (ibid.).

If warships can be regarded as floating palaces, the parallel to the *fluit* on dry land are the houses with the characteristic *halsgevel* facade that we meet in any Dutch town with continuity from the 1600s. The decorations on these facades follow patterns that are just as predictable as the sterns of *fluits*. The two categories of the material culture of the Golden Age reveal many similarities. Irrespective of size, the facades contain quite the same ingredients arranged and assorted in a very similar way, even if there are of course occasional exceptions.

Most of the sculptures are to be found in the uppermost part of the gable. As an extension of the ridge of the roof we find a crane girder, used for lifting goods into the building. Access to the loft is provided by a hatch located right underneath a crane girder. Today, these hatchways are fitted with windows, as the result of the loft being converted into apartments. The ornamentation on both sides of the hatch that leads into the loft may be shaped in a variety of forms and different sculptural themes. A common arrangement is to have pilasters run vertically on both sides of the hatch, forming a rectangular field. The space between the pilasters and the curved outer contour of the *halsgevel* is filled with various ornaments.

The storey underneath the loft usually has one larger, square opening in the middle, flanked by two small windows towards the sides. The height on this storey is reduced by the pitch of the roof hence the limited size of the flanking windows. These small windows are often elliptic or round surrounded by elaborate frames. Between the floors there is often a sign with the year the building was constructed.

In Figure 7.11 a *halsgevel* facade is placed beside a *fluit*'s stern. One may first of all note that the silhouette of the *fluit*, with its characteristic narrow transom and the wide, round stern below, is very reminiscent of the outline of the gable. The curved outline of the gable corresponds to the 'tumble home' of the *fluit*'s stern and quarters. The pilasters that flank the hatch leading to the loft on the facade define a rectangular shape that resembles the *fluit*'s transom. The small windows of the stern cabins of the *fluit*s have their perfect counterparts on the gable. The year of construction is placed on the same spot on both the *fluit* and the house.

But there are also many differences, and these are perhaps even more revealing than the similarities. What symbols are present on the house that are not present on the ship? On the ship, as described already, the home port is often shown through a city weapon, placed high up on the transom. For obvious reasons, there is no need to reveal such information to the people passing the house on the street. Instead we may sometimes find the owner's coat-of-arms on the facades, as is the case with the wealthiest patricians, like for instance those who built their homes at Herengracht, one of the fancier streets in Amsterdam, during the 1600s (cf. Schama 1988:311). A coat-of-arms referring to a specific family could prove problematic on a merchant ships as these ships were often joint property within a group of ship-owners. To own shares in several ships was a way to spread the risks (cf. Ahlström 1997:85–110).

The sculptures that reveal the ship's name are of course redundant on a house. Besides, where it should be located is the hatch into the loft. But one important ingredient of the *fluit*'s stern is missing on the house, namely the *hoekman*. It obviously cannot be excluded that somewhere there are houses with such sculptures. During the sixteenth century and earlier full-length figures are fairly common on timber-framed town houses (cf. Thomasson 1997:715f). But these sculptures usually depict biblical or Roman motifs, and thus do not relate to the owner in the same way as the *hoekman* on the *fluit* (see for instance Binding et al. 1984 for examples). Whereas these sculptures are more or less compulsory on *fluits*, this is definitively not the case on houses.

I think part of the explanation to why they do not appear on house facades may be that the urban context already reveals that the property belongs to a specific category of citizen. There is no reason to attach a sculpted fashionista to the façade when such individuals actually inhabited the house or might be found strolling in the street beneath it. The proud burghers who invested in urban houses and shares in *fluits* gained an increased social influence during the 1600s, especially in Sweden, as we shall return to below. Perhaps, anyone who met a *fluit* outside its urban context would have needed some help understanding the connections and networks the ship belonged in.

Fluits in Stockholm

In the previous chapters it has been argued that possibly the most important difference between ships and houses is the ability to move of the former. As pointed out by architectural historian Badeloch Noldus, with respect to Dutch influences on Swedish architecture and culture in the 1600s, classicism is always more or less regional. There is always an adaptation to current standards, materials, resources, climate and similar (Noldus 2005:5, 45). This includes the sculptural decoration which was adjusted to the ideological climate. As has been described by Frederic Bedoire, the sculptural decoration on buildings should be seen in the light of, but also as active components in, the propaganda for a republic which flourished among the nobility during the seventeenth century (Bedoire 2001).

Ships do not adapt to the local circumstances as they move and enter new harbours, towns and roadsteads. The semiotic message expressed through the sculptures is the same whether the ship is moored in Lisbon,

Amsterdam or Stockholm. Ships may in this way be regarded as uncensored architecture that do not adjust to the surrounding environment. The uniform exterior of the *fluits* may be likened to copies of books or leaflets that communicate their unedited messages worldwide. When Sweden began trading with the Dutch Republic, then suddenly dozens of Dutch buildings were moored along the quays of Stockholm.

Wolfgang Hartmann's engraving of Stockholm has been mentioned above (Fig. 7.1) and the phenomenon is visible on other **seventeenth**-century engravings of the city as well, like for instance Erik Dahlberg's well known *Suecia antiqua et hodierna* and other contemporary images. Rows of more or less identical *fluits*, each with a set of carved messages upon them, occupied central places in the capital cities at this time.

As described in chapter 5, moored merchant ships formed **continu**-ously changing city blocks (Gawronski 2009:17). The characteristic exterior of the *fluits*, with the pear-shaped stern, and the set of carved symbols upon them, revealed the presence of Dutch merchants in town. Essentially, the *fluits*, densely packed along Skeppsbron, like the *halsgevel* facades of a Dutch town, formed a floating wooden Amsterdam in the middle of Stockholm!

Swedish attitudes towards trade

Even if the Dutch Republic formed Sweden's prime trading partner in the seventeenth century (Barbour 1930, Fahlborg 1923, Müller 1998, Noldus 2002, 2005 van Zanden and van Tielhof 2009: 389–403) the attitudes to commerce and merchandise were essentially different in the two countries. This has been described by various scholars from different disciplines before, but I find it relevant to recapitulate some of the aspects in the different perspectives in order to understand *fluits* in context.

In the seventeenth century Sweden was a society that relied heavily on the estates as a kind of God-given order (see for instance Englund 1989 or Stadin 2009 for overview). Affiliation to a certain estate was due to descent, and thus was something you were born into. The ideology was conservative to the extreme, in order to maintain what was regarded as harmony and balance. Changes should be done slowly and preferably not at all. The society was often likened to analogies such as a body, or a ship at sea in order to underline that it was a system in which each element (position) had its proper function. As a consequence people who, out of self-interest, came to act outside their estates, their God-given role, were threatening the entire societal organism. No member would benefit from all members being equal.

In 1640, a delegation from the Dutch Republic came to meet the Swedish Council of State. The objective from the Dutch side was to try to convince the Swedes to loosen their restrictive regulations for trade. This meeting has become famous and is commonly used as an example to illustrate the differences between the two countries (Noldus 2005:7). The Swedish Chancellor Axel Oxenstierna explained to the Dutch that the Swedish society was built up out of well-defined estates, and that the nobility did not trade:

Our state is not like theirs (the Dutch) founded on commerce. Each estate here has their privileges. The nobility is separated from the burghers, and live out of their country estates. The priests achieve their allotted salary. The burghers trade and do this within certain defined harbours and locations (Axel Oxenstierna 1640, cited in Englund 1989:68, my translation).

As noted by historian Peter Englund, the statement contains a subtle antithesis that gives a rough but equally revealing picture of the ideal society, from the nobility's point of view. Sweden was a country built up of privileges, whereas the Dutch was built out of commerce. Behind these two systems, we can see a feudal system set against a capitalistic one. It is obvious that the contrasts between the two were already fully perceivable during the first half of the seventeenth century. The statement also reveals that there was a conflict between the two (Englund 1989:131ff).

Those within the Swedish bourgeoisie who conducted foreign trade accounted for a relatively small group, especially during the 1600s before half and this activity was consequently largely dominated by foreign players who were more skilful. Or, as historian György Nováky put it, there was a fundamental conflict between the 'dumb' domestic and knowledgeable foreign merchants (1993:215–232). The Florentinian diplomat, Lorenzo Magalotti, visited Sweden in 1674. His claims about trade are assumed to be heavily coloured by his English informants, but all the same he argues that the shrewd Dutchmen repeatedly took advantage of the Swedes' stupidity, as they did not understand what trade was (Magalotti 1912:44,117).

Such assertions must be understood against the background that the Dutch economic story of success aroused envy among other nations.

While the rest of Europe had to struggle with a crippling shortage of capital, the Republic was constantly flooded with new wealth. The detractors argued that the Dutch, by their cunning in business, only usurped what others had worked together to achieve with toil and sweat (Fahlborg 1923:208f). Hence a wide range of biases and hearsay circulated around the Dutch merchants. For example, Magalotti records that they bought rolls of English cloth, stretched it, and sold it for the same price per metre as it was purchased for (Magalotti 1912:56).

What is interesting here is that such attitudes spilled over onto the Dutch ships. It was customary for other seafaring nations, especially the English, to accuse the Dutch of cutting corners in their shipbuilding specifications through using green timber and the like (Schama 1988:31).

In fact, such attitudes also shine through in Åke Rålamb's book on shipbuilding, where he praises the English way of shipbuilding and criticizes that of the Dutch:

What these (English Master Shipbuilders) after a certain dimension and proportion perfected, this (Dutch Masters) did at approximate and about, which I found very unsatisfying' (*i dhet/ att hwad desse efter wist Mått och Storleek giorde/ det giordes af denna* (holländska mästare) *på höfft och ungefähr/ så att detta mig heelt och hållet intet behagade*) (Rålamb 1943, introduction).

Despite such disparaging statements, the Dutch influences on Swedish society came to be considerable. Around the mid seventeenth century an increased number of ennoblements took place, and the more recently ennobled were generally more compliant to mercantile matters, even highlighting the Dutch as exemplary. Axel Oxenstierna, however, still argued to maintain restrictions on such activities, and that the Dutch model was not applicable to Swedish conditions (Englund 1989:131ff).

During the seventeenth century the burghers gained an increased economic position in Swedish society. Their sons were sent to the universities and achieved an education that previously has been reserved for the nobility. Dutch universities were popular among Swedes (Noldus 2002:16), and an aspect of sending the youth to this country was the opportunity to learn something about the Dutch mercantile system (Englund1989:133). The increased number of ennoblements in the mid seventeenth century was partly the result of attitude changes. In the early seventeenth century ennoblement were inherited together with the position. There were two paths to choose, the pen or the sword (for instance Asker 1993).

From the mid-century it became the other way around, that is, ennoblement followed the position, which led to various controversies between the old and the new nobility (for an overview see Englund 1989).

Magalotti makes fun of the ennobled merchants when he comments that:

> If a merchant by chance manages to collect a fortune, he immediately becomes ennobled, and if it is possible for this recently ennobled person to continue trading, it can only be undertaken with difficulty. The reason is that the money that should be used in the business is instead used for the maintenance of the new status, for construction of buildings, purchase of property or all those other things required in order to appear as a nobleman (Magalotti 1912:46, my translation).

A large number of Dutch families settled in Sweden. The contacts with relatives on the continent were of prime importance when forming trading networks, not least as credit required reliable partners (see for instance Müller 1998). Strategic marriages were an important ingredient in the creation of networks for business (compare Stadin 2004:238ff). The Dutch influences in Swedish art, architecture, culture, trade and industry were considerable during the seventeenth century.

The influence is still visible today, inspiring expressions like 'Dutch Stockholm' (Van Ufford 1943: 261–272) which describe the still enduring palaces of families like Van Der Noot, Mooma-Renstierna, De Geer and the work of architects trained in the Netherlands (see for instance Noldus 2005).

The *fluit* was amongst the first Dutch buildings, the first *things* that arrived to Sweden. The ideas, goods, knowledge and other aspects that were imported from the republic to Swedish society, but most of these were brought to Sweden on board ships, with the *fluit* being the most common among these. But the *fluit* was not a mere container of goods. It was a billboard for a Dutch view of trade. Moored into capitals such as Stockholm the *fluits*, with their specific set of commercial symbols, promulgated a specific attitude towards commerce. Having another look at Hartmann's engraving (Fig.7.1), we see that in the very centre of

Stockholm there are quite a few *fluits* delivering this message. As mentioned above, the attitudes towards the Dutch commerce within the Swedish nobility was lukewarm to say the least. But the situation changed over the century, and trade became more and more accepted, even within the noble circles. Perhaps the ever-present *fluits* in the urban centres of Sweden worked as silent mediators in this process?

As discussed in chapter 5 the *fluit*, or any ship for that matter, was not solely constructed for being under sail. It was just as much meant for being moored, to be waiting in a harbour. It was during this state of waiting that the exteriors of *fluits* were perceived, not just by persons on board other ships, but also by anyone else who happened to pass by. In their moored state they become more or less a part of the city, and as these ships sailed between different markets that in reality were synonymous with different urban ports, *fluits* are urban ships, urbanism under sail.

8. Conclusions

Lorenzo Magalotti's account from his visit to Stockholm in 1674 has been referred to several times above. His report touches upon several maritime themes. Apart from mentioning famous warships, such as *Svärdet* and *Kronan*, he also provides a detailed description of Sweden's overseas trade. Time and again he returns to the dominance of the Dutch. The ships used in this trade, the *fluits*, are not even mentioned. This does not mean that he did not *see* them during his visit, but rather that he did not *register* seeing them (Eriksson 2014b). These ships had become a fixture: so numerous and self-evident so comprehensively integrated into everyday life in the Early Modern period that there was no reason to comment upon them. They may as well have been invisible.

This is tied to the idea that the most important objects are the ones we barely perceive. As discussed in chapter 3, these things warrant no attention as long as they are 'ready-to-hand' (cf. Olsen 2010:63–88, Trentmann 2009:289). Only as the unexpected happens, when these ordinary things for some reason go outside everyday routines and fail to be ready-to-hand, do they surface. For instance, this may occur with the introduction of an innovation, a new thing, which attracts special awareness when we are learning to deal with it. That the *fluit* initiated such a stir when the first example was built in the late 1500s can be regarded as one such case (see introduction of chapter 1). The raised eyebrows on the puzzled, curious people who visited the city of Hoorn to see the creation with their own eyes may be held as an indication that the ship's design was outside the ordinary. When *fluits* had become established ingredients in the early modern world, when thousands of nearly identical ships sailed the important trades routes, people barely registered them anymore. They fell into a ready-to-hand slumber and were blind to the ubiquitous *fluits*.

In a similar way once common objects achieve attention when for some reason they are no longer ready-to-hand. Perhaps they are lost or they break down. The two identified shipwrecks in the study are both examples where *fluits* have gone outside their 'ready-to-hand' mode. Written accounts exist concerning these ships because they were involved in unexpected and extraordinary events. The *Anna Maria* was icebound and sank due to a fire, while the armed *fluit Constantia* was sunk by its own crew during a fight against an unbeatable enemy. If these events had never taken place, the two ships would have sailed more or less unnoticed into oblivion. The traces left to posterity would have been no more than perhaps manning and crew lists, notes in the Toll registers that the ship has passed through the Sound or similar.

Quite paradoxically, the ships that have sunk through dramatic events are possibly the most important sources to reveal the mundane aspects of everyday life, now several hundred years later. From an archaeological point of view, things that are preserved in the soil or on the seabed are early modern 'ready-to-hand' things which still endure today.

As stressed, most notably in the first three chapters, this study has tried to take wrecks seriously. Not to limit wrecks to being illustrations of a narrative retold through history and written sources nor to dwell within 'text-free zones', but to highlight the lived experience of ships – as *things*! With the conviction that human life is always intimately entangled with things, I have tried to grasp what people did with *fluits* and what *fluits* made people do.

In their capacity as enduring physical everyday structures, the study of wrecks can provide renewed insights into the early modern Being-in-the-world, which perhaps can be regarded as the very opposite of drama. It is the ordinary elements of everyday life that are left when all the layers - big moments, unique events, disasters, persons, revolutions, breakthroughs and so forth – have been peeled off. Such an approach, however, presupposes that the remains are properly recorded. As mentioned above, specifically in chapter 2, this is seldom the case when dealing with historical shipwrecks, where the written sources tend to overshadow other sources, and the material remains may be dismissed, or regarded as auxiliary or even unnecessary (cf. Harpster 2013).

With this said I would like to summarize the results of this thesis by highlighting three outcomes which I find particulary important:

Firstly, it has been shown that an archaeology that considers shipwrecks as buildings actually works. Through highlighting the lived experience of space and the arrangement of the facilities used on an everyday basis, an understanding of a past society which is not directly accessible from other sources may be gleaned. But in order to really 'get at' such aspects it is crucial to engage with things in and of themselves. In this case, to record and reconstruct shipwrecks.

8. CONCLUSIONS

Studies of material culture from periods where both written and iconographical material are abundant, in addition to the more specific archaeological sources, offer the opportunity to move between the sources. The different categories are sometimes argued to complement each other, but perhaps most importantly they may reinforce some specific aspects. The supply of new information, for example through surveying a shipwreck, provides the means to change the focus within the already existing material. Light falls in a new way and previously neglected or trivialized elements become visible. Through recording, measuring, sketching, drawing plans of and writing about wrecks, the gaze will reach already available and existing sources and uncover previously unlit aspects.

Archaeological fieldwork on wrecks is a way of bringing forth forgotten 'ready-to-hand' things of the past. The sculptures, discussed in chapter 7, are a prime example of this. Sculptures on *fluits* are depicted in paintings, engravings and drawings. But even so, and the information is largely already available, the urban and mercantile connotations have not been considered in the analysis of embellishments on *fluits* (Peters 2013:69ff, also Eriksson 2014b).

A second result of this research has been to reveal the specific characteristics and idiosyncrasies of *fluits* in different ways. One such aspect is the arrangement of space; the wrecks clearly demonstrate that the facilities necessary for maintaining the daily routines of human life on board the Baltic merchant *fluits* are located under the quarterdeck. This may seem minor at first glimpse, but as the discussion established, the relocation had a crucial impact on all those small acts and routines that came together to form the everyday lived experiences a whole.

Of course this thesis does not provide a complete account of what the everyday life aboard *fluits* consisted of, such as how interpersonal relations were created, how the differences in rank, hierarchy and similar were maintained and so on. These less tangible aspects are not possible to grasp with any real confidence under the circumstances. But an engagement with the wrecks themselves does provide some insights into the material part of everyday life, which to paraphrase Fernand Braudel, sets 'The Limits of the Possible' (1981).

The analysis has been based either on non-intrusive surveys, or excavations carried out with limited contextual and stratigraphical recording. It is plausible that more detailed archaeological excavations can provide more information regarding social conditions on board *fluits*. But still I think such aspects are far from self-evident.

In any case, the present work has shown that some general statements can be made. Most importantly, that the arrangement differs from some previous attempts to reconstruct such interiors, with the crew under the forecastle deck, before the mainmast, and the Captain's quarter in the stern (chapters 4 and 5). The discrepancy between previous statements and the situation as revealed through the study of wrecks, is important for two reasons. First, wrecks reveal that the private sphere occupied by the person in command was not distant from the rest of the crew. Order was maintained through means *other* than spatial distancing. This means that the social order on board the merchant *fluits* was of a different character, one that was created without the powerful and tricks known to have been widely implemented and mediated through the architecture of ships elsewhere; like, for instance, maintaining a distance, separate movement patterns, stringent differences in living conditions and everyday routines and similar.

The second reason the discrepancy between the spatial situation (as revealed from wrecks) and the well-established assumption (where the crew was lodged before the mainmast) is important to note is that it underlines the impact of popular beliefs regarding shipboard life. Some argue that a sailor's identity, to have served on board a sailing ship, is something that penetrates deeper into the soul than any other profession, such as the industry or railroad (Aubert & Arner 1959: 213, Genrup 1990). Regardless of the substance of such claims it is obvious that there is a deeply-rooted romantic image surrounding the life of a sailor. Consider the plethora of artistic and literary depictions of life at sea made with such overtones, from Patrick O'Brien to Eric Newby.

There is also the tendency discussed in chapter 5, which archaeologist Joe Flatman has dubbed 'Hornblower syndrome', that is, that archaeologists and historians assume that there is always the worst kind of hierarchy and abuse of power on board ships. Flatman points out that it is just the worst examples that are remembered and that life on board the ship was not always as hard as many fictional accounts contend. Again, it is usually the worst examples, stories that go outside the ordinary, that are remembered (cf. Flatman 2003:148).

Certainly there is a considerable difference between being one among several hundred others on board a naval vessel during wartime and being with six to ten other persons on board a *fluit* on the Baltic, with the task of shipping grain, iron or tar.

Another pecularity of the *fluit*, which I think has been demonstrated through this study, is what *fluits* added to the surrounding environment. The unusual shape of the hull has been recognized since the first *fluits* were built at the end of the sixteenth century, but here the set of sculptures, so characteristic for *fluits*, have also been possible to examine in more detail. Again, wrecks are seen to contribute to our understanding regarding aspects of ordinary everyday life, as these sculptures, communicating messages of mercantile ideology, described in chapter 7, were indeed ever-present in the early modern public space.

A third aspect to stress is the relation between ships and the rest of the world. Many researchers studying ships, irrespective of disciplinary background, have a tendency to focus on pinpointing that which is particular to ships. The more interesting question is: to what extent should ships be isolated as something peculiar and to be contrasted with life in a more general sense? The fact that ships contain everything needed to sustain life (at least for a limited period) makes them excellent metaphors and thought experiments concerning a separate world inside the hull-planking.

Le Corbusier thought of the Atlantic steamer as a model for society in a more general sense (Peter & Dawson 2009:145ff, Råberg 1998:142–153), as mentioned in chapter 3. Thoughts revolving around the relationship between ships and the rest of the world have a much longer tradition than that. Think of Noah's Ark, or Plato's 'ship of state' in book VI of the *Republic*. Plato likened the governance of a city-state to the command of a naval-vessel. A thousand years later Swedish Chancellor Axel Oxenstierna (1583–1654) described his view of the ideal state organized like a ship, steered with the firm hand of the king at the top, nobles beneath and the people at the bottom (Adams 2003:33 2013a:28ff, Englund 1989:28, 46, Rönnby and Adams 1994:68).

In a similar way, archaeologists have described the ship variously as a 'society in miniature' (Einarsson 1997:210, Soop 2001:14ff), a 'micro society' (Pomey 2011:30) or a 'microcosm' (Einarsson 1997:210, also Muckelroy 1978:99). Such wordings attempt to describe a ship's, and most notably a warship's, ability to contain individuals from the entire social gamut, and thus such a range is reflected in the material remains. The study of one particular wreck could with such a logic be argued to unveil a mirrored version of society at large. However, as noted by Rönnby and Adams, women are undoubtedly underrepresented (1994:67).

No doubt, ships may be used as metaphors in rhetorical arguments for miniature versions of a much larger world outside the hull-planking. This does not mean that they *are* miniature societies, though! It is perhaps stating the obvious, but rather than being reflections, representations or miniature versions of society, they are simply parts of it. As noted by Jonathan Adams, the roles and values performed by the people on board were:

> ...related in various ways to the organization and activities of wider society. Not as passive reflections which one can 'read off' what wider society must have been like, but as translations of social attitudes to a shipboard situation in pursuit of those aims and needs that underpinned the construction of the vessel in the first place (Adams 2003:33).

This is why some archaeologists prefer to be a bit more nuanced and refer to ships as 'closed communities' (Adams 2003:31, Muckelroy 1978:221ff) to emphasize that ships are isolated from life ashore.

Important to note, I believe, is that the idea of a sailor's culture, or a ship resembling society in miniature, has resulted in a tendency to focus on the peculiarities of ships, isolating some kind of 'maritime essence', like in maritime archaeology, maritime ethnology, maritime cultural landscapes and so on. There may of course be multiple reasons to label different things, persons, activities or academic sub-disciplines 'maritime', but a point this investigation has made, and which I hope the reader has noted, is that ships can hold other qualities as well, besides just that; they are a vital part of the rest of the world.

I, too, am responsible for emphasizing maritime aspects of *fluits*. The research background in chapter 2 firmly establishes the study in the maritime research field. Perhaps it would be more innovative to downplay the maritime and emphasize other more general aspects of ships? *Fluits* were an essential part of early modern *maritime* life; but, as Hartmann's engraving of Stockholm (Fig. 7.1) reveals, they were at the same time an important component of *urban* life.

The fact that key elements of early modern urban environments are now present in the middle of the Baltic Sea requires some antiquarian-topographical reconsideration of what an archaeological context is. As

8. CONCLUSIONS

shown in chapter 7 the study of wrecked *fluits* provides insights into sculptural decorations which were part of public space in many early modern cities.

That the long rows of moored *fluits* formed a kind of billboard for Dutch attitudes regarding commerce has not made its mark in written sources. Depictions from the period do not reveal the content of the sculptural message, nor do often cited travels accounts from visiting foreigners (Magalotti 1912, Ogier 1914, Oscarsson 2013). The study of wrecks has thus revealed some long fortgotten aspects of everyday life which have otherwise simply been ignored or taken for granted.

Contemporary observations that have become central to the way seventeenth-century Sweden is presented today, such as Axel Oxenstierna's statement on how Sweden is based on the idea of Estate society, unlike that of the Dutch, which is based on commerce, can now be read with a nuanced understanding when the image is complemented by the idea of the *fluits* as a form of ideological placard. When these statements were made, rows of *fluits* were already moored along the ship's bridge in Stockholm. The wrecked *fluits*, resting on the seabed in the Baltic and elsewhere, are dispersed fragments of long lost early modern cities.

Sammanfattning (Swedish Summary)

Kapitel 1, Introduktion

I slutet av 1500-talet utvecklades i Nederländerna en typ av fartyg som kallades flöjt. De blev mycket uppskattade då de var enkla och billiga att bygga och kunde seglas med små besättningar, ofta färre än tio personer. Fram till omkring mitten av 1700-talet var de lastdryga flöjterna de vanligaste handelsfartygen i norra Europa och Östersjön.

Flöjterna var mycket standardiserade och det var främst storleken som varierade. De minsta var runt 20 och de största över 40 meter mellan för- och akterstäv. De användes till allt från ostindiefart till valfångst och som örlogsfartyg.

Under 1600-talet var Nederländerna Sveriges viktigaste handelspartner. Trä- och metallråvaror skeppades ut från Östersjöområdet medan förädlade produkter och salt importerades. Dessa transporter genomfördes i stor utsträckning med just flöjtskepp, som då i allmänhet var helt obestyckade.

Trots att tusentals mer eller mindre identiska flöjter byggts finns förvånansvärt få detaljerade beskrivningar av hur de egentligen såg ut. De tycks ha varit så vanliga att de nästan blev osynliga.

Under de senaste 50 åren har flera vrak efter flöjter påträffats på Östersjöns botten. Nere i det kalla bräckta bevaras trä förvånansvärt väl, tack vare avsaknad av skeppsmask. Det är sådana välbevarade vrak efter flöjter som är utgångspunkten för denna studie.

Vraken utgör kvardröjande beståndsdelar av dagligt liv för flera hundra år sedan. Det är detta vardagsliv som studien diskuterar. Det är inte de stora händelserna, de dramatiska förlisningarna, den ekonomiska utvecklingen eller sjöfartens konjunkturer som är i fokus i denna studie.

Med inspiration från framförallt fenomenologi syftar avhandlingen till att beskriva hur olika miljöer påverkar och strukturerar människors agerande i eller i aslutning till flöjter. Sådana fenomenologiskt inspirerade analyser har tidigare förekommit inom bland annat landskaps- och byggnadsarkeologin, men när det gäller skeppsvrak är det en tämligen oprövad ingång. Utöver nya inblickar i vardagsliv kring flöjtskeppen syftar avhandlingen också till att bidra med ett delvis nytt sätt att studera skepp och vrak.

Kapitel 2, Historisk arkeologi kring Östersjön

Under 1800-talet och långt in på 1900-talet genomförde olika dykerifirmor bärgningsarbeten på sjunkna örlogsfartyg från stormaktstiden. Det var vrak vars historia redan var känd från tradition och historiska dokument. Kanoner, riggdetaljer, keramik, skeppstimmer av svartnad ek och annat lyftes ur djupet och såldes; antingen till privatpersoner eller till vad som senare kom att utvecklas till museisamlingar. Arbetet understöddes i de flesta fall av intresserade personer inom marinen. En del av dessa fynd användes i utställningar och som illustrationer i olika publikationer.

När sportdykning med lätt dykutrustning blev populärt under 1960-talet påträffades flera tidigare okända vrak efter handelsfartyg. Successivt växte också den antikvariska medvetenheten och 1967 kom de gamla trävraken att skyddas av kulturminneslagen, vilket kan ses som ett incitament för såväl den antikvariska som den akademiska marinarkeologin i Sverige. En liknande utveckling ägde samtidigt rum i många andra länder runt Östersjön.

De stora vraken efter handelsfartyg från historisk tid kom nu att bli föremål för flera arkeologiska pionjärundersökningar. Arbetet genomfördes ofta med den uttalade ambitionen att samla in information som kunde härleda skeppets ursprungliga identitet i historiska källor.

Forskningen kring handelsfartygen motiverades delvis som ett sätt att utmana och nyansera de stora historieberättelserna om kungar och krig, vilket de tidiga bärgningsaktiviteterna kan anses vara uttryck för. Genom att föra fram bortglömda vrak och fartygsöden kom berättelser ur handelsjöfartens historia i dagen.

Även om man kan urskilja en viss polarisering mellan de som intresserade sig för den traditionella historieskrivningen och de som belyste "vanligt" folk och handelsfartyg, så hanterade båda lägren skriftligt, historisk källmaterial och arkeologiska fynd på ett delvis likartat sätt. De skriftliga källorna användes för att förklara de till synes stumma skeppsvraken på havets botten. Den arkeologiska dokumentationen och analysen av de stora sammanhängande skroven, var tämligen sparsam och spelade en ganska underordnad roll. Forskningen kring vraken i

SAMMANFATTNING (SWEDISH SUMMARY)

Östersjön har i stor utsträckning haft en historisk prägel, genom att skriftliga källor förklarat och gett mening till de till synes stumma materiella lämningarna.

Inom den internationella skeppsarkeologin är det emellertid i högre grad tekniska frågeställningar som varit i fokus. Spörsmålen har ofta kretsat kring de metoder och tekniker som använts när fartyget byggts, liksom manöveregenskaperna hos det färdiga skeppet. De tidigmoderna vraken i östersjöområdet förekommer sparsamt inom denna forskning, även om viktiga undantag finns. En bidragande orsak till detta är att mer nedbrutna vrak, som påträffats på land eller som noggrant grävts ut under vatten och bärgats, ofta lämpar sig väl för tekniska analyser. Sammanhängande skeppsvrak som undersökts under vatten, erbjuder däremot sällan möjligheter att samla in den information som behövs för diskussioner kring byggnadsteknik, skrovform eller segelegenskaper.

Oidentifierade men välbevarade vrak placerar sig därmed i ett glapp mellan olika forskningstraditioner. De är för intakta för att användas i den tekniskt inriktade skeppsarkeologin och de är för ord- och textlösa för att användas i den historiskt inriktade forskningen, där fokus ligger på identifiering. Den här studien tar sin utgångspunkt i att de erbjuder möjligheten att studera något annat, nämligen den fysiska inramningen för alla de till synes obetydliga aktiviteter och rutiner som format livet ombord.

Kapitel 3, Från vrak till vardagsliv

Att förstå människor genom att studera ting kan sägas utgöra själva kärnan av arkeologiskt resonerande. Många olika strategier har prövats för att ta sig an detta problem. Ting har en förmåga att rikta och dirigera livet och förmå människor att agera på olika sätt. De förmedlar till synes banala budskap som "sitt här", "gå igenom här", "stanna här", "ät här" och så vidare. Sammantaget bildar de ett slags materiellt ramverk för livet i stort. Men merparten av tillvarons alla ting är så vardagliga att vi knappt förnimmer dem. De är mest uppenbara och samtidigt bäst gömda. När allt fungerar som det ska, när skeppet inte förliser, när besättningen anländer på avtalad tid med livet i behåll, med sin vanliga last ombord på ett vanligt flöjtskepp, finns ingenting att kommentera. Dessa resor har satt sparsamma avtryck.

Välbevarade skeppsvrak kan rekonstrueras till mer eller mindre hela skepp och kompletta miljöer. Detta förutsätter dock att det finns någon slags arkeologisk dokumentation att utgå ifrån. Arkeologiskt arbete till havs och i synnerhet under vatten, innebär alltid att tiden är begränsad. Att arbeta med till stor del intakta skeppsvrak som reser sig flera meter ovan sjöbottnen har däremot den fördelen att de kan dokumenteras utan åverkan. Utgrävning, bärgning och andra förstörande ingrepp kan i stor utsträckning undvikas.

I den här studien har många aspekter av skeppsvraken utelämnats av prioriteringsskäl (Det ska dock understrykas att eftersom ingen åverkan gjorts på lämningarna är det fullt möjligt att inhämta eventuell saknad information). Den dokumentation som utförts har fokuserat på de detaljer som ansetts viktiga för att beskriva skeppet som vardagsmiljö, till exempel skrovets form, däcksnivåer, storlek och läge för luckor, härdar, fönster och andra detaljer som format inramning och riktning åt det mänskliga livet i och omkring dessa skepp. Den insamlade informationen har bearbetats till tvådimensionella ritningar i plan och genomskärning, vilka bildar stöd för analysen genom att redovisa vilka rum som funnits och var olika vardagliga göromål genomförts.

Kapitel 4, Vardagliga flöjter

Det finns flera exempel från facklitteraturen kring flöjter där detmer eller mindre i förbigående redovisas uppfattningar om hur rummet organiserats ombord på dessa skepp. Enligt dessa är de ombordvarande separerade, med befälhavare i aktern och manskap i skeppets för. Detta trots att flera bevarade ritningar av *Katschips* och andra skeppstyper som är snarlika flöjten redovisar ett annat rumsligt arrangemang.

Fyra vrak efter flöjtskepp redovisas i detalj avseende rumsindelning och användning. Det så kallade "Jutholmsvraket" påträffades redan på 1960-talet. Större delen av skrovet grävdes ut i metodutvecklingssyfte under 1970-talet och ett stort antal fynd bärgades. Ambitiösa försök att identifiera skeppet i skriftliga källor har gjorts, men utan framgång. När vraket undersöktes på nytt år 2008 insamlades information för rekonstruktion av skeppets rumsliga arrangemang. Intressant nog kontrasterar denna rekonstruktion med hur skeppets interiör beskrivits tidigare. Den statusskillnad mellan hög och låg som omtalas i vissa tidigare publikationer om vraket kan i stor utsträckning avfärdas. Sammantaget visar analysen av skrov, tillsammans med det fyndmaterial som tillvaratogs vid den tidigare undersökningen, att de ombordvarande var inhysta tillsammans i skeppets akter.

SAMMANFATTNING (SWEDISH SUMMARY)

Det andra vraket är det stora flöjtskeppet *Anna Maria* som fastfrusen i isen fattade eld och sjönk i Dalarö hamn i februari 1709. Under 1980- och 90-talen genomfördes arkeologiska punktinsatser, som bland annat ledde till att skeppets ursprungliga identitet kunde fastställas. Sedan detta genombrott har vraket främst beskrivits utifrån historiska källor. Under 2010 gjordes en uppmätning av det sammanhängande skrovet. Tillsammans med bland annat rättegångsprotokoll har stora delar också av *Anna Marias* rumsindelning och rummensanvändande kunnat fastställas. Även i detta fall kontrasterar resultatet mot hur *Anna Maria* rekonstruerats tidigare, då man också här har menat att manskapet varit inhyst i förkastellet och befäl i aktern. Vare sig vraket eller de tillgängliga skriftliga källorna stödjer ett sådant påstående.

Det så kallade "Spökskeppet" påträffades på nära 130 meters djup ost om Gotska sandön år 2003. Även om skeppet är i det närmaste komplett medför det stora djupet att tillgängligheten är begränsad. Med hjälp av tekniska lösningar som bland annat omfattar fjärrstyrda undervattensrobotar har det ändå varit möjligt att dokumentera vraket i något sånär detalj. Förutom att en rumsindelning som motsvarar de ovan nämnda skeppen, så erbjuder "Spökskeppet" en inblick i hur ett sådant fartyg var invändigt organiserat och

möblerat, med en välbevarad spis, sittbänkar och bord inne i den gemensamma kajutan i skeppets akter. Vraket har också flera välbevarade skulpturer (se nedan).

Det sista mer i detalj redovisade vraket är det så kallade "Lejonvraket" som påträffades så sent som 2009 i skärgården norr om Stockholm. Skeppet har endast översiktligt dokumenterats, men ger trots allt en god inblick i hur det fungerat som bostad åt de ombordvarande och hur en liten flöjt varit dekorerad.

Allt sammantaget ger de undersökta vraken en samstämmig bild av hur dessa flöjter varit invändigt organiserade. Uppgifter om detta har tidigare saknats. Vraken visar att samtliga ombordvarande var inhysta i skeppets akter och den var här som den enda kabyssen fanns. Det var här de åt och det var i detta utrymme som den enda toaletten ombord var placerad. Flera mer nedbrutna och endast översiktligt besiktigade vrak av flöjtskepp förstärker denna bild.

Kapitel 5, Ombord på flöjter.

Konsekvenserna av denna rumsliga ommöblering blir tydlig när man rekonstruerar de ombordvarandes vardagliga rutiner. En fenomenologisk rumsanalys tar sin utgångspunkt i den mänskliga erfarenheten och mer eller mindre medvetna upplevelsen av rummet, genom sinnliga intryck och genom handling. Rumsuppfattningen påverkas bland annat av möjligheten att röra sig. Som undersökningen visat var de ombordvarande på flöjterna inhysta under halvdäcket i aktern. Om detta utrymme var uppdelat i mindre hytter är okänt. Oavsett vilket så visar vraken med önskvärd tydlighet ändå att merparten av vardagens aktiviteter genomfördes i gemensamma utrymmen.

Relationer och hierarkier formas och omförhandlas utifrån vardagliga praktiker. Dessa i sin tur dirigeras och påverkas av tingen och rummet. Vraken ger ingående upplysningar om hur det fysiska ramverket för olika aktiviteter organiserats. Till återkommande rutiner hör sådant som rör mat och ätande. Måltiden är något om aktivt formerar en grupp genom att inkludera eller exkludera. Som framkommit av undersökningen är kabyssen vanligtvis placerad i det förligaste rummet under halvdäcket, medan maten intogs i det aktre rummet som kallas kajutan. Detta indikeras bland annat av möblemanget funnet ombord på det så kallade "Spökskeppet" och skedarna funna på "Jutholmsvraket".

Till de inrättningar som används på daglig basis hör även toaletten. Flera av flöjterna har denna placerad längst akterut åt babord inne i kajutan. Denna enda toalett har varit ämnad för samtliga ombordvarande. Situationen skiljer sig från arrangemanget på örlogsfartyg. Där finns i allmänhet fler avträden, givet det större antalet människor ombord. Men där finns dock också en uppdelning mellan inrättningarna ämnade för befäl och manskap, vilket alltså saknas ombord på de handelsflöjter som undersökts inom ramen för denna studie.

Allt sammantaget visar det rumsliga arrangemanget ombord på flöjterna att de vardagliga aktiviteterna i stor utsträckning ägde rum i utrymmen som delades av samtliga ombordvarande. Skriftliga källor i form av lönelistor visar att ersättningen varierar kraftigt med befattning. Här erbjuder således de materiella lämningarna en delvis kontrasterande bild. Därmed inte sagt att tillvaron ombord på ett flöjtskepp karaktäriserades av en egalitär struktur och avsaknad av hierarki. Att detta inte satt avtryck i det rumsliga arrangemanget kan ha olika orsaker. Att skott, mellanväggar, personliga tillhörigheter inte bevarats eller observerats kan

SAMMANFATTNING (SWEDISH SUMMARY)

givetvis skeva bilden. Samtidigt finns det många andra sätt att upprätthålla status än genom fysiskt avstånd. Genom civilstånd, tilltal, vem som anförtros läsa bordsbön och liknande rutiner kan liknande förhållanden upprätthållas, men detta är givetvis svårt att bekräfta utifrån studier av vrak.

Kanske ska det gemensamma utrymmet ombord förstås mot bakgrund av att skeppare mönstrade sin besättning från deras omedelbara geografiska och sociala närhet. Men även om så inte alltid var fallet menar många forskare att den nederländska kulturen under det som kommit att betecknas som "guldåldern" (*Gouden Eeuw*) inte karaktäriserades av skarpa gränser mellan hög och låg. På liknande sätt inkluderades tjänstefolk på familjeporträtt vid tiden, där de bar kläder motsvarande herrskapet. Vissa menar att detta bottnar i en kalvinistisk mentalitet, där människans öde är predestinerat. Är du utvald finns ingen anledning att förhäva sig. Tvärtom är allt som kan betecknas som överflöd och frosseri en säker väg till fördärvet.

Den kanske största skillnaden mellan skepp och de flesta andra byggnader är att skepp är mobila. De rör sig i det geografiska rummet och måste fungera i olika situationer och miljöer, där de kanske mest uppenbara är *till sjöss* eller *i hamn*. För att tydliggöra skillnaderna mellan ett skepp som är till sjöss och ett förtöjt vid en hamn kan de beskrivas i termer av aktör-nätverk. Ett fullt fungerande skepp består av skrov, rigg, segel, proviant, besättning och mycket annat. Allt som ingår i detta aktörnätverk måste hålla samman till en fungerande enhet för att inte skeppet ska förlisa, besättningen svälta ihjäl, myteri ska bryta ut eller liknande. När skeppet anländer till hamn löses nätverket delvis upp och omformas för att även inkludera aktörer i land. Det är fortfarande samma skepp men får en delvis ny funktion. Skeppet utgör en bostad som ändrar karaktär utifrån det sammanhang det uppträder i.

Skepp kunde bli liggande i hamn under ganska långa perioder. De som anlände till Stockholm under november månad kunde inte räkna med att kunna segla därifrån förrän kommande maj på grund av is. Under sådana perioder fungerade flöjten ungefär som ett boningshus och utrymmet under halvdäck som en slags lägenhet för besättningen. Flöjtskeppets avlånga rektangulära skrov, med de två ljusinsläppen i aktern (på gaveln), var förtöjdes sida vid sida med andra flöjter. Tillsammans bildade dessa hamnkvarter där byggnaderna, det vill säga skeppen, hela tiden byttes ut.

Rättegångsprotokollen från det fastfrusna skeppet *Anna Marias* förlisning ger mot en sådan bakgrund en intressant inblick i hur besättningarna socialiserade i dessa miljöer.

Med detta sagt finns anledning att återerinra tidigare rekonstruktioner av flöjtskeppsinteriörer som gör rumslig skillnad mellan befäl i skeppets akter och manskap i skeppets för. Ett sådant rumsligt arrangemang rimmar illa med vad som ovan anförts och är i grund och botten inget annat än en ganska dåligt underbyggd hypotes. En sådan rumsindelning hör hemma på örlogsfartyg.

Kapitel 6, Flöjtskepp i strid

Det som är karaktäristiskt med handelsflöjternas rumsliga arrangemang framträder än tydligare när man kontrasterar dem mot örlogsfartyg. Från mitten av 1600-talet erhöll kraftigt byggda handelsfartyg som kunde bestyckas med minst 14 kanoner skattelättnader mot att de fick användas av flottan i händelse av krig. Bland dessa skepp återfinns flera flöjter. Att förändra ett handelsfartyg till krigsfartyg handlar inte endast om att lägga till kanoner, officerare, båtsmän och knektar. Allt detta måste också arrangeras, inte minst rumsligt, för att samspela och fungera som en sådan enhet som kan kallas krigsfartyg.

Den av svenska flottan inhyrda och bestyckade flöjten *Constantia*, sattes i brand av sin egen besättning för att inte falla i fiendehänder i april 1676. Även om såväl eld som våg- och isrörelser som svarteksbärgning gått hårt åt vraket så är det tydligt att skeppets rumsliga arrangemang skiljer sig från de mer renodlade handelsflöjter som diskuterats ovan. Den i sammanhanget mest iögonfallande olikheten är kabyssen. På örlogsflöjterna återfinns den stora tegelkabyssen som i skeppets mitt, medan andra flöjter har en mindre kabyss placerad högre upp och längre akterut. Placeringen och inte minst dimensioneringen av kabyssen ombord på *Constantia* motsvaras av andra samtida örlogsfartyg i den svenska flottan och skall således förstås mot det för ändamålet anpassade tillstånd skeppet befanns i då det sjönk.

Även om endast de nedre delarna av *Constantias* skrov bevarats kan den rumsliga organisationen ombord på en kraftigt bestyckad flöjt rekonstrueras med stöd av bilder, litteratur och samt bevarade ritningar. Medan de för handel ämnade flöjterna inte visar på någon egentlig rumslig uppdelning mellan olika kategorier eller grupper av människor

SAMMANFATTNING (SWEDISH SUMMARY)

ombord är situationen den motsatta när det gäller dessa för krig konverterade flöjter. Ombord på *Constantia* fanns hela 137 personer, vilket kan jämföras med den betydligt större *Anna Maria*, som när hon seglade i handelsjöfart hade 22 personer ombord – vilket i sig är ovanligt många för en flöjt.

I konverteringen av flöjtskepp från handel till örlog ingick således också att rumsligt inrätta skeppet med särskilda områden för officerare och gemena, med separerade, parallellt existerande rörelserum för vardagliga praktiker. Officerare förblev officerare genom att vara inhysta i de högre belägna delarna i skeppets akter och genom att äta officersmat bland andra officerare. Båtsmän och soldater förmåddes uppträda som sådana genom att vistas i det för dem avdelade området i skeppets förliga del. Upplevelsen av underordning förstärktes, genom en arkitektur som invaggade manskapet i tron att de var konstant iakttagna. Skillnaden mellan handels- och örlogsflöjter låg i det aktiva samspelet mellan människor, skepp, kanoner, rum, mat, toaletter, rigg, ankare och kojplatser.

Kapitel 7, Flöjtskeppets exteriör

På samma sätt som flöjterna påverkat de ombordvarandes vardagliga praktiker hade de påverkan på de miljöer de uppträdde i. I likhet med andra tidigmoderna skepp och byggnader var flöjterna dekorerade med skulpturer. Även här var utformningen förvånansvärt uniform, för att inte säga förutsägbar. Skeppens namn uttrycktes vanligtvis genom en symbolframställning på den smala akterspegeln. Skeppen bar ofta namn som *Vintunnan*, *Bruna hästen*, *Vita svan*, *Pärlan* och liknande benämningar som kan uttryckas genom symboler. Utöver dessa förekom ofta bekanta episoder ur bibeln, såsom *Jonah och valfiken* eller *Abrahams offer*, som skeppsnamn. Ovanför namnskulpturen återfinns vanligtvis ett vapen som avslöjade skeppets hemmahamn. Akterspegeln flankerades av två skulpterade män, antingen i helfigur eller som hermpilastrrar. Från bevarade bilder och även enstaka arkeologiska fynd är det tydligt att dessa ofta avbildar män klädda i ganska typiska 1600-talskläder, motsvarande dem som vid den aktuella tiden bars av stadsbor i såväl Sverige som Nederländerna.

Vid jämförelse med samtida örlogsfartyg framstår flera tydliga skillnader i motivval. Allegoriska framställningar av kungamakten, liksom romerska krigare och götiska sagokungar, som återfinns i till exempel *Vasas* (1628) exteriör, lyser helt med sin frånvaro på flöjterna. Dessa pryds i stället av blomster- och ymnighetsmotiv i kombination med de urbana modelejon som till det yttre liknar den grupp som ägde och handlade med skeppen. Medan örlogsfartygen, med deras överdådigt utsmyckade akterspeglar ganska välfunnet har beskrivits i termer av flytande palats, kan flöjten snarast ses som en pendang till den urbana bebyggelsen; ett flytande köpmanshus. Rakt akterifrån har flöjtskrovets yttre kontur stora likheter med de halsgavelfasader som återfinns i Amsterdam, Lieden, Enkhuisen och andra Nederländska städer med tidigmoderna anor.

Även om de Nederländska influenserna på det svenska samhället verkade såväl ideologiskt, estetiskt, kommersiellt och på andra sätt så har alltid en anpassning till det rådande förhållandena inom landet ägt rum. Arkitekturstilar blir alltid mer eller mindre regionalt anpassade. Halsgavlarna slog till exempel aldrig igenom i Sverige. Som framförs på flera ställen i avhandlingen är den kanske största skillnaden mellan skepp och hus att de förra rör på sig. Helt krasst innebär detta att någon regional anpassning i ett skepps arkitektur knappast kan ske när det anträder främmande hamnar. När flöjtskeppen ankrade upp i en lång rad utmed skeppsbron i Stockholm utgjorde de ett stycke nederländsk arkitektur i koncentrat. De bildade ett slags flytande stadskvarter med motsvarighet i Amsterdam eller Lieden. Som sådana utgjorde de också reklampelare för nederländsk kultur och attityd gentemot kommers.

Kapitel 8, Slutsatser

En av avhandlingens viktigaste slutsatser är att en byggnadsarkeologi som betonar rum och brukande är fullt genomförbar på skeppsvrak, och då i synnerhet stora fortfarande sammanhängande lämningar av den karaktär som ibland påträffas i Östersjön. Sådana undersökningar kan vara ett sätt att föra fram bortglömda aspekter av tidimodern tid.

Ett belysande exempel är resultatet att att samtliga ombordvarande på flöjterna bodde i aktern. Vraken visar att maktutövning genom att skapa grupper med strikt separerade rörelserum inte förekommit ombord på handelsflöjter, medan det varit en viktig del av disciplineringen ombord på ett örlogsskepp. Denna bild kontrasterar med en tidigare uppfattning om att strikt maktordning och hierarki alltid är rådande ombord på skepp.

SAMMANFATTNING (SWEDISH SUMMARY)

Studien visar också att flöjtskeppens exteriörer hade en repertoar med skulpterade symboler som tycks ha varit ganska specifik för denna kategori fartyg. Dessa symboler intog en central plats i det offentliga rummet i städer som handlade med Nederländerna. Flöjterna har på det viset utgjort ett markant inslag det urbana rummet.

Med detta i åtanke kan man dra den generella slutsatsen att skeppsvrak rimligtvis inte behöver vara föremål för *marin*arkeologi. Skepp är delar av samhället i stort. Vrak efter förlista flöjtskepp kan på det viset betraktas som geografiskt utspridda fragment av tidigmoderna städer.

Glossary

Beakhead. A platform or projecting structure forward of the stem. Usually decorated with ornaments and a figurehead.

Beam. Heavy athwartship timber, strongly fastened to the hullside, which contributes to the stiffness of the hull. In most vessels they are set along specific levels in the hull to support decks. These are called *deckbeams*.

Bilge pump. Pump used to evacuate water from the hull. On *fluits* the pump-barrel is usually made out of a drilled-through tree-trunk. Connected to the pump is the *pump-dale*.

Bow. The forward part of the hull, from where the sides curve towards the stem.

Bowsprit. Part of the rig, which consists of a spar projecting forward upwards, often fitted with a small sail.

Bulkhead. A wall on board a ship.

Bulwark. The part of the hullside that rises above the upper deck level.

Cable-tier. A compartment for storing the anchor cable.

Capstan. A device used for moving heavy loads using ropes, such as hoisting anchors, lifting yards or careening vessels. They consist of a spool-shaped vertical cylinder, mounted on a spindle and bearing and turned round levers. On board the *fluits* they are usually found abaft the mainmast.

Carlings. Timbers fitted in between *deckbeams* in the ships lengthwise direction. Their purpose is to provide extra strength around hatches or masts.

Carvel-built. Where the strakes of planking are placed side by side so that the hullside is smooth, as opposed to **clinker-built**.

Caulking. Moss, animal hail or other fibrous material driven into seams between planks.

Clinker-built. Where the strakes of planking are overlapping. The uppermost part of the hull in the bow and stern of *fluits* have clinker-laid strakes of planking.

Deckbeam. *See beam.*

Forecastle. A structure or small room over the forward part of the upper deck.

Foremast. The foremost mast on the *fluit*.

Galley. The compartment of a vessel where the food is prepared.

Gunport. Opening in a hull through which a gun could be fired.

Gunroom. Aft part of the lower deck where the master gunner had his compartment. The Dutch term is *Konstapels Kamer*, whereas the Swedish is *Arkliet*.

Hatch, main-. The main loading hatch on a *fluit* is located before of the main mast.

Helmsman's stand. The place or compartment where the helmsman stood when steering the vessel.

Hennegat. Dutch word for the low space between the quarterdeck and inner roof of the main-cabin on board a *fluit*, aimed for the *tiller*.

Hoekman. Dutch term, literary meaning 'corner man' to designate the sculpture placed in the corner between the transom and the hull-side. The English term is usually *Strongman*.

Hold. The lowest space in the hull, used for cargo, stores and ballast when required.

Katschip. A simpler version of the *fluit*.

Knee. L-shaped timber used for additional strength, for instance between deck and hullside.

Knightshead. Vertically oriented timbers placed on the deck, with sheaves for running rig, occasionally with carved heads upon them.

Lateen. Triangular sail set on a long yard that was slung from its mast at *c.* 45-degree angle. On *fluits* lateen sails are set on the mizzen.

Lower Deck. Deck-level oriented parallel to the main or upper deck.

Mainmast. On a *fluit*, this is the highest of the three masts, placed just abaft amidships.

Mizzenmast. The aftermost mast on a three-masted ship, such as the *fluit*.

Pinnace. A Dutch fine-lined ship with flat stern. Usually employed as a warship or armed trading vessel.

Planking. The outer layer of a ship's hull.

Poop. Deck above the quarterdeck.

Port. Left side of the hull, when standing in the *stern* and nose is pointing towards the *stem*. **Pump,** see *Bilge Pump*.

Pump-dale. A dale which transports bilge-water from the pump overboard. On a *fluit*, this dale usually consist of a hollowed *deckbeam* (see *beam*).

Quarterdeck. After deck, above the main or weather deck, and beneath any *poop*. The station of the officer(s) conning the ship.

Sheer. The upward curve towards the ends of the hull in the profile of a ship.

Shelf clamp. (Also shelf, clamp or beamshelf). A thick internal plank oriented longitudinally and onto which the *deckbeams* rest.

Square Sail. Canvas which is square and is set from yards that at rest are carried horizontally.

Starboard. The right side of the hull when standing in the stern and the nose is pointing towards the *stem*.

Stem. The large curved timber scarfed onto the keel that largely determines the shape of the bow and into which the ends of the outer planking are rabbeted.

Stern. Aftermost part of the ship.

Sternpost. The near-vertical extension of the keel aft off which the rudder was hung.

Strongman, see *Hoekman*.

Tiller. A lever attached to the rudder to facilitate steering.

Top timber. The uppermost element in a frame.

Transom. Flat part of a ship's stern.

Tumblehome. The inward slope of the sides of the upper hull.

Wale. Thick strake of hull *planking*.

Whipstaff. A vertical lever at the end of the *tiller*, used by the helmsman to steer the ship.

Windlass. A form of horizontal *capstan* favoured by merchant ships and small crafts as it requires less space than a capstan.

Quarter. The after part of a vessel's side.

Quarter gallery. Ornamental balcony on the sides of the stern.

References

Adams, J., 2003, *Ships, Innovation and Social Change. Aspects of Carvel Shipbuilding In Northern Europe 1450–1850*. Diss. Stockholm University.

Adams, J., 2013a, *A Maritime Archaoleogy of Ships: Innovation and Social Change in Medieval and Early Modern Europe*. Oxford & Oakville: Oxbow Books

Adams, J., 2013b, Experiencing Shipwrecks and the Primacy of Vision, In: Adams, J. and Rönnby, J. (eds.). *Interpreting Shipwrecks: Maritime Archaeological Approaches*. Southamton & Stockholm: Highfield Press (Södertörn Academic Studies 56, Southampton Archaeology Monograph New Series 4), pp. 85–96.

Adams, J. and Rule, N., 1991, A comparison of the application of a three dimensional survey system on three underwater archaeological sites, In: Reinders, R. & Oosting, R. (ed.). *Scheepsarcheologie: prioriteiten en lopend onderzoek*. Lelystad: Rijksdienst Ijsselmeerpolders, (Flevobericht, nr 322), pp. 145–154.

Adams, J. and Rönnby, J., 1996, *Furstens fartyg. Marinarkeologiska undersökningar av en renässanskravell*. Uppsala: Almqvist & Wiksell. (Sjöhistoriska museets rapportserie 32).

Adams, J. and Rönnby, J., 2012, One of His Majesty's *'Beste Kraffwells'*: the wreck of an early carvel-built ship at Franska Sternarna, Sweden, *IJNA*, 42.1: 103–117.

Ahlström, C., 1995, *Spår av hav, yxa och penna – historiska sjöolyckor i Östersjön avspeglade i marinarkeologiskt källmaterial*. Diss. Helsinki: The Finnish Academy of Science and Letters.

Ahlström, C., 1997, *Looking for Leads – shipwrecks of the past revealed by contemporary documents and archaeological record*. Helsinki: The Finnish Academy of Science and Letters.

Almevik, G., 2012, *Byggnaden som kunskapskälla*. Diss. Göteborg: Göteborgs universitet, 2012.

Almevik, G., 2014, Byggnaden som kunskapskälla. in: Forssberg, A. M. & Sennefelt, K. (eds.) *Fråga föremålen: Handbok till historiska studier av materiell kultur*. Lund: Studentlitteratur, pp. 71–88.

Alopaeus, H., 1995, Ship archaeological recording techniques as applied under water in Nordic waters, In: Cederlund, C. O. (ed.) *Medieval Ship Archaeology, Documentation, Conservation, Theoretical aspects – the management perspective*. Stockholm: Stockholm University (SMAR – Stockholm Marine Archaeology Reports) pp. 39–46.

Andrén, A., 1997, *Mellan ting och text. En introduktion till de historiska arkeologierna*. Stockholm: Stehag.

Andrén, A., 1998, *Between Artefacts and Texts: Historical Archaeology in Global Perspective*. Translated by Crozier, A., New York: Plenum Publishing.

Arnshav, M., 2008, *VA-ledningar mellan Dalarö och Dalarö skans särskild arkeologisk utredning: Södermanland, Dalarö socken, Haninge kommun*. Stockholm, SMM (Report 2008:1).

Arnshav, M., 2011,*"Yngre vrak" – samtidsarkeologiska perspektiv på ett nytt kulturarv*. Huddinge: Södertörn University (Södertörn Archaeological Studies 8).

Asker, B., 1993, Från godsägarstat till ämbetsmannastat, In: Dahlgren, S., Florén, A., Karlsson, Å. (eds.). *Makt & vardag, Hur man styrde, levde och tänkte under svensk stormaktstid*. Stockholm: Atlantis, pp. 68–85.

Aubert, V. and Arner, O., 1959, On the Social Structure of the Ship, *Acta Sociologica*, 3: 200–201.

Barbour, V., 1930, Dutch and English Merchant Shipping in the Seventeenth Century, *The Economic History Review*, Vol 2.2, pp. 261–290.

Barker, R., 1991, Design in the Dockyards, about 1600, In: Reinder, R. and Kees, P. (eds.) *Carvel construction Technique, Fifth International Symposium on Boat and Ship Archaeology, Amsterdam 1988*. Oxbow Monograph 12, Oxford, pp 61–69.

Bass, G., 1966, *Archaeology under Water*. London: Thames & Hudson.

Bass, G., (ed.) 1972, *A history of Seafaring, based on underwater archaeology*. London: Thames & Hudson.

Bass, G., 2011, The Development of Maritime Archaeology, In: Catsambis, A., Ford, B., Hamilton, D. L. (eds.) *The Oxford Handbook of Maritime Archaeology*. Oxford & New York: Oxford University Press, pp. 3–22.

Bedoire, F., 2001, *Guldålder: slott och politik i 1600-talets Sverige*. Stockholm: Bonnier.

Bentham, J., 1995, *The Panopticon Writings*. Edited by Miran Bozovic, London: Verso.

REFERENCES

Bentham, J., 2002, *Panopticon: en ny princip för inrättningar där personer övervakas.* Nora: Nya Doxa.

Berg, J., 1968a., *Votivskepp 1.* Inventeringen, Stockholm: SMM.

Berg, J., 1968b, Votivskeppsinventeringen, In: Berg, J. & Ohrelius, B. (eds.) *Sjöhistorisk Årsbok 1967-1968.* Stockholm: SMM.

Binding, G., Mainzer, U., Wiedenau, A. 1984, *Kleine Kunstgeschichte des deutschen Fachwerkbaus.* 3. unveränd. Aufl. Darmstadt: Wissenschaftliche Buchgesellschaft.

Björklund, A., (ed.) 1989, *Sjöhistoriska museet 50 år, Sjöhistorisk Årsbok 1988-1989.* Stockholm: SMM.

Bollnow, O. F., 1994, Vara-i-rum och ha-rum. Swedish translation by William Fovet and Björn Sandmark, chapter 1 in part V, in Mench und Raum, *Nordisk Arkitekturforskning*, nr 1, pp. 111-120.

Bollnow, O. F., 2011, *Human space.* London: Hyphen.

Borgersen, T. and Ellingsen, H., 1994, *Bildanalys: Didaktik och metod.* Lund: Studentlitteratur.

Braudel, F., 1981, *Civilization and Capitalism 15th-18th Century, Vol. 1 The Structures of Everyday Life.* Berkley, Los Angeles: University of California Press.

Bruseth, J. E. and Turner, T. S., 2005, *From a Watery Grave: The Discovery And Excavation of La Salle´s Shipwreck.* College Station: Texas A&M University Press.

Burke, P., 1990, *The French Historical Revolution; The Annales School 1929-89.* Stanford: University Press.

Börjeson, H., 1932, *Stockholms segelsjöfart: minnesskrift 1732-1932.* Stockholm: Sjökaptens.societeten i Stockholm.

Cederlund, C. O., 1988. Flöjt, *Longitud*, nr 24, pp. 45-55.

Cederlund, C. O., 1981a, Pionjärer: Harald Åkerlund – en banbrytare inom svensk marinarkeologi, *Marinarkeologisk tidskrift*, nr 2, pp. 33-35.

Cederlund, C. O., 1981b, *Vraket vid Älvsnabben – fartygets byggnad.* Stockholm: SMM (Statens Sjöhistoriska museum. Rapport 14).

Cederlund, C. O., 1982a., Bara örlogsskepp?, *Meddelanden från Marinarkeologiska Sällskapet*, nr 4, pp. 3-5.

Cederlund, C. O.,1982b, *Vraket vid Jutholmen – fartygets byggnad.* Stockholm: SMM. (Statens Sjöhistoriska museum. Rapport 16).

Cederlund, C. O., 1983, *The Old Wrecks of the Baltic Sea.* Oxford: BAR (Intern. Ser. 186).

Cederlund, C. O., (ed.) 1985, *Postmedieval Boat and Ship Archaeology, Papers based on those presented to an International Symposium on Boat and Ship Archaeology in Stockholm in 1982*. Oxford: BAR (Intern. Ser. 256).

Cederlund, C. O., 1992, The Ships of Scandinavia and the Baltic, In: Gardiner R. & Bosscher P. (eds.) *The Heyday of Sail: The Merchant Sailing Ship 1650–1850*. London: Conway Maritime Press (Conways History of the Ship), pp. 55–76.

Cederlund, C. O., 1994, The Regal Ships and divine kingdom, *Current Swedish Archaeology*, Vol. 2: 47–86.

Cederlund, C. O., 1997, *Nationalism eller Vetenskap, svensk marinarkeologi i ideologisk belysning*. Stockholm: Carlssons.

Cederlund, C. O. and Hocker, F. M., 2006, *Vasa I: the archaeology of a Swedish warship of 1628*. Stockholm: SMM.

Cederlund, C. O., 2012, Ett oskrivet kapitel i skeppet Vasas historia, *Forum navale*, Vol. 86.

Cederlund, C. O. and Ingelman-Sundberg, C., 1973, The excavation of the Jutholmen wreck, 1970–71, *IJNA*, vol. 2.2, pp. 301–327.

Clarke, D. L. 1968. *Analytical Archaeology*, London: Methuen.

Counihan, C. M. and Van Esterik, P., 1997. *Food and Culture: A Reader*. New York: Routledge.

Crumlin-Pedersen, O. and Olsen, O., 2002, *The Skuldelev Ships I: Topography, Archaeology, History, Conservation and Display*. Roskilde: Viking Ship Museum/National Museum of Denmark (Ships and Boats of the North, 4.1).

Dahlman, S., Kenas, J., Pettersson, P.-A., 1986, *Projektet Saltskutan. Rapport från 1986 års marinarkeologiska undersökning av flöjtskeppet Anna Maria*. Unpublished Report, SMM Archive.

Dahlman, S., Kenas, J., Pettersson, P.-A., 1990, *Projektet Saltskutan. Rapport från 1988 års marinarkeologiska undersökning av flöjtskeppet Anna Maria*. Unpublished Report, SMM Archive.

Deetz, J., 1977, *In Small Things Forgotten: The Archaeology of Early American Life*. New York: Anchor Books.

De Vries, J. and Van Der Woude, A., 1997, *The First Modern Economy: Success, failure, and perseverance, 1500–1815*. Cambridge: Cambridge University Press.

Dixelius, M., Oskarsson, O., Nilsson, O., Rönnby, J., 2011, The Ghost Ship Expedition, *Hydro International*, No 1, vol 15.

REFERENCES

Dolwick, J. S., 2009, 'The Social' and Beyond: Introducing Actor-Network Theory, *Journal of Maritime Archaeology*, Vol. 4, pp. 21–49.

Edberg, R., 2002, *Färder i österled: experiment, källor, myter och analogier*. Stockholm: Dept. of Archaeology.

Einarsson, L., 1997, Artefacts from the Kronan (1676): cathegories, preservation and social structure, In: Redknap, M. (ed.) *Artefacts from Wrecks: Dated assemblages from the Late Middle Ages to the Industrial Revolution*. Oxford: Oxbow (Oxbow Monograph 84), pp. 209–218.

Ekman, C., 1934, *Rapport till Marinmusei nämnd*. Unpublished Report, SMM Archive.

Ekman C., 1942, Stora Kraveln Elefanten, In: Lybeck, O. (ed.) *Svenska flottans historia: örlogsflottan i ord och bild från dess grundläggning under Gustav Vasa fram till våra dagar*. Band 1. Malmö: Allhem: Allhem, pp. 89–98.

Ellmers, D., 1994, The Cog as Cargo Carrier, In: Gardiner, R. and Unger, R., (eds.) *Cogs, Caravels and Galleons: The Sailing Ship 1000–1650*. London: Conway Maritime Press (Conways History of the Ship), pp. 29–46.

Emke, C., 2001, Fluitschip '*Anna Maria*': Een reconstructie, part 1. *de Modelbouwer*, published by Nederlanse Vereniging van Modelbouwers, nr 7, pp. 376–382.

Emke, C., 2004, Anna Maria: A late seventeenth-century fluyt, *Model Shipwright*, vol. 126, pp. 6–24.

Englund, P., 1989, *Det hotade huset: adliga föreställningar om samhället under stormaktstiden*. Stockholm: Atlantis.

Englund, P., 1991, *Förflutenhetens landskap: Historiska essäer*. Stockholm: Atlantis.

Eriksdotter, G., 2005, *Bakom fasaderna: Byggnadsarkeologiska sätt att fånga tid, rum och bruk*. Diss. Stockholm: Almqvist & Wiksell (Lund Studies in Medieval Archaeology 36).

Eriksdotter, G., 2009, Rum för rörelse: byggnadsarkeologi i virtuella miljöer, In: Mogren, et al. (eds.) *Triangulering – historisk arkeologi vidgar fälten*. Lund (Lund Studies in Historical Archaeology 11), pp 85–96.

Eriksson, N., 2004, Västeråsskeppet – framgrävt för andra gången, In: *Marinarkeologisk tidskrift*, nr 2, pp.15–17.

Eriksson, N., 2010, *Jutholmsvraket – ett handelsfartyg från sent 1600-tal*, Stockholm: SMM (Report 2010:1).

Eriksson, N., 2012a, Recording a large Three-dimensional ship-structure – thoughts rendered from the Dalarö-wreck project, In: J.C. Henderson (ed.) *Beyond Boundaries. The 3rd International Congress on Underwater Archaeology, IKUWA 3, London 2008.* Römisch-Germanische Kommission, pp. 193–198.

Eriksson, N., 2012b, The *Lion Wreck*: a survey of a seventeenth-century Dutch merchant ship – an interim report. *IJNA*, Vol. 41.1, pp. 17–25.

Eriksson, N., 2013, Sailing, sleeping and eating on board seventeenth century ships: Tapping the Potential of Baltic Sea shipwrecks, with regard to the Archaeology of Space, In: Adams, J. & Rönnby, J. (eds.) *Interpreting Shipwrecks: Maritime Archaeological Approaches* Southampton: Highfield Press. (Södertörn Academic Studies 56, Southampton Archaeology Monograph New Series 4), pp. 97–109.

Eriksson, N., 2014a, The Edesö Wreck: the hull of a small, armed ship wrecked in the Stockholm archipelago in the latter half of the seventeenth century, *IJNA*, Vol. 43.1, pp. 103–114.

Eriksson, N., 2014b, Seglande halsgavelhus: om skulpturer på flöjtskepp i Sverige och Nederländerna under tidigmodern tid, *Historisk tidskrift*, vol.134.3, pp. 385–408.

Eriksson, N., forthcoming, Being lodged in a *fluit* ship; the material setting of everyday life onboard *Anna Maria* of 1694, In: *Journal of Maritime Archaeology*.

Eriksson, N., During, C., Holmlund, J., Rönnby, J., Sjöblom, I. Ågren, M. 2013. *Resande mannen (1660), Marinarkeologisk rapport 2012.* Stockholm: Södertörn University (Södertörn arkeologiska rapporter och studier).

Eriksson, N. and Rönnby, J. 2012a. 'The *Ghost Ship*'. An Intact *Fluyt* from c.1650 in the Middle of the Baltic Sea, *IJNA*, Vol. 41, nr 2, pp 350–361.

Eriksson, N. and Rönnby, J., 2012b, Svärdet: Marin slagfältsarkeologi, In *Marinarkeologisk tidskrift*, nr 1, pp. 4–7.

Eriksson, U., 1995, *Historien om Briggen Severn av Carlskrona.* Nynäshamn: Marinarkeologiskt utbildningscentrum (Marinarkeologisk rapport 1).

Erixon, S., 1947, *Svensk Byggnadskultur: Studier och skildringar belysande den svenska byggnadskulturens historia.* Stockholm: Aktiebolaget Bokverk.

Fahlander, F., 2010, The Nose, the Eye, the Mouth and the Gut: Social Dimensions of Food-Cravings and Commensality, In: Fahlander, F. & Kjellström, A. 2010 (eds.) *Making Sense of Things: Archaeologies of Sensory Perception.* Stockholm: Stockholm University, (Stockholm Studies in Archaeology 53), pp. 35–50.

Fahlander, F. and Kjellström, A., 2010, (eds.) *Making Sense of Things: Archaeologies of Sensory Perception*, Stockholm: Stockholm University, (Stockholm Studies in Archaeology 53).

Fahlborg, B., 1923, Ett blad ur den svenska handelsflottans historia (1660–1675), *Historisk Tidskrift*, Vol. 43, Issue 3, pp. 205–281.

Fahlström, J-M., 1947, Till belysning av holländarnas ekonomisk-historiska insats, *Forum Navale*, Vol. 8, pp. 73–97.

Ferreiro, L. D., 2007, *Ships and Science: The Birth of Naval Architecture in the Scientific Revolution, 1600-1800*. Cambridge, Massachusetts, London: The MIT Press.

Fischer, A., 1983, *Riddarholmsskeppet: en skeppsarkeologisk beskrivning och bedömning*. Stockholm.

Fischler, C., 2011, Commensality, society and culture, *Social Science Information*, Vol. 50, pp. 528–548.

Flatman, J., 2003, Cultural biographies, cognitive landscapes and dirty old bits of boat: 'theory' in maritime archaeology, *IJNA*, Vol. 32. 2 pp. 143–157.

Foucault, M., 1995, (1977). *Discipline and punish: the birth of the prison*. 2nd Vintage Books ed. New York: Vintage Books.

Franklin, J., 1989, *Navy Board Ship Models, 1650-1750*. London: Conway Maritime Press.

Franzén, A., 1981, *HMS Kronan The search for a great seventeenth century warship*. Stockholm: Royal Institute of Technology (Stockholm papers in history and philosophy of technology).

Franzén, A., 1982, Varför forska i örlogsskepp?, *Marinarkeologisk Tidskrift*, nr 4, Stockholm, pp. 6–8.

Franzén, A., 1985, De tolv skeppen, In: Johansson, B. A. (ed.). *Regalskeppet Kronan*, Höganäs: Bra böcker, pp. 14–15.

Freud, S., 2003, *The uncanny*. London: Penguin.

Gardiner R. and Bosscher P., (eds.) 1992, *The Heyday of Sail: The Merchant Sailing Ship 1650-1850*. London: Conway Maritime Press (Conways History of the Ship).

Gardiner, R. and Unger, R. W., (eds.) 1994, *Cogs, caravels and galleons: the sailing ship 1000-1650*. London: Conway Maritime Press (Conways History of the Ship).

Gardiner, R. and Lavery, B., (eds.) 1992, *The Line of Battle: The Sailing Warship 1650-1840*. London: Conway Maritime Press (Conways History of the Ship).

Garfinkel, S., 2006, Recovering Performance for Vernacular Architecture Studies, Perspectives, *Vernacular Architecture*, Vol. 13, No. 2, pp. 106–114.

Gawronski, J., 2009, *Amsterdam, een maritieme stad?*. Amsterdam: University of Amsterdam.

Genrup, K., 1990, När och hur upptäckte etnologerna sjömanskulturen? Om Gunnar Jonssons maritimetnologiska forskning, In: *Bottnisk kontakt v*, Raumo, pp.104–106.

Giles, K., 2007, Seeing and Believing: Visuality and Space in Pre-Modern England, *World Archaeology*, Vol. 39.1, Viewing Space, pp. 105–121.

Glassie, H., 1983, *Folk Housing in Middle Virginia: a structural analysis of historic artefacts*. Tennessee: The University of Tenessee Press.

Glete, J., 2010, *Swedish Naval Administration 1521–1721, Resource Flows and Organisational Capabilities*. Lieden & Boston: BRILL.

Gould, R. A., 2000, *Archaeology and the Social history of Ships*. Cambridge: University Press.

Goodwin, L., 2002, Everyday Life, In: Orser, C. (ed.) *Encyclopedia of Historical Archaeology*. London & New York: Taylor & Francis, pp. 188–190.

Goodwin, P., 1987, *The Construction and Fitting of the English Man of War, 1650–1850*. London.

Griffiths, S., 2012, The use of Space Syntax in Historical Research: current practice and future possibilities, In: Greene, M. Reyes, J. Castro, A. (eds.) *Proceedings: Eighth International Space Syntax Symposium*, Santiago de Chile: PAPER REF # 8193.

Granlund, L., 1992, I hygienens tjänst, In: Granlund, L. & Skeri, K. (eds.) *Renlighet och Bekvämlighet på Skokloster*. Skokloster (Skoklosterstudier nr 25), pp. 6–14.

Gøthche, M. and Rieck, F., 1990, Skuden er ladet med?: Et 1600-tals vrag fra Mariager Fjord, In: *Nationalmuseets arbejdsmark*. Copenhagen, pp. 157–171.

Hacking, I., 1999, Making up people, In: Biagioli, M. (ed.) *The Science Studies reader*. London and New York: Routledge, pp.161–171.

Hamilton, E., 1957, En marinarkeologisk undersökning utförd av Statens Sjöhistoriska museum, In: Albe, G., (ed.) *Sjöhistorisk årsbok 1955–1956*. Stockholm: Föreningen sveriges sjöfartsnuseun, pp. 163–183.

Hammar, A., 2014, *Mellan kaos och kontroll: Social ordning i svenska flottan 1670–1716*. Diss. Lund: Nordic Academic Press.

Hansson, H., 1960, *Med tunnelbanan till medeltiden: vad fynden berättar om Stockholms historia*. Stockholm: Bonnier.

Hansen, E., 2000, Fra malerisk til analytisk – opmålingens historie i Danmark, In: Sjömar, P., Hansen, E., Ponnert, H., Storsletten, O. (eds.) 2000. *Byggnadsuppmätning, Historik & praktik*. Stockholm: Central Board of National Antiquities, pp. 7–19.

Hansson, S., 2002, *Den skapande människan: Om människan och tekniken under 5000 år*. Lund: Studentlitteratur.

Hanson, J., (ed.) 2003, *Decoding homes and houses*. Cambridge: Cambridge University Press.

Harland, J., 2011, The Whipstaff, *The Mariner's Mirror*, Vol. 97.1, pp. 97–102.

Harpster, M., 2013, Shipwreck Identity, Methodology, and Nautical Archaeology, *Journal of Archaeological Method and Theory*, Vol. 20.4, pp. 588–622.

Harris, D. G., 1989, *Chapman: The First Naval Architect – His Work*. London: Conway Maritime Press.

Hasslöf, O., 1972, Maritime ethnology and its associated disciplines, In: Hasslöf, O., Henningsen, H. and Christensen, A. E., (eds.) 1972. *Ships and Shipyards, sailors and fishermen: an introduction to maritime ethnology*. Copenhagen: Copenhagen University Press, pp. 9–19.

Hasslöf, O., Henningsen, H. and Christensen, A. E. (eds.) 1972, *Ships and Shipyards, sailors and fishermen: an introduction to maritime ethnology*. Copenhagen: Copenhagen University Press.

Hædersdal, E., 1999a, *Om att förstå ett hus, Den dynamiska modellen, dokumentationsmetoder, vårdplan och restaureringsideologi*. del 1, Lund: Lunds tekniska högskola.

Hædersdal, E., 1999b, *Om att förstå ett hus, Den dynamiska modellen, dokumentationsmetoder, vårdplan och restaureringsideologi*. del 2, Lund: Lunds tekniska högskola.

Heckscher, E. F., 1940, *Den svenska handelssjöfartens ekonomiska historia sedan Gustav Vasa*. Uppsala: Almqvist & Wiksell (Skrifter utgivna av Sjöhistoriska samfundet 1).

Hicks, D., 2010, The Material-Culture Turn: event and effect, In. Hicks, D. and Beadry, M. 2010 (eds.) *The Oxford Handbook of Material Culture Studies*. Oxford: Oxford University Press, pp. 25–98.

Hicks, D. and Beadry, M., 2010 (eds.) *The Oxford Handbook of Material Culture Studies*. Oxford: Oxford University Press.

Hillier, B. and Hanson, J., 1989, *The Social Logic of Space*. Cambridge: Bell & Bain.

Hocker, F. M., 1991, *The Development of a Bottom-Based Shipbuilding Tradition in Northwestern Europe and the New World*. Diss., Texas A&M.

Hocker, F. M and Vlierman, K., 1996, *A small cog wrecked on the Zuiderzee in the early fifteenth century*. Lelystadt: NISA (Excavation report 19. Flevobericht 408).

Hocker, F. M., 2003, Maritime Archaeology and the ISBSA – Where to go in the 21st Century?, In Beltrame, C. (ed.) *Boats, Ships, and Shipyards, Proceedings of the ninth International Symposium on Boat and Ship Archaeology, Venice 2000*. Oxford: Oxbow, pp. 1–6.

Hocker, F. M., 2004, Shipbuilding: Philosophy, Practice, and Research, In: Hocker, F. M & Ward, C. (eds.) *The Philosophy of shipbuilding: conceptional approaches to the study of wooden ships*. College Station: Texas A & M University Press, pp. 1–6.

Hocker, F. M., 2011, *Vasa*. Stockholm: Medströms bokförlag (Forum Navales skriftserie 39).

Hocker, F. M and Ward, C., (eds.) 2004, *The Philosophy of shipbuilding: conceptional approaches to the study of wooden ships*. College Station: Texas A & M University Press.

Hocker, F. and Wendel, P. 2006. Site formation processes, In: Cederlund, C. O. and Hocker, F. M. (eds.) *Vasa 1: the archaeology of a Swedish warship of 1628*. Stockholm: Statens maritima museer, pp. 146–170.

Hoving, A., 1995, Seagoing Ships of the Netherlands. In: Gardiner R. and Bosscher P. (ed.) *The Heyday of Sail: The Merchant Sailing Ship 1650–1850*. London: Conway Maritime Press (Conways History of the Ship), pp. 34–54.

Hoving, A., 2012, *Nicolaes Witsen and Shipbuilding in the Dutch Golden Age*. College Station: Texas A & M University Press.

Hoving, A. and Emke, C., 2000, *The Ships of Abel Tasman*. Hillersum: Verloren.

Höglund, P., 1997, Vasa – arkeologiska fynd och ett fartygssamhälle: spåren efter folk ombord. *Forum Navale*, 52, pp. 34–68.

Ingelman-Sundberg, C., 1976, Preliminary report on finds from the *Jutholmen* wreck. *IJNA*, Vol. 5.1, pp. 57–71.

Jahnson, Å., 1971, *Constantia*. Unpublished report, SMM Archive.

Jakobsson, H., 1999, Tekniska influenser och central normer i svenskt skeppsbyggeri – Lübeck 1664–1667, *Forum Navale*, Vol. 55, pp. 26–43.

Jakobsson, H., 2000, The warship in Swedish seventeenth society – a cultural construction? *Scandinavian journal of history*, Vol. 24, pp. 225–243.

Johnson, M., 1993, *Housing Culture: Traditional architecture in an English landscape*. London: UCL Press.

Johnson, M., 1996, *An Archaeology of capitalism*. Oxford: Blackwell Publishers.
Johnson, M., 2002, *Behind the castle gate: from Medieval to Renaissance*. London & New York: Clarendon Press (The Oxford History of Early Modern Europe).
Kaijser, I., 1981, *Vraket vid Älvsnabben: Dokumentation last och utrustning*. Stockholm: SMM (Statens Sjöhistoriska museum. Rapport 13).
Kaijser, I., 1983, *Vraket vid Jutholmen: Dokumentation last och utrustning*. Stockholm: SMM (Statens Sjöhistoriska museum. Rapport 17).
Ketting, H., 2006, *Fluitschepen voor de VOC, balanceren tussen oncostelijckheijt en duursaemheijt*. Zaltbommel: Aprilis.
Kirby, D. and Hinkkanen, M.-L., 2000, *The Baltic and the North Seas*. New York: Routledge.
Kleiner, F., 2009, *Gardner's Art through the Ages: The Western Perspective, Vol. II*, Boston: Wadsworth.
Knappet, C. and Malafouris, L., (eds.). 2008. *Material Agency: Towards a Non-Anthropocentric Approach*. New York: Springer.
Knappet, C., 2008, The Neglected Networks of Material Agency: Artefacts, Pictures and Texts, In: Knappet, C. and Malafouris, L. (eds.). *Material Agency: Towards a Non-Anthropocentric Approach*. New York: Springer, pp. 139–156.
Koehler, L., Domínguez-Delmás, M. Megens, L.. du Mortier, B., de Keijzer, M. van Keulen, H. Manders, M., and van Tilburg, B. 2012, Tracing the Ghost Ship: Can the *hoekman* reveal her construction date and origin?, *Poster at ISBSA 13*, Amsterdam.
Landon, D., 2002, Food and foodways, In: Orser, C. (ed.). *Encyclopedia of Historical Archaeology*. London & New York: Taylor & Francis, pp. 220–221.
Larsson, S., 2009, Mellan Birger Jarl och Burger King – Urban arkeologi, In: Mogren, et al (eds.) *Triangulering – historisk arkeologi vidgar fälten*. Lund (Lund studies in historical archaeology 11), pp. 147–160.
Latour, B., 1990, 'Drawing Things Together', In: Michael Lynch and Steve Wolgar (eds.) *Representation in Scientific Practice*. Cambridge: MIT Press, pp. 19–68.
Latour, B., 2005, *Reassembling the Social, An introduction to Actor-Network-Theory*. Oxford: University Press.
Laughton, L. G. C., 2001, (1925), *Old ship figure-heads & sterns: with which are associated galleries, hancing-pieces, catheads and ad divers other matters that concern the "grace and counterance" of old sailing-ships*. Mineola, New York: Dover Publications.

Lavery, B., 1987, *The Arming and Fitting of English Ships of War, 1600–1815*. London: Naval Institute Press.

Lavery, B., (ed.) 1981, *Deane's Doctrine of naval architecture, 1670*. London: Naval Institute Press.

Lavery, B., 1992, Support Craft, In: Gardiner, R. & Lavery, B. (eds.) *The Line of Battle: The Sailing Warship 1650–1840*. London: Conway Maritime Press (Conways History of the Ship), pp. 106–115.

Law, J., 2000, *Objects, Spaces and Others*, published by the Centre of Science Studies, Lancaster University, Lancaster LA1 4 YN, UK, at http://www.comp.lancs.ac.uk/sociology/papers/Law-Objects-Spaces-Others.pdf

LeeDecker, C. H., 1994, Discard Behaviour on Domestic Historic Sites: Evaluation of Contexts for the Interpretation of Household Consumption Patterns, *Journal of Archaeological Method and Theory*, Vol. 1.4, pp. 345–375.

Lefebvre, H. and Levich, C., 1987. The Everyday and Everydayness, *Yale French Studies*, Vol. 73, pp. 7–11.

Lemée, C., 2006, *The Renaissance Shipwrecks from Christianshavn, An archaeological and architectural study of large carvel vessels in Danish waters 1580–1640*. Roskilde: Viking Ship Museum/National Maritime Museum of Denmark (Ships and Boats of the North, Vol 6).

Lenihan, D., 1983, Rethinking Shipwreck Archaeology: A history of Ideas and Considerations for New Directions. In: Gould, R. (ed.) *Shipwreck Anthropology*. Albuquerque: University of New Mexico, pp. 37–64.

Little, B., 1994, People with History: An Update on Historical Archaeology in the United States, *Journal of Archaeological Method and Theory*, Vol.1, pp. 5–40.

Lisberg-Jensen, O., 1972, Caritas och Constantia, In: *Aktuellt från föreningen marinmusei vänner i Karlskrona*. Karlskrona, pp. 32–47.

Lovén, C., 1999, *Borgar och befästningar i det medeltida Sverige*. Stockholm: Kungliga Vitterhets-, historie- och antikvitetsakademien.

Lucassen, J. and Unger, R. W., 2011, Shipping Productivity and Economic Growth, In. Unger, R. W. (ed.) *Shipping and Economic Growth 1350–1850*. Lieden & Boston: BRILL (Global Economic History Series 7), pp. 3–46.

Lybeck, O., (ed.) 1942, *Svenska Flottans Historia 1521–1679, Vol. 1*. Stockholm: Allhem

Maarleveld, T., 1994, Double Dutch Solutions in Flush-planked Shipbuilding, In: Westerdahl, C. (ed.).*Crossroads in Ancient Shipbuilding, Proceedings of the Sixth International Symposium on Boat and Ship Archaeology, Roskilde 1991*. Oxford: Oxbow (Oxbow Monograph 40), pp.153-163.

Maarleveld, T. J. and Van Ginkel, E. J. 1990. *Archeologie onder water: Het verleden van een varend volk*, Amsterdam: Muelenhoff.

Magalotti, L., 1912, *Sverige under år 1674, från italienskan med 23 samtida bilder, utgifven av Stenbock, C. M.* Stockholm: Nordstedts.

Marsden, P., 2003, *Sealed by time: The loss and recovery of the Mary Rose*. Portsmouth: The Mary Rose Trust (The Archaeology of the Mary Rose, vol.1).

Mc Grail, S., 2011, Boats, Ships and Wrecks: Maritime archaeology and The Mariner's Mirror, *The Mariner's Mirror*, Vol. 97:1, pp. 37-62.

Mogren, M., Roslund, M., Sundnér, B. and Wienberg, J., (eds.) 2009, *Triangulering: Historisk arkeologi vidgar fälten*. Lund (Lund Studies in Historical Archaeology 11).

Moreland, J., 2001, *Archaeology and Text*. London: Duckworth.

Muckelroy, K., 1978, *Maritime Archaeology*. Cambridge: Cambridge University Press.

Munday, J., 1978, Heads and tails: The Necessary seating, In: Annis, P. G. W. *Ingrid and other studies*. Greenwich: NMM (Maritime Monographs and Reports 36), pp. 120-145.

Müller, L., 1998, *The Merchant Houses of Stockholm, c. 1640-1800: A Comparative study of Entreprenneural Behaviour*. Diss. Uppsala University.

Nagbøl, S., 1983, Makt och arkitektur – försök till en upplevelseanalytisk arkitekturtolkning, *Magasin Tessin: Tidskrift för arkitektur, estetik och miljökritik*, nr 2, pp. 39-52.

Noldus, B., 2002, *Palats och herrgårdar: nederländsk arkitektur i Sverige = Stadspaleizen en Buitenplaatsen: Nederlandse bouwkunst in Zweden*. Stockholm: Ambassade van het Koninkrijk der Nederlanden.

Noldus, B., 2005, *Trade in Good Taste: Relations in Architecture and Culture between the Dutch Republic and the Baltic World in the seventeenth Century*. Turnhout:Brepols (Architectura Moderna 1).

Nordliner, G., 1988, Sjöhistoriska museet 50 år, In: Björklund, A. (ed.) *Sjöhistoriska museet 50 år*. Stockholm (Sjöhistorisk Årsbok), pp. 25-35.

Nordberg, O. T., 1930, Die Schiffsfunde im Riddarholmskanal, Stockholm. Vorfläufige Mitelung. *Acta Archaeologica 1*, pp. 263-273.

Nordberg, O. T., 1931, Riddarholmsskeppen – minnen från unionstidens svensk-danska fejder kring Stockholm, In: Thordeman, B., Schück, A., Nerman, B. (eds.) *Jorden ger – svenska forskningar och fynd under senare år.* Stockholm: Svenska fornminnesföreningen, pp. 193–208.

Nováky, G., 1993, Den ansvarsfulle handelsmannen, In: Dahlgren, S., Florén, A., Karlsson, Å. (eds.). *Makt och vardag, hur man styrde, levde och tänkte under svensk stormaktstid.* Stockholm: Atlantis, pp. 215–232.

Nurmio-Lahdenmäki, A. (ed.) 2006, *St. Michael 1747.* Helsingfors: Fingrid Oyj.

Oertling, T., 1996, *Ship's Bilge Pumps; A History of their Development, 1500–1900.* College Station: Texas A&M University Press (Studies in Nautical Archaeology).

Ogier, C., 1914, *Från sveriges storhetstid: Franske legationssekreteraren Charles Ogiers dagbok under ambassaden in Sverige 1634–1635, från latinet med inledning och noter utgiven av Sigurd Hallberg.* Stockholm: Nordstedts.

Olsen, B., 2003, Material culture after text: re-membering things, *Norwegian Archaeological Review*, Vol. 36:2, pp. 87–104.

Olsen, B., 2010, *In Defense of Things: Archaeology and the Ontology of Objects, Archaeology in society Series.* Lanham, New York, Toronto, Plymouth UK: Altamira Press (Archaeology in society series).

Olsen, B., Shanks, M., Webmoor, T., Witmore, C., 2012, *Archaeology: The Discipline of Things.* Berkley, Los Angeles, London: University of Carlifornia Press.

Olsen, O. and Crumlin-Pedersen, O., 1978, *Five Viking ships from Roskilde fjord.* Roskilde: Viking ship museum.

Olsson, M., 1957, Borgerlig möblering i Stockholm på 1600-talet, *Fataburen: Nordiska museets och Skansens årsbok 1957.* Stockholm, pp. 137–146.

Oosting, R., 1991, Preliminary results of the research on the seventeenth century merchantman found at lot E 81 in the Noordoostpolder Netherlands, In: Reinders, R. & Kees, P. (Eds.) *Carvel Construction Technique, Fifth International Symposium on Boat and Ship Archaeology, Amsterdam 1988.* Oxford: Oxbow (Oxbow Monograph 12), pp. 72–76.

Oosting, R. and van Holk, A., 1994, The Excavation of a Peat-Barge found at Lot LZ 1 in Zuiderlijk Flevoland, In: Westerdahl, C. (ed.) *Crossroads in Ancient Shipbuilding, Proceedings of the Sixth International Symposium on Boat and Ship Archaeology, Roskilde 1991.* Oxford: Oxbow (Oxbow Monograph 40), pp. 215–221.

Ossowski, W., 2008, Archaeological underwater excavation of wreck W-32, In: Ossowski, W. (ed.) *The Genereal Carleton Shipwreck, 1785*. Gdansk: Polish Maritime Museum in Gdansk, pp. 35–64.

Oscarsson, I., (ed.) 2013, *Den franske kammartjänarens resa: minnen från länderna i norr på 1660-talet*. Stockholm: Atlantis.

Partesius, R., 2005. Preliminary Report on the Excavation of the seventeenth century Anglo-Dutch East-Indianman Avondster in Bay of Galle, Sri Lanka, *IJNA*, 34.2, pp. 216–237.

Pedersen, R. K., 1996. *Waterschip ZN 42': a clenched-lap fishing vessel from Flevoland, the Netherlands*. Lelystad: ROB (NISA), (Excavation Report 17).

Peter, B. and Dawson, P., 2009, Modernism at Sea: Ocean Liners and the Avant-garde, In: Feigel, L. & Harris, A. (eds.) *Modernism on Sea: Art and Culture at the British Seaside*. Oxfordshire: International Academic Publishers, pp. 145–158.

Petersen, B-M., 1987. The Dutch Fluitship *Anna Maria*, foundedred I Dalarö Harbour in 1709. *IJNA*, vol. 16. pp. 293–304.

Petersen, B-M., 1993, *Identifieringen av flöjtskeppet Anna Maria förlist i Dalarö 1709 – En modell för identifiering av vrak efter handelsfartyg under ny tid*. Uppsats i påbyggnadskurs i arkeologi. Stockholms universitet.

Petrejus, E. W., 1967, The Dutch Flute, seventeenth century, In: Jobé, J., (ed.) *The Great Age of Sail*. Edita: Lausanne, pp. 81–131.

Pipping, O., 2003, Whipstaff and Helmsman. An Account of the Steeringgear of the Vasa, In: Beltrame, C. (ed.) *Boats, Ships and Shipyards: Proceedings of the Ninth International Symposium on Boat and Ship Archaeology, Venice 2000*. Oxbow: Oxford, pp. 329–333.

Pollock, S., 2012. Towards an Archaeology of Commensal Spaces. An Introduction, *Topoi Journal of Ancient Studies*, Vol. 2, pp. 1–20.

Pomey, P., 2004., Principles and Methods of Construction in Ancient Naval Architecture, In Hocker, F. & Ward, C. (eds.), *The Philosophy of Shipbuilding: Conceptional approaches to the study of wooden ships*. College Station: Texas A & M University Press, pp. 25–36.

Pomey, P., 2011, Defining a ship: Architecture, function and human space, In. Catsambis, A. Ford, B., Hamilton, D. L. (Eds.) *The Oxford Handbook of Maritime Archaeology*. Oxford: University Press, pp. 25–46.

Van Ufford, W. C. A., 1943, Det holländska Stockholm, *Jorden runt: magasin för geografi och resor*, pp. 261–272.

Ransley, J., 2005, Boats are for Boys: Queering Maritime Archaeology, *World Archaeology*, Vol. 37.4, pp. 621–629.

Reinder, R and Kees, P., (eds.) 1991, *Carvel Construction Technique, Skeleton-first, Shell-first; Fifth International Symposium on Boat and Ship Archaeology, Amsterdam 1988*. Oxford: Oxbow Books.

Riis, S., 2008, The Symmetry Between Bruno Latour and Martin Heidegger: The Technique of Turning a Police Officer into a Speed Bump, *Social Studies of Science*, Vol. 38:2, pp. 285–301.

Roche, D., 2000, *A History of Everyday Things: The birth of consumption in France, 1600–1800*. Cambridge: Cambridge University Press.

Rosén, S. and Wetter, B., 1970, Bidrag till hemlighusets historia, In. Axel-Nilsson, C., Bæhrendtz, N.-E., Jansson, S. O., Nilsson, S. T. (eds.) *Fataburen: Nordiska museets och Skansens årsbok 1970*. Stockholm: Nordiska museet, pp. 169–186.

Rosenhane, S., 1944, *Oeconomia, Utgiven av Torsten Lagerstedt*. Nyköping: Sörmlands hembygdsförbund (Sörmländska handlingar).

Rådberg, J., 1998., Atlantångaren och den moderna staden – maskinmetaforen som ledbild i stadsbyggandet, In: Pettersson R./Sörlin S. (eds.) *Miljön och det förflutna – landskap, minnen, värden*. Umeå (Idéhistoriska skrifter), pp. 142–153..

Rålamb, Å. C., 1943 (1691), *Skepsbyggerij – eller Adelig öfvings tionde Tom*. Stockholm: Sjöhistoriska museet.

Rönnby, J., 1989, *Marinarkeologisk undersökning Högskärsvraket, Oxelösund, Södermanland, Undersöknigsetapp 3*. Stockholm University.

Rönnby, J., 2003, En flygande holländare i Oxelösund, In Åkerlund, A. (ed.) *Kulturell mångfald i Södermanland, 2*. Nyköping: Länsstyrelsen i Södermanlands län, pp. 123–130.

Rönnby, J., 2013, The Archaeological Interpretation of Shipwrecks, In: Adams, J. and Rönnby, J. (eds.) *Interpreting Shipwrecks: Maritime Archaeological Approaches*. Southampton: Highfield Press (Södertörn Academic Studies 56, Southampton Archaeology Monograph New Series 4), pp. 9–24.

Rönnby, J. and Adams, J., 1994, *Östersjöns sjunkna skepp. En marinarkeologisk tidsresa*. Stockholm: Tiden.

Schama, S., 1988, *The Embarrasment of riches*. London: University of California Press.

Sigmond, P. and Wouter, K., 2007. *Sea battles and naval heroes in the Seventeenth century Dutch Republic*, Amsterdam: Rijksmuseum.

Simmons, J., 1998, *Those Vulgar Tubes: External Sanitary Accommodations aboard European Ships of the Fifteenth through seventeenth Centuries*,

Second edition. College Station: Texas A&M University Press (Studies in Nautical Archaeology 1).

Sjömar, P., 2000, Byggnadsundersökning och uppmätning, In: Sjömar, P., Hansen, E., Ponnert, H., Storsletten, O. (eds.) 2000. *Byggnadsuppmätning, Historik & praktik.* Stockholm: Central Board of National Antiquities, pp. 63-84.

Sjömar, P., Hansen, E., Ponnert, H., Storsletten, O. (eds.) 2000. *Byggnadsuppmätning, Historik & praktik.* Stockholm: Central Board of National Antiquities.

Skeri, K., 1992, Inventarieförteckningar – en källa till kunskap, In Granlund, L. and Skeri, K., (eds.) *Renlighet och Bekvämlighet på Skokloster.* Skokloster (Skoklosterstudier nr 25), pp. 15-35.

Smolarek, P., 1985, The development of the archaeology of boats and ships in Poland, In: Cederlund, C. O. (ed.) *Postmedieval Boat and Ship Archaeology, Papers based on those presented to an International Symposium on Boat and Ship Archaeology in Stockholm in 1982.* Oxford: BAR (Intern. Ser. 256), pp. 421-436.

Soop, H., 1978, *Regalskeppet Vasa, Skulpturer.* Stockholm: Liber.

Soop, H., 1992 (1986), *The power and the glory: the sculptures of the warship Wasa.* Stockholm: Kungl. Vitterhets-, historie- och antikvitetsakad.

Soop, H., 2001, *Silver, brons, mässing, tenn: bruksföremål från örlogsskeppet Vasa.* Lund: Signum.

Soop, H., 2007, *Flytande palats: utsmyckning av äldre svenska örlogsfartyg.* Stockholm: Signum.

Sorokin, P., 2005, Researches of 2003 at Underwater Arxhaeological Sites in the Gulf of Finland and Lake Ladoga, In: *Stady on the Maritime Archaeology Vol. 5,* St. Petersburg, pp. 42-57.

Spens, E., 1942, Livet ombord och till lands under äldre Vasatid, In: Lybeck, O. (ed.). *Svenska flottans historia, Vol. I,* Malmö: Allhem, pp.137-154.

Stadin, K., 2009, *Stånd och genus i stormaktstidens Sverige.* Lund: Nordic Academic Press.

Sténuit, R., 1974, Early Relics of the VOC trade from Shetland, The wreck of the flute *Lastdrager* lost off Yell, 1653, *IJNA* Vol. 3.2, pp. 213-256.

Steffy, J. R., 1994, *Wooden ship building and the interpretation of shipwrecks.* College Station: Texas A&M Univ. Press.

Sutherland, W., 1711, *The Ship-builders Assistant: Or some essays Towards Compleating the ART of Marine Architecture.* London.

Sutherland, W., 1717, *Britain's Glory: Or Ship-building unvail'd, being A General Director, for Building and Completing the said Machines.* London.

Söderlind, U., 2006, *Skrovmål: Kosthållning och matlagning i den svenska flottan från 1500-tal till 1700-tal.* Diss. Stockholm: Carlssons (Forum Navales skriftserie 17).

Thomasson, J., 1997, Private Life Made Public, In: Andersson, H., Ersgård, L., Carelli, P. (eds.) *Visions of the past: trends and traditions in Swedish medieval archaeology.* Stockholm: Central Board of National Antiquities, pp. 671–698.

Tilander, G., 1980 (1968), *Stång i vägg och hemlighus: Kulturhistoriska glimtar från mänsklighetens bakgårdar.* Avesta: FABEL.

Tilley, C., 1994, *A Phenomenology of landscape, Places, Path and Monuments.* Oxford: Berg.

Tornqvist, C. G., 1788, *Utkast till swenska flottans sjö-tåg.* Stockholm: C. G. Tornqvist.

Trentmann, F., 2009, Materiality in the Future of History: Things, Practices, and Politics, *Journal of British Studies,* Vol. 48.2, pp. 283–307.

Triewald, M., 1734, *Konsten att lefwa under Watn.* Stockholm: facsmile: Anders Engwall.

Troels-Lund, T. F., 1903, *Dagligt liv i Norden i det 16:de aarhundrede,* Vol 5/6, *Fødemidler; Hverdag og fest.* København: Gyldendal.

Unger, R. W., 1978, *Dutch shipbuilding before 1800. Ships and guilds.* Assen/Amsterdam: Van Gorcum.

Unger, R. W., 1994, The Fluit: Specialist Cargo Vessels 1500 to 1650, In: Gardiner, R. (ed.) *Cogs, Caravels and Galleons, the sailing ship 1000–1650.* London: Conway Maritime Press (Conway's History of the Ship), pp. 115–130.

Unger, R. W., (ed.) 2011, *Shipping and Economic Growth 1350–1850.* Lieden & Boston: BRILL (Global Economic History Series 7).

Ufkes, T., 2001, Nederländska skeppare på stockholmska handelsskepp 1685–1700, *Forum Navale.* Vol. 56, pp. 35–59.

Upton, D., 2002, Architecture in Everyday Life, *New Literary History,* Vol. 33. 4, pp. 707–723.

Van Beylen, J., 1970, *Schepen van de Nederlanden.* Amsterdam: van Kampen & Zoon.

Van Holk, A. F. L., 1997, Family Life on board: the Dutch boat people between 1600 and 1900, In: Redknap, M. (ed.) *Artefacts from Wrecks:*

Dated assemblages from the Late Middle Ages to the Industrial Revolution. Oxford: Oxbow (Oxbow Monograph 84), pp. 219-228.

Van Royen, P. C., 1992, Seamen and the Merchant Service, 1650-1830, In: Gardiner, R. and Bosscher (eds.) *The Heyday of Sail: The Merchant Sailing Ship 1650-1830*. London: Conway Maritime Press (Conway's History of The Ship), pp.152-159.

Van Tielhof, M., 2002, *The 'Mother of all Trades': The Baltic Grain Trade in Amsterdam from the Late 16th to the Early 19th Century*. Lieden, Boston, Köln: BRILL (The Northern World).

Van Tielhof, M. and Van Zanden, J. L., 2011, Productivity Changes in Shipping in the Dutch Republic: The Evidence from Freight rates, 1550-1800, In: Unger, R. W. (ed.) *Shipping and Economic Growth 1350-1850*. Lieden & Boston: BRILL (Global Economic History Series 7), pp. 47-80.

Van Zanden, J. L. and Van Tielhof, M., 2009, Roots of growth and productivity change in Dutch shipping industry, *Explorations in Economic History*, Vol. 46, pp. 389-403.

Vlierman, K., 1997a, The Ijsselmeerpolders: a 'source book' for late medieval and early post-medieval wreck inventories, In: Redknap, M. *Artefacts from Wrecks: dated Assemblages from the Late Middle Ages to the Industrial Revolution*. Oxford: Oxbow (Oxbow Monograph 84), pp. 15-36.

Vlierman, K., 1997b, The galley, galley utensils and cooking, eating and drinking vessels from an armed 'Tjalk' wrecked on the Zuiderzee in 1673: a preliminary report, In: Redknap, M. *Artefacts from Wrecks: dated Assemblages from the Late Middle Ages to the Industrial Revolution*. Oxford: Oxbow (Oxbow Monograph 84), pp.157-166.

Vlierman, K., 2003, Late medieval fishing vessels from the Zuiderzee, In: Pieters, M, F.,

Verhaeghe, G., Gevaert, J., Mees and J. Seys (eds.) *Colloquium: Fishery, trade and piracy – fishermen´s settlements in and around the North Sea area in the Middle Ages and later*. Museum Walraversijde, Oostende.

Von Baumhauer, E. H., 1878, The Teredo and its Depredations, *Popular Science Monthly*, Vol. 13, September 1878, pp. 545-558.

Wallace, S., 2010, *An Interpretative Study of Knightheads: What do human heads carved on the end of rigging bitts symbolize?* Unpublished Report: Södertörn University.

Weber, M., 1978 (1934), *Den protestantiska etiken och kapitalismens anda*. Lund: Argos.

Wegener Sleswyg, A., 2003, *De Gouden Eeuw van het Fluitschip*. Van Wijnen.

Westbeck, O. J., 1829, *Beskrifning öfver de af Undertecknad upfunne Bergnings-Instrumenter, eller Förklaring öfver de bifogade Plancherne A. och B.; jemte en Kort Berättelse om bergningen af sjunkna Fregatt-Skeppet NADESDHAS laddning.* Göteborg: S. Nordberg.

Westin, J., 2012, *Negotiating 'culture', Assembling a Past: the visual, the nonvisual and the voice of the silent actant*. Diss. Göteborg (Gothenburg Studies in Conservation 28).

Wetterholm, C.-G., 1994, *Vrak i svenska vatten*. Stockholm: Rabén Prisma.

Wijkander, K., 2007, The role of the traditional museum, In: Satchell, J and Palma, P. (eds.) *Managing the Marine Cultural Heritage: Defining accessing and managing the resource*. Oxford: Council for British Archaeology (Research Report 153), pp. 65–68.

Winfield, R., 2010, *First Rate: The Greatest Warships of the Age of Sail*. Annapolis, Maryland: Naval Institute Press.

Witsen, N., 1979 (1671), *Aeoloude en scheeps-bouw en bestier*. Alphen aan den Rijn: Canaletto.

Zettersten, A., 1903, *Svenska flottans historia: åren 1635–1680*. Norrtelje: Norrtelje tidnings boktr.

Åkerhagen, A., 2008, *Kritpipor funna i Sverige*. (CD) Haninge: A. Åkerhagen.

Åkerlund, H., 1951, *Fartygsfynden i den forna hamnen i Kalmar*. Uppsala: Almqvist & Wiksells.

REFERENCES

Abbreviations

IJNA, The International Journal of Nautical Archaeology.
ISBSA, International Symposium on Boat and Ship Archaeology.
MARIS, Maritime Archaeological Research Institute at Södertörn University.
MAS, Marinarkeologiska sällskapet (Swedish Maritime Archaeological Society).
MMR, Maritiem Museum Rotterdam.
MMT, Marin mätteknik.
NMM, National Maritime museum, London.
SMM, Swedish National Maritime Museum.
SU, Stockholm University.

Södertörn Doctoral Dissertations

1. Jolanta Aidukaite, *The Emergence of the Post-Socialist Welfare State: The case of the Baltic States: Estonia, Latvia and Lithuania*, 2004
2. Xavier Fraudet, *Politique étrangère française en mer Baltique (1871– 1914): de l'exclusion à l'affirmation*, 2005
3. Piotr Wawrzeniuk, *Confessional Civilising in Ukraine: The Bishop Iosyf Shumliansky and the Introduction of Reforms in the Diocese of Lviv 1668– 1708*, 2005
4. Andrej Kotljarchuk, *In the Shadows of Poland and Russia: The Grand Duchy of Lithuania and Sweden in the European Crisis of the mid-17th Century*, 2006
5. Håkan Blomqvist, *Nation, ras och civilisation i svensk arbetarrörelse före nazismen*, 2006
6. Karin S Lindelöf, *Om vi nu ska bli som Europa: Könsskapande och normalitet bland unga kvinnor i transitionens Polen*, 2006
7. Andrew Stickley. *On Interpersonal Violence in Russia in the Present and the Past: A Sociological Study*, 2006
8. Arne Ek, *Att konstruera en uppslutning kring den enda vägen: Om folkrörelsers modernisering i skuggan av det Östeuropeiska systemskiftet*, 2006
9. Agnes Ers, *I mänsklighetens namn: En etnologisk studie av ett svenskt biståndsprojekt i Rumänien*, 2006
10. Johnny Rodin, *Rethinking Russian Federalism: The Politics of Intergovernmental Relations and Federal Reforms at the Turn of the Millennium*, 2006
11. Kristian Petrov, *Tillbaka till framtiden: Modernitet, postmodernitet och generationsidentitet i Gorbačevs glasnost´ och perestrojka*, 2006
12. Sophie Söderholm Werkö, *Patient patients?: Achieving Patient Empowerment through Active Participation, Increased Knowledge and Organisation*, 2008
13. Peter Bötker, *Leviatan i arkipelagen: Staten, förvaltningen och samhället. Fallet Estland*, 2007
14. Matilda Dahl, *States under scrutiny: International organizations, transformation and the construction of progress*, 2007
15. Margrethe B. Søvik, *Support, resistance and pragmatism: An examination of motivation in language policy in Kharkiv, Ukraine*, 2007
16. Yulia Gradskova, *Soviet People with female Bodies: Performing beauty and maternity in Soviet Russia in the mid 1930–1960s*, 2007
17. Renata Ingbrant, *From Her Point of View: Woman's Anti-World in the Poetry of Anna Świrszczyńska*, 2007
18. Johan Eellend, *Cultivating the Rural Citizen: Modernity, Agrarianism and Citizenship in Late Tsarist Estonia*, 2007

19. Petra Garberding, *Musik och politik i skuggan av nazismen: Kurt Atterberg och de svensk-tyska musikrelationerna*, 2007
20. Aleksei Semenenko, *Hamlet the Sign: Russian Translations of Hamlet and Literary Canon Formation*, 2007
21. Vytautas Petronis, *Constructing Lithuania: Ethnic Mapping in the Tsarist Russia, ca. 1800–1914*, 2007
22. Akvile Motiejunaite, *Female employment, gender roles, and attitudes: the Baltic countries in a broader context*, 2008
23. Tove Lindén, *Explaining Civil Society Core Activism in Post-Soviet Latvia*, 2008
24. Pelle Åberg, *Translating Popular Education: Civil Society Cooperation between Sweden and Estonia*, 2008
25. Anders Nordström, *The Interactive Dynamics of Regulation: Exploring the Council of Europe's monitoring of Ukraine*, 2008
26. Fredrik Doeser, *In Search of Security After the Collapse of the Soviet Union: Foreign Policy Change in Denmark, Finland and Sweden, 1988–1993*, 2008
27. Zhanna Kravchenko. *Family (versus) Policy: Combining Work and Care in Russia and Sweden*, 2008
28. Rein Jüriado, *Learning within and between public-private partnerships*, 2008
29. Elin Boalt, *Ecology and evolution of tolerance in two cruciferous species*, 2008
30. Lars Forsberg, *Genetic Aspects of Sexual Selection and Mate Choice in Salmonids*, 2008
31. Eglė Rindzevičiūtė, *Constructing Soviet Cultural Policy: Cybernetics and Governance in Lithuania after World War II*, 2008
32. Joakim Philipson, *The Purpose of Evolution: 'struggle for existence' in the Russian-Jewish press 1860–1900*, 2008
33. Sofie Bedford, *Islamic activism in Azerbaijan: Repression and mobilization in a post-Soviet context*, 2009
34. Tommy Larsson Segerlind, *Team Entrepreneurship: A process analysis of the venture team and the venture team roles in relation to the innovation process*, 2009
35. Jenny Svensson, *The Regulation of Rule-Following: Imitation and Soft Regulation in the European Union*, 2009
36. Stefan Hallgren, *Brain Aromatase in the guppy, Poecilia reticulate: Distribution, control and role in behavior*, 2009
37. Karin Ellencrona, *Functional characterization of interactions between the flavivirus NS5 protein and PDZ proteins of the mammalian host*, 2009
38. Makiko Kanematsu, *Saga och verklighet: Barnboksproduktion i det postsovjetiska Lettland*, 2009
39. Daniel Lindvall, *The Limits of the European Vision in Bosnia and Herzegovina: An Analysis of the Police Reform Negotiations*, 2009
40. Charlotta Hillerdal, *People in Between – Ethnicity and Material Identity: A New Approach to Deconstructed Concepts*, 2009
41. Jonna Bornemark, *Kunskapens gräns – gränsens vetande*, 2009

42. Adolphine G. Kateka, *Co-Management Challenges in the Lake Victoria Fisheries: A Context Approach*, 2010
43. René León Rosales, *Vid framtidens hitersta gräns: Om pojkar och elevpositioner i en multietnisk skola*, 2010
44. Simon Larsson, *Intelligensaristokrater och arkivmartyrer: Normerna för vetenskaplig skicklighet i svensk historieforskning 1900–1945*, 2010
45. Håkan Lättman, *Studies on spatial and temporal distributions of epiphytic lichens*, 2010 [report]
46. Alia Jaensson, *Pheromonal mediated behaviour and endocrine response in salmonids: The impact of cypermethrin, copper, and glyphosate*, 2010
47. Michael Wigerius, *Roles of mammalian Scribble in polarity signaling, virus offense and cell-fate determination*, 2010
48. Anna Hedtjärn Wester, *Män i kostym: Prinsar, konstnärer och tegelbärare vid sekelskiftet 1900*, 2010
49. Magnus Linnarsson, *Postgång på växlande villkor: Det svenska postväsendets organisation under stormaktstiden*, 2010
50. Barbara Kunz, *Kind words, cruise missiles and everything in between: A neoclassical realist study of the use of power resources in U.S. policies towards Poland, Ukraine and Belarus 1989–2008*, 2010
51. Anders Bartonek, *Philosophie im Konjunktiv: Nichtidentität als Ort der Möglichkeit des Utopischen in der negativen Dialektik Theodor W. Adornos*, 2010
52. Carl Cederberg, *Resaying the Human: Levinas Beyond Humanism and Antihumanism*, 2010
53. Johanna Ringarp, *Professionens problematik: Lärarkårens kommunalisering och välfärdsstatens förvandling*, 2011
54. Sofi Gerber, *Öst är Väst men Väst är bäst: Östtysk identitetsformering i det förenade Tyskland*, 2011
55. Susanna Sjödin Lindenskoug, *Manlighetens bortre gräns: Tidelagsrättegångar i Livland åren 1685–1709*, 2011
56. Dominika Polanska, *The emergence of enclaves of wealth and poverty: A sociological study of residential differentiation in post-communist Poland*, 2011
57. Christina Douglas, *Kärlek per korrespondens: Två förlovade par under andra hälften av 1800-talet*, 2011
58. Fred Saunders, *The Politics of People – Not just Mangroves and Monkeys: A study of the theory and practice of community-based management of natural resources in Zanzibar*, 2011
59. Anna Rosengren, *Åldrandet och språket: En språkhistorisk analys av hög ålder och åldrande i Sverige cirka 1875–1975*, 2011
60. Emelie Lilliefeldt, *European Party Politics and Gender: Configuring Gender-Balanced Parliamentary Presence*, 2011
61. Ola Svenonius, *Sensitising Urban Transport Security: Surveillance and Policing in Berlin, Stockholm, and Warsaw*, 2011
62. Andreas Johansson, *Dissenting Democrats: Nation and Democracy in the Republic of Moldova*, 2011

63. Wessam Melik, *Molecular characterization of the Tick-borne encephalitis virus: Environments and replication*, 2012
64. Steffen Werther, *SS-Vision und Grenzland-Realität: Vom Umgang dänischer und „volksdeutscher" Nationalsozialisten in Sønderjylland mit der „großgermanischen" Ideologie der SS*, 2012
65. Peter Jakobsson, *Öppenhetsindustrin*, 2012
66. Kristin Ilves, *Seaward Landward: Investigations on the archaeological source value of the landing site category in the Baltic Sea region*, 2012
67. Anne Kaun, *Civic Experiences and Public Connection: Media and Young People in Estonia*, 2012
68. Anna Tessmann, *On the Good Faith: A Fourfold Discursive Construction of Zoroastrianism in Contemporary Russia*, 2012
69. Jonas Lindström, *Drömmen om den nya staden: stadsförnyelse i det postsovjetisk Riga*, 2012
70. Maria Wolrath Söderberg, *Topos som meningsskapare: retorikens topiska perspektiv på tänkande och lärande genom argumentation*, 2012
71. Linus Andersson, *Alternativ television: former av kritik i konstnärlig TV-produktion*, 2012
72. Håkan Lättman, *Studies on spatial and temporal distributions of epiphytic lichens*, 2012
73. Fredrik Stiernstedt, *Mediearbete i mediehuset: produktion i förändring på MTG-radio*, 2013
74. Jessica Moberg, *Piety, Intimacy and Mobility: A Case Study of Charismatic Christianity in Present-day Stockholm*, 2013
75. Elisabeth Hemby, *Historiemåleri och bilder av vardag: Tatjana Nazarenkos konstnärskap i 1970-talets Sovjet*, 2013
76. Tanya Jukkala, *Suicide in Russia: A macro-sociological study*, 2013
77. Maria Nyman, *Resandets gränser: svenska resenärers skildringar av Ryssland under 1700-talet*, 2013
78. Beate Feldmann Eellend, *Visionära planer och vardagliga praktiker: postmilitära landskap i Östersjöområdet*, 2013
79. Emma Lind, *Genetic response to pollution in sticklebacks: natural selection in the wild*, 2013
80. Anne Ross Solberg, *The Mahdi wears Armani: An analysis of the Harun Yahya enterprise*, 2013
81. Nikolay Zakharov, *Attaining Whiteness: A Sociological Study of Race and Racialization in Russia*, 2013
82. Anna Kharkina, *From Kinship to Global Brand: the Discourse on Culture in Nordic Cooperation after World War II*, 2013
83. Florence Fröhlig, *A painful legacies of World War II: Nazi forced enlistment: Alsatian/Mosellan Prisoners of war and the Soviet prison camp of Tambov*, 2013
84. Oskar Henriksson, *Genetic connectivity of fish in the Western Indian Ocean*, 2013
85. Hans Geir Aasmundsen, *Pentecostalism, Globalisation and Society in Contemporary Argentina*, 2013

86. Anna McWilliams, *An Archaeology of the Iron Curtain: Material and Metaphor*, 2013
87. Anna Danielsson, *On the power of informal economies and the informal economies of power: rethinking informality, resilience and violence in Kosovo*, 2014
88. Carina Guyard, *Kommunikationsarbete på distans*, 2014
89. Sofia Norling, *Mot "väst": om vetenskap, politik och transformation i Polen 1989–2011*, 2014
90. Markus Huss, *Motståndets akustik: språk och (o)ljud hos Peter Weiss 1946–1960*, 2014
91. Ann-Christin Randahl, *Strategiska skribenter: skrivprocesser i fysik och svenska*, 2014
92. Péter Balogh, *Perpetual borders: German-Polish cross-border contacts in the Szczecin area*, 2014
93. Erika Lundell, *Förkroppsligad fiktion och fiktionaliserade kroppar: levande rollspel i Östersjöregionen*, 2014
94. Henriette Cederlöf, *Alien Places in Late Soviet Science Fiction: The "Unexpected Encounters" of Arkady and Boris Strugatsky as Novels and Films*, 2014
95. Niklas Eriksson, *Urbanism Under Sail : An archaeology of fluitships in early modern everyday life*, 2014

www.ingramcontent.com/pod-product-compliance
Lightning Source LLC
Chambersburg PA
CBHW072042160426
43197CB00014B/2601